D1049148

LIVING ABROAD IN
IRELAND

CHRISTINA McDONALD

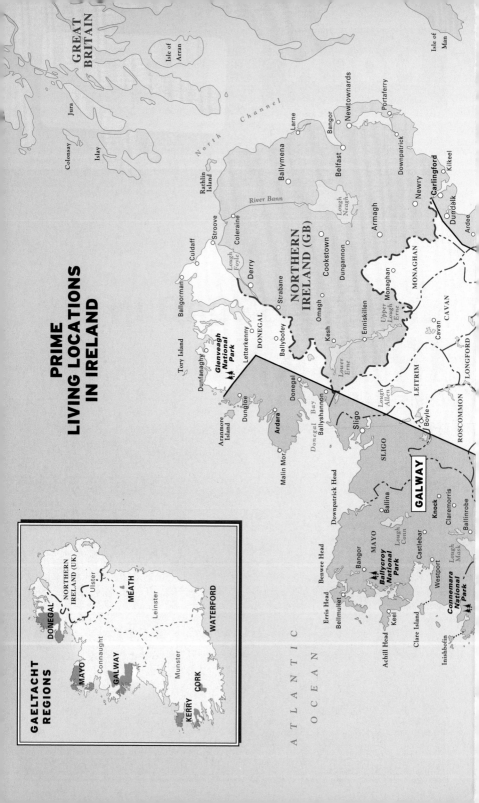

PRIME
LIVING LOCATIONS
IN IRELAND

GAELTACHT
REGIONS

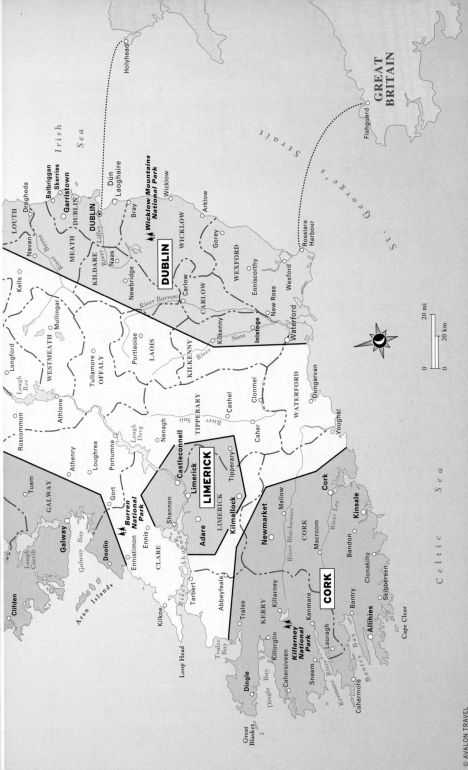

Contents

At Home in **Ireland**

Very few countries are as plagued by cliché as Ireland, Éireann in Irish. People still have images of a weathered old man wearing an Aran Island sweater alternatively knocking back pints of frothy, black Guinness and playing the fiddle, as well as energetic leprechauns dancing to Irish music next to a pot of gold perched beneath a sparkling rainbow. They think of Ireland as synonymous with rain-drenched greenery, the friendliest people in the world, and gifted poets who sparked a literary tradition. Ireland is steeped in stereotypical perceptions that range from the insightful to the truly inane.

So how much did these clichés color my idea of Ireland? Well, a lot. I entirely expected the friendly people, the colorful pub scenes, the gifted poets, and the unceasing rain resulting in emerald green fields. What I didn't expect were people with a fiery passion for their country, offset with a laid-back attitude that sometimes made it difficult to get anything accomplished. I didn't expect the modern rush of Dublin city center to so perfectly accent the staid, peaceful setting of lakes and mountain peaks in Wicklow, or the smell of horses competing for attention with car exhaust on Dublin's Dame Street.

I didn't expect the people to be so friendly that they would give you their umbrella in the rain and honestly believe that you would bring it back if they just gave you their address. My second day in Galway I went with some newly acquired friends into a wine and cheese shop. It was one of those pristine days when the sun was shining in a bright blue sky and the water sparkled like diamonds in the harbor. The shopkeeper lent us wine glasses and plates after simply extracting a promise that we would bring

them back. We drank our wine and ate our cheese on a handkerchief-size patch of grass near the water, just below the Spanish Arch, and, simply because we had said we would, brought back our borrowed goods later in the day. This sort of sincere openness – completely trusting that a stranger would honor their word – made me fall in love with Ireland.

Since first arriving in Ireland in 2001, I have experienced more versions of Irish hospitality than I can count: while chatting with shopkeepers at the weekly market, looking for an excellent bottle of red in the wine shop, enjoying a cup of tea or a pint at the local pub, or riding a bicycle down the winding, grassy knolls of Inis Mór, one of the Aran Islands. Ireland is still the only country I have ever been where even the officers at Immigrations in the airport are friendly and welcoming.

Of course there are the downsides to living in Ireland – the relaxed attitude means bureaucracy is even more of a drag than in most other countries; the narrow, cobbled streets mean constant traffic in the city centers; the incessant rain can get even the sunniest person down at times – but the small minority of negatives is offset by a plethora of positives.

Despite a huge shift in social and economic factors in recent years, Ireland still retains a timeless charm offset by historic traditions. Spectacular landscapes of dramatic coasts, majestic mountains, and charming villages captivate your heart, and the warmth and hospitality of the Irish people still persist.

► WHAT I LOVE ABOUT IRELAND

- The easygoing, laid-back atmosphere and attitude.

- The Irish sense of *craic* (good times) lends an intoxicating edge to any social atmosphere.

- The lyrical quality of the Irish accent.

- Ireland is so compact, you can get almost anywhere in the Republic in 3–4 hours.

- The Irish are fiercely proud of their Irish heritage but are always willing to accept an outsider.

- The juxtaposition of a cosmopolitan vibe in the city with a sense of the Old World in the country.

- Tea in Ireland makes everything better, from a simple sore throat to a broken heart.

- The ease with which complete strangers will talk to you.

- Everybody seems related by just six degrees of separation (at most). You can be with an Irish friend in the store, and they will strike up a conversation over the apples and find out that person is their uncle's third cousin's wife.

- The stunning beauty of the country, from quaint villages to jaw-dropping vistas, from sheer cliffs to rolling, lush green hills.

- Thatched-roof cottages still abound in the countryside.

- Nobody thinks twice if you have a glass of wine or a pint of beer at lunch. Or even if you have two.

- The Irish work to live, instead of living to work: Consider four working weeks (20 days) vacation leave, nine public holidays, and six months of paid maternity leave.

- When you go out to a pub or club with a group of friends, you buy in rounds, not individually.

- Subsidized health care. We don't have it in America, so I was able to really appreciate affordable health care in Ireland.

- The changeable weather means you may wake up to rain, but you'll probably also see the sun a few times.

WELCOME TO IRELAND

COURTESY OF TOURISM IRELAND

INTRODUCTION

Americans have a love affair with everything Irish. We love the green, rolling hills, the legend of the leprechaun, the idea of a pot of gold beneath a brilliant rainbow, the frothy black Guinness, the lyrical accent. We have always had a close relationship with this nation. In 1492 an Irishman named Patrick Maguire is said to have been the first man to set foot from Columbus's ship onto American soil. By 1855, nearly a quarter of Ireland's population had emigrated to the United States after the devastation of the potato famine. During the Civil War, the Union Army had four times as many Irish soldiers as the Confederates, spilling their blood to ensure the country stayed unified. This rich and historic relationship is reflected in the high amount of people claiming Irish descent that now live in the United States. President Barack Obama best summed this relationship up in his speech at College Green, Dublin, in May 2011: "Never has a nation so small inspired so much in another country. Irish signatures are on our founding documents. Irish blood was spilled on

© SUSAN LEGG

our battlefields. Irish sweat built our cities. You can say there has always been a little green behind the red, white, and blue."

To some, Ireland still exists as a misty land from fairy tales, where the grass is lush green and the people end each day with a pint of Guinness at their local pub. While these preconceptions are accurate to an extent, there is more to the Emerald Isle than just the intransigent notions that foreigners have. The eight million or so tourists who flock to Ireland each year can attest to that. These tourists descend on Ireland hoping for a glimpse of the spectacular landscape, the historic archaeology, the old-world charm, and the friendly people famed throughout the world. In fact, Ireland was named the favorite holiday destination in the world by Frommers in 2011.

But those who actually move to Ireland can dig deeper and experience more than just the scenery, more than just the archaeology. As an expatriate, you will experience the generous nature of the people, feel the texture of silence wrap around you in the evenings, and encounter the dynamic spirit that comes from a historic heritage and a unique culture. You will have the opportunity to go where the grass actually is greener, and you will have the opportunity to savor the energetic vibe and the flavor of everyday life that will color your experience and create a life worth reaching for.

Ireland is a land of contrasts, with jagged cliffs on the west coast and peaceful harbors on the east coast. The thrum of cosmopolitan life vibrates throughout Dublin, but the sleepy harbor of Dun Laoghaire (Dun-LEER-ee) or the quaint village of Enniskerry contrast sharply. Beaches with some of the largest surfing waves crash on the northwest coast, while ancient limestone paves the land around the Burren in the southwest.

This land of contrasts also holds true in today's social and economic structure. After years of hardship, the Celtic Tiger—a time of fantastic economic success—roared through Ireland in the 1990s, giving the country a much needed face-lift and injecting cash into a previously poor country. The Irish lived high, spent large, and celebrated their good luck. Because the new generation of people hadn't had to grow up pinching pennies, this caused frivolousness with money that would have made any Irish person's great grandparents roll in their graves. This excessive spending, on the part of the government and the banks, as well as businesses and individuals, led the country to a crater-size recession that threatened to demolish their precariously balanced accomplishments.

The previous social and economic changes that occurred in Ireland over the last few decades brought new races, new cultures, and new ideas flocking to Ireland. This influx of migrant workers is sometimes fuel for old-timers who still cling to racist beliefs that Ireland is for the Irish and the rest should keep out.

There are, unfortunately, still prevailing opinions that asylum seekers and other immigrants are taking "Irish" jobs and "Irish" social welfare benefits. Despite this, the overall attitude of the Irish is accepting, particularly in the younger, open-minded generation. As long as you pay your taxes and pay your own way, they are willing to welcome you into their culture with open arms.

But what about the people? The Irish are a fiercely nationalistic race, proud of their heritage and proud of their legacy. Not only are they proud of being Irish, they are proud of the region they come from, the sports team that hails from their region, and what school they went to. You can identify where an Irish person is from based on her accent—with widely different accents from Cork to Dublin, Galway to Donegal—and this is like wearing a flag on your head that says you are proud of where you come from.

The Irish buy Irish products rather than imported products simply because they have the label "Irish" on it. This is a country that has gone through a lot of hardship in the past—two famines, mass emigration, poverty, colonization by the English, a civil war, and a crippling recession—and as a result, they look at themselves as survivors and have the attitude that they are all in it together, during the good times and the bad. As such, the people of this great nation possess a camaraderie with each other that is apparent no matter where in the world they may be. In fact, I would wager that you would be hard-pressed to find a race of people more proud of who they are.

While the Irish do enjoy their drink, it is more the spirit of *craic* (good times) that is central to their gatherings. They are proud of their heritage as a friendly race, and their race represent a warmth and coziness, a sense of togetherness, and a feeling a belonging that is difficult to find in other countries. Perhaps due to their heritage of mournful poets, the Irish enjoy a bit of melancholy, but they always offset this with their traditional saying, "Sure, it will be grand." But whether you are just starting on this journey to Ireland or returning, the intoxicating beauty and warm spirit of the land will grasp you, permeate you, and leave you wanting more. And, as the breastplate of St. Patrick proclaims:

Hills as green as emeralds, cover the countryside,
Lakes as blue as sapphires are Ireland's special pride,
And rivers that shine like silver make Ireland look so fair,
But the friendliness of her people is the richest treasure there.

Lay of the Land

Ireland is a tiny little island perched on the edge of the Atlantic Ocean and surrounded by 34 other islands. The island is politically divided between the Republic of Ireland in the south and Northern Ireland in the north. The land mass of Ireland only covers about 27,000 square miles, making this compact island roughly the size of Maine. It is situated in the far west of Europe, surrounded by the Atlantic Ocean to the north and west, the Celtic Sea to the south, and the Irish Sea to the east, from which the United Kingdom lies beyond. Ireland is often called the "Emerald Isle" due to its lush, green vegetation, a result of its rainy weather and mild climate.

Ireland's landscape consists of a ring of coastal mountains that encircles a relatively flat midland composed of rolling limestone plains, fertile farmland, and raised bogs. Technically, Ireland has no mountains, only hills. The tallest hill, Carantuohill, is located in County Kerry and only reaches 1,020 meters (3,400 feet) high. The River Shannon, Ireland's longest and largest river, flows 273 kilometers (230 miles) south and west from its origins in Cuileagh Mountains in County Cavan down to County Limerick, separating the west of Ireland from the marshy midlands.

The country is dotted with limestone plains that have remained untouched for centuries, as well as prehistoric bogs from which the industrious Irish gather peat to use as fuel for their fires. Today there has been a concerted effort by the

© SUSAN LEGG

peat bog drying in a field in County Mayo

Irish government to create forest parks around the island in order to further preserve the bogland.

Ireland's Aran Islands—Inis Mór, Inis Meáin, and Inis Oírr—are three limestone islands situated on the island's west coast, on the mouth of Galway Bay. All three possess a stark, almost lonely beauty, featuring rugged, windswept cliffs, grassy knolls, and rocky fields divided by low-hanging stone walls. The impressive Dún Aenghus, an Iron Age fort, sits 300 miles above the Atlantic, on a jagged cliff side, on the western side of Inis Mór.

COUNTRY DIVISIONS

In ancient times, Ireland was divided into provinces. Each of these provinces was ruled by a king who protected and fought for its borders. These four provinces still have the same names today: Leinster, Ulster, Connacht, and Munster, with Ulster located in Northern Ireland.

The *dinnseanchas* (lore of notable places) poem entitled *Ard Ruide* (Ruide Headland) poetically describes the kingdoms of Ireland:

> Connacht in the west is the kingdom of learning, the seat of the greatest and wisest druids and magicians; the men of Connacht are famed for their eloquence, their handsomeness and their ability to pronounce true judgment.

> Ulster in the north is the seat of battle valour, of haughtiness, strife, boasting; the men of Ulster are the fiercest warriors of all Ireland, and the queens and goddesses of Ulster are associated with battle and death.

> Leinster, the eastern kingdom, is the seat of prosperity, hospitality, the importing of rich foreign wares like silk or wine; the men of Leinster are noble in speech and their women are exceptionally beautiful.

> Munster in the south is the kingdom of music and the arts, of harpers, of skilled ficheall (a type of chess) players and of nimble horsemen. The fairs of Munster were the greatest in all Ireland.

Leinster, Cúige Laighean in Irish, is the eastern province of Ireland, encompassing both the Midlands and the southeast of the island. Ireland's capital, Dublin, is the only actual city in the province of Leinster, but it contains approximately 40 percent of the Republic's population. Dublin is the cultural center of Ireland, offering a wide range of art, culture, and education, and within just one hour's drive are a handful of rivers, lakes, charming coastal villages, prehistoric ruins, and the verdant Wicklow Mountains.

Munster, or Cúige Mumhan in Irish, is Ireland's largest province and refers to the southernmost province of Ireland. This is the greenest, most verdant of the provinces, providing breathtaking scenery and a large supply of archaeological remains. Munster derived its name from the Celtic goddess Muma. Cork City, Limerick City, and Waterford City are the major towns in Munster, with the popular tourist sights of the Ring of Kerry, Blarney Castle, and the Cliffs of Moher located here.

The western province of Ireland is called Connacht, or Cúige Chonnacht, and is composed of the counties of Galway, Leitrim, Mayo, Roscommon, and Sligo. Connacht is situated on the west coast of Ireland and comprises Ireland's coastline, with thousands of bays, inlets, and islands. The name Connacht comes from the mythical king Conn of the Hundred Battles. Galway City and Sligo are the only major towns in this ancient province, but the area features many stunning sites, such as Galway City, the Aran Islands, Connemara National Park, Kylemore Abbey, Clifden, and the Gaeltacht.

The province of Ulster, Cúige Uladh, encompasses the counties in Northern Ireland. All but three of these counties—Cavan, Donegal, and Monaghan— are part of Great Britain.

The provinces of Ireland were further divided into counties by the Tudors of England in the 16th century, and in 1920, under the Government of Ireland Act 1920, the English Parliament completed the division, establishing 26 counties in the Republic of Ireland and six counties in Northern Ireland. This was finalized by the 1922 Anglo-Irish Treaty, which left the Republic as a separate, sovereign country. The central government is based in Dublin, handling foreign and local policy, as well as national affairs.

Ireland's 32 counties, grouped under the four provinces of Ireland, are listed here:

- Munster: Clare, Cork, Kerry, Limerick, Tipperary, and Waterford.

- Leinster: Dublin, Carlow, Kildare, Kilkenny, Laois, Longford, Louth, Meath, Offaly, Westmeath, Wexford, and Wicklow.

- Connacht: Sligo, Mayo, Galway, Roscommon, and Leitrim.

- Ulster: Cavan, Donegal, and Monaghan in the Republic; Antrim, Armagh, Derry, Down, Fermanagh, and Tyrone in Northern Ireland.

ACCENTS

There are numerous groups of accents throughout Ireland, which can make it difficult for an expat to understand what an Irish person is saying from one coast to the next. These accents break down into those within and surrounding Dublin; the accents of the west, midlands, and the south (Connacht, Leinster, and Munster); and the widely different accent of Northern Ireland. Just within Dublin there are a number of different accents that give listeners a hint at whether the person was raised in a working-class, middle-class, or an upper-class neighborhood. The posh "D4" accent (an accent from Dublin 4, an area in Dublin) is Irish with a hint of upper-class British thrown in, while the lower-class accent features a more drawn-out whine to the pronunciation. These accents tend to break down with upper-middle-class accents falling in the Southside, and lower working-class tending toward the Northside or inner-city areas. Of course, this is a broad generalization, and there are some working-class areas in the Southside and upper-class areas in the Northside.

The accents in Laois, Kildare, and Offaly feature a flat tone. The Cork and Kerry accents possess a lyrical quality, with Corkonians pronouncing words with an upward lilt on the last word, and an emphasis is put on the "brrr" sound on the letter *r*. The word *are* in Cork would sound almost like a pirate's "arrrgh." The Kerry accent is similar, but heavier, with even more emphasis on the "brrr" sound, almost sounding Scottish. Mayo and Galway have soft accents with hard *t*'s, with "sh" replacing many *s* sounds; for example, *stop* becomes "shtop."

IRISH LANGUAGE

Irish (Gaelic) and English are the two official languages of Ireland. The Irish language—along with Welsh and Breton—is among the oldest living languages in Europe, arriving in Ireland before 300 B.C. Irish is one of three Gaelic languages—along with Manx Gaelic and Scots Gaelic—and is a subdivision of the Goidelic branch of the Celtic language. All three branches of Gaelic are different, featuring various local dialects and influences that the English language has imparted on them. In modern Ireland, there are now three main dialects of Irish: Munster in the southwest, Connacht on the northern coast of Galway Bay, and Ulster in Northern Ireland.

The history of this beautiful language is rich and diverse, and falls into three periods: Old Irish (7th–9th century A.D.), Middle Irish (10th–16th century A.D.), and Modern Irish (16th century A.D.–present day). Historically, pockets of Irish-speaking people have congregated along the western coast of Ireland. In modern-day Ireland, this is where the Gaeltacht borders are.

© SARAH-JANE SWEENEY

street sign in Dublin

Until 1871, the Irish language was prohibited as a part of Great Britain's efforts to implement English language and customs. This repression was enforced during a time of natural and economic tragedies that led to social collapse and migration out of the country, resulting in a decline in the Irish language. Since Ireland became a free state, the loss of Irish has been compounded by economic pressures, changes brought about by industrialization, government laxity, and poor attitudes that plagued the language. Today Irish is the only Gaelic language that is on the UNESCO Interactive Endangered Languages list.

Despite this, much has been done throughout the island to revive, promote, and teach the Irish language. There are numerous newspapers that print exclusively in Irish, including *Lá Nua,* a daily newspaper; *Foinse,* a weekly newspaper; and *Saol,* a monthly newspaper. A number of magazines are printed in Irish, including *An tUltach, Comhar,* and *Feasta.* TG4 television broadcasts exclusively in Irish. Raidió na Gaeltachta, the island's Irish radio station, broadcasts in Irish. Adult- or child-oriented immersion classes are available in the local Gaeltacht. And, perhaps most importantly, Irish is taught in all public schools in Ireland, and a certain degree of proficiency is required in order to get accepted into university. While most students do not graduate fluent in Irish, they still have a rudimentary grasp of the language, much the way an American who studied Spanish in high school would be able to grasp Spanish. In 2007, the Irish language became officially recognized as a working language by the European Union.

All of this work has been paying off, with approximately 1.4 million of

IRISH IDIOMS

While the Irish speak English, it is not always exactly the same English as we speak in North America. They speak the Irish vernacular, a local version of English that has been influenced by centuries of tradition as well as the Irish language. Some words used in Ireland we wouldn't use in North America, yet they are used extravagantly in Ireland, coloring their conversation and their expressions in a distinct way. The following are a few of them.

- On the rip or on the tear: going on the drink, going to the pub
- On the piss: getting drunk
- Taking the piss: making fun of
- Langered or langers: drunk
- *Céad míle fáilte:* one hundred thousand welcome
- *Culchie:* a shortening of the word *agricultural*; refers to anybody born and bred outside of Dublin

- Deadly: very good or a great time
- Soft old day: a wet day
- Yoke: a broad term referring to just about anything: "that yoke there"
- Yer man: that man there (whose name is unknown)
- Yer one: that woman there (whose name is unknown)
- Jammers: packed
- Shattered or wrecked: tired
- Knackered: very tired
- Lose the head or lose me head: to lose control in anger
- Talking shite: not making much sense
- Blather: to talk excessively
- *Craic* or crack: fun
- Having the *craic:* having a good time

Ireland's population saying they are able to speak Irish. Now the Irish use their knowledge of the language—no matter how basic—as a source of nationalistic pride. At work conferences, social gatherings, sports events, and even in everyday language, you will hear Irish phrases dropped into conversation. I quite regularly had to decipher what my friends meant when saying, "*slán*" (goodbye), "He is such a *me feiner*" (he is so selfish), or "*Go raibh maith agat*" (thank you).

This symbol of nationalism began during the development of Irish nationalism in the 19th century and became hugely symbolic when Ireland became a free state in the 20th century. Irish is still a paramount symbol of the Irish state and nation, and remains an important method of communication in governmental, educational, literary, and cultural circles. However, there is no worry for an expatriate landing in Ireland being confused by the language. The Irish speak predominantly English on everyday occasions, even if it is sprinkled colorfully with Irish phrases.

- What's the *craic*: Hello or what's up?
- Eejit: idiot
- Jammy: lucky
- Scallywag: someone who gets up to mischief
- *Sláinte:* cheers
- Arseways: making a mess of things
- *Slán:* goodbye
- Bucketing or lashing: raining hard
- Crisps: potato chips
- Chips: fries
- Cute hoor: a sly or untrustworthy person
- Dodder: waste time
- Dosser: lazy person
- Fag: cigarette
- Fair play: well done
- *Feck:* used instead of the other F word; used commonly as an adjective and isn't meant to offend
- Gone in the head: mad, crazy
- Nappy: diaper
- Snog, shift: to make out or kiss
- Gas: funny
- Give out to: scold
- Yonks: a long time
- Queue: line (standing in a line)
- I'm going to my *leaba:* I'm going to bed
- He or she is such a *me feiner:* he or she is so selfish
- Did he throw the gob?: Did he try to kiss you?
- Bog: toilet
- It will be grand: things will be fine
- *Ceilidh* or *ceili* (KAY-lee): a social evening or dancing session

IRISH SYMBOLISM

With Ireland's ancient history and rich heritage, it is no surprise that there has been an emergence of symbols that represent Ireland. The most famous of these is, undoubtedly, the shamrock. The shamrock, originating from the Irish word *seamrog,* is a three-leaf clover that grows throughout Ireland. Legend says that St. Patrick used the shamrock to demonstrate the Christian Trinity.

The Celtic cross is another Irish symbol that is synonymous with Ireland. The symbol is a traditional Christian cross combined with a ring surrounding the intersection. The theory is that St. Patrick combined the sun cross with the Christian cross to show the pagan followers of ancient Ireland how important the cross was.

The Irish flag represents a source of nationalistic pride, which still remains intense. The Irish flag is composed of three vertical bands of green, white, and orange, all equal in size. The green band, on the far left of the flag, is a symbol for the Catholic majority. The orange band, on the far right of the flag, represents the Protestant minority. The middle white band represents their unity.

The Irish harp is the oldest official symbol of Ireland. It is widely used on Ireland's passport, Irish coins, state seals, the presidential flag, uniforms, and official documents. Guinness adopted the Irish harp as its trademark in 1862, and the harp has been associated with it ever since.

The Claddagh is a symbol that originated in Claddagh, a small fishing village just outside of Galway. The symbol—composed of two hands holding a crowned heart—is often worn on a ring as a representation of love, friendship, or loyalty. Legend says that the right hand represents Dagda, the father of Celtic Gods, and the left hand represents Anu, the mother goddess. The mystical Celtic spirit Beathauile represents the crown.

WEATHER

There is an old saying, "You don't go to Ireland for the weather." Another one says, "The usual way to tell the difference between winter and summer in Ireland is to measure the temperature of the rain." You get the idea. It rains a lot in Ireland. Nowhere else in the world do meteorologists classify rain so enthusiastically. In fact, the national costume could be the raincoat with a pair of Wellies (rain boots). Rain can fall in thick droves, which the Irish refer to as "lashing," or it can fall in fine mists that give way to dazzling rainbows. It can "spit" rain, where a few isolated raindrops fall, or it can "shower," lasting only a few minutes and often occurring when the sun is shining. Only when it is a steady downpour of rain, worthy of a *brolly* (an umbrella), do the Irish classify it as true rain. All of this rain is due to Ireland's oceanic climate, which is ruled by the Atlantic Ocean. This means the temperature across the island remains fairly moderate throughout the year, dominated by rain that is accumulated from the ocean. But this rain is what keeps the grass a lush green and the temperamental sea off its coast a deep, steel blue.

However, the weather in Ireland can also be quite changeable, so even if you awaken to clouds and rain in the morning, you are likely to see at least a peekaboo sun, especially during the summer months. On the flip side of this, don't be fooled by bright morning sunshine, as the clouds and rain can roll in and start lashing at any second. Storms blow in from the Atlantic without a moment's notice, drenching the land and then leaving before you know what hit you.

Even still, while most foreigners have the impression that it rains nonstop in Ireland, two out of three hourly observations do not have any measurable rainfall at all, according to The Irish Meteorological Service. Rainfall varies greatly, depending on the area of the country you are in. The average hourly rainfall in Ireland ranges 0.04–0.08 inch (1–2 millimeters). Much of the eastern half of Ireland receives 74–99 centimeters (29–39 inches) of rain a year, while the traditionally wetter west of Ireland receives 99–124 centimeters (39–49 inches) a year.

Temperatures in Ireland rarely get below 0°C (32°F) in the winter, although there have definitely been exceptions to this. When the weather does turn freezing or even a sprinkling of snow falls, the country typically grinds to a halt and people panic. Generally, however, the temperatures hover right around 4–10°C (40–50°F). In the summer months the temperature is typically between 16–21°C (60–70°F), with July and August being the warmest months, and May and June the sunniest months.

FLORA AND FAUNA

Ireland has a less diverse animal and plant species than Continental Europe or Great Britain, due to rising sea levels that isolated the island after the Ice Age. There are 55 mammal species, with only 26 species that are native to Ireland. Since civilization began to expand, Ireland lost its bear, wolf, native cattle, wildcat, and beaver. However, the island still retains many species of small rodents in the woods and fields, and there are 400 bird species that roam the skies, most of which come from Africa, Greenland, and Iceland. In the sea, species such as sharks, turtles, and dolphins abound.

© SARAH-JANE SWEENEY

wildflowers growing in the Irish fields

THE IRISH MILE AND IRISH TIME

Some things in Ireland are beyond the comprehension of a foreigner. Two such things are the concepts of the Irish mile and Irish time, which are both flexible and fluid. The Irish mile can mean to the next post box or the next town and can roughly be translated as a "country mile." It is vague and adaptable, changing to accommodate any distance that the speaker may wish. If you ask for walking directions from a local, he may downplay the distance or send you on a scenic route, assuring you it is just an Irish mile away. He may also throw in random suggestions, such as "down the hill, around two bends, and beyond a rock positioned at the third farm." Trust me. Get a map. I was sucked into this when I first moved to Ireland and ended up walking for two hours.

The Irish view time totally different than we do in North America. Being on time is only sometimes viewed seriously; simply arriving is the goal. If you arrive on time for a dinner reservation, you may end up waiting on your own for quite a while. While this may be inconvenient, it is also part of Irish charm.

strolling down an Irish *boreen* (lane)

They are just happy to be living in the moment. The saying "so laid-back he was nearly horizontal" probably originated to fit an Irish person. I once asked an Irish friend of mine about "clocking in" when you get to work, and he actually laughed at the idea.

No snakes can be found anywhere in Ireland, with the only indigenous reptile the common lizard. Legend has it that St. Patrick drove the snakes from Ireland, standing on a hill and using his staff to herd the slithering reptiles into the sea, banishing them for all of eternity. However, this probably has more to do with geography and temperature than anything St. Patrick did. Hundreds of millions of years ago, Ireland was entirely submersed beneath water. Since the most recent ice age began, about three million years ago, glaciers have advanced and retreated more than 20 times, often blanketing Ireland with ice. Ireland only thawed out for the first time about 15,000 years ago. Snakes, being cold-blooded creatures, are not able to survive where the ground freezes. Since Ireland first thawed out, it has been separated from Scotland—which does have a few snakes—by 12 miles of cold water, so the snakes simply were never able to get there.

Although Ireland was at one time almost entirely forested with pine, oak, and birch trees, these trees were cleared by the English to provide timber for their shipbuilders. In fact, only 1 percent of the hardwood forests survived, and Ireland has had to import wood for the past 200 years. Ireland is now dotted with soft green pasture land, which is blanketed by many species of wildflowers, gorse (a wild evergreen shrub), and various types of ferns. Ireland's mild climate allows the growth of many subtropical species, such as the palm tree, although they remain quite short and stumpy compared to what you would find on the beaches of the Caribbean.

Social Climate

Europe has historically been a place where many have sought immigration status. Despite this, immigration is relatively new to Ireland. From the 17th century onward, Ireland has been plagued by economic hardship and religious persecution that has resulted in waves of emigrants exiting the country. In fact, in 1995 Mary Robinson, then president of Ireland, often referred to the "Fifth Province" of Ireland, speaking of the 30 million people worldwide who claim Irish as their heritage.

It has only been since the Celtic Tiger in the 1990s that Ireland's economy has become so strong that an influx of immigrants, mostly from North Africa and Eastern Europe, began arriving. Since then, Ireland has experienced one of the fastest increases in immigration rates in history. In less than 10 years, Ireland's immigration population has increased from just below 1 percent to approximately 12 percent.

While Ireland's recent recession, the credit crunch, and the high cost of living have caused immigration to drop, there are still approximately half a million non-Irish people that live in a country with a population of about four and a half million people. As a result, the face of Ireland has begun to change, with Polish bars, Chinese shops, and Indian markets a common sight, particularly in the larger, more cosmopolitan cities like Dublin, Cork, and Galway.

Immigration still remains a volatile issue in Ireland, with some people feeling that any and all jobs should go to the Irish. This is exacerbated by the recession and the continuing high cost of living in Ireland. However, the overall attitude of the Irish is a general acceptance of immigrants and their contribution to the economy and social fabric of Ireland.

While Ireland is a place that many love to visit as a tourist, I did not

FAMOUS IRISH PEOPLE

Thanks to years of tumultuous history, an often unstable economy, oppression by the English, and exploitation by the Catholic Church, the Irish have fled to the corners of the world, leaving their mark everywhere they go. Here are just a few of the most famous people that claim Irish roots.

- **U2** are a famous Irish rock band. On vocals and guitar is Bono; guitar, keyboards, and vocals is The Edge; Adam Clayton performs bass guitar; and Larry Mullen Jr. is on drums and percussion. U2 have remained successful since their debut in 1976, selling more than 150 million records worldwide and winning 22 Grammy Awards.

- Actor **Pierce Brosnon,** born in 1952, is an Irish actor and producer. He trained at the Drama Centre in London, from which followed a stage acting career, followed by a television acting career, before breaking into films. He is most well-known for his role as James Bond in several movies.

- Comedian **Conan O'Brien,** the host of late-night talk show *Conan,* is a famous comedian in America. While born in Brookline, Massachusetts, he was raised in an Irish Catholic family.

- **Enya** – her real name is Eithne Ní Bhraonáin – is an Irish singer and songwriter who began her musical career in 1980 when she joined her family's band, Clannad. She left to begin a solo career and has sold approximately 70 million albums as of 2009. She has earned four Grammys and one Academy Award nomination.

- **Sinéad O'Connor** is another successful Irish singer and songwriter. She became famous in the late 1980s with the release of her first album, *The Lion and the Cobra,* and achieved worldwide

encounter many Americans who had actually made the move to Ireland. Perhaps this is because America is such a large country that if somebody is looking for a change, they can simply move a few states away. Americans who do move to Ireland are typically looking for their ancestors or their heritage and then end up staying, or, like me, are college students who end up staying after graduation. Despite the relatively few Americans who live in Ireland, there are small circles of expats that congregate in the larger cities of Dublin, Cork, and Galway.

IRELAND AND FOREIGNERS

Overall, the Irish are open and accepting of foreigners. They will help somebody who looks lost on the street, give directions if necessary, recommend the best hotels to stay at or restaurants to visit, and even invite you for a pint in the local pub. Then they will pepper you with questions about your experience in Ireland, where you're from, how you got to Ireland, and what your perception is so far. By the end of your third Guinness you will be waxing fame when she covered the song "Nothing Compares 2 U."

- A new indie rock band named **Two Door Cinema Club** formed in Ireland in 2007, giving the country a fresh, new sound and winning the Choice Music Prize for Irish Album of the Year 2010.

- **Oscar Wilde** (1854–1900) is a famous Irish author who published *The Happy Prince* (1888), *The Picture of Dorian Gray* (1891), and *The Importance of Being Earnest* (1895).

- **George Bernard Shaw** (1856–1950) was an Irish playwright who cofounded the London School of Economics. He wrote more than 60 plays, including *Widowers' Houses* (1892) and *The Devil's Disciple* (1897).

- **Samuel Beckett** (1906–1989) was born in Foxrock, Dublin, but lived most of his years in Paris. He wrote his trilogy of novels, *Molloy, Malone Dies,* and *The Unnameable,* and the play *Waiting for Godot.* In 1969 he was awarded the Nobel Prize for Literature.

- Irish novelist and poet **James Joyce** (1882–1941) is considered one of the most influential writers of the 20th century. He is most well-known for writing *Ulysses* (1922) but also wrote *Dubliners* (1914), *A Portrait of the Artist as a Young Man* (1916), and *Finnegans Wake* (1939).

- Diverging from Ireland's theme of artists and scholars is **Robert Boyle** (1627–1691). Boyle was a 17th-century scientist who was educated in chemistry, physics, and theology. He is regarded as the father of chemistry due to establishing Boyle's law, which states that the volume of a gas decreases with increasing pressure, and vice versa.

lyrical about the wonders that are James Joyce, and this Irish person you met on the street a few hours ago will be your new best friend.

The Irish are overall a friendly and welcoming bunch, with socializing the biggest part of their society. Pubs are the main place for socializing, particularly in the small towns. They are typically cozy, welcoming spots where the locals haunt, families congregate, and foreigners hang out. You can drink a few (or more) pints, eat pub grub, dance, and sometimes listen to live music by local musicians.

That being said, there is a complex layer of feelings toward Americans. *The Simpsons* is adored by almost everyone, *Sex and the City* house parties still crop up, and the golden arches of McDonald's dot numerous streets, even in the rural areas. However, while the Irish will certainly love you and be willing to chat with you over a pint, you must be careful when discussing politics or U.S. foreign policy, for fear of offending or even angering them. Some Irish adamantly disagree with some American policies: citizens being allowed to have guns, the death penalty, and the war in Iraq, to name a few.

But despite any disagreements with America's policies, the Irish are pragmatic in their knowledge that Ireland's economy is highly dependent on the U.S. market. In fact, the Irish have a saying: "When America sneezes, we get pneumonia." The global recession of 2008–2011 was an eye-opener for the Irish people, and they continue to learn how to be self-sufficient in a world that is precariously balanced on the edge of depression.

Despite the prevailing liberal, left-leaning attitude of the Irish, some vestiges of their Catholic upraising still hold true. While overall the new economies and industries of the 21st century are being embraced, many view Ireland as a refuge for morality, where traditional values are still upheld. Many Irish abhor abortion (it is, in fact, still illegal in Ireland), divorce only became legal in Ireland in 1997, homosexuality was only decriminalized in 1993, and family values are still quite strong there. Every single one of my friends in college still went home to their parents' house on Sundays for the traditional roast dinner.

The Catholic Church continues to wield some influence over Irish society, but this is slowly weakening, in part due to the scandals that have rocked the Church, causing some Irish people to lose their faith in Catholicism and the values it upholds. The Catholic Church no longer controls the legislature or the government of Ireland, and the younger generation is moving further and further away from the establishment of the Church.

praying at Knock Shrine

HISTORY, GOVERNMENT, AND ECONOMY

The nation of Ireland evolved over two millennia, with powerful internal and external forces that shaped the Ireland we know today. While there were people inhabiting the island throughout early civilization, the Celtic migrations during the first millennium brought the origins of Ireland's language and culture. The 5th century A.D. saw the beginning of Irish Christianity and the Irish monks, who did much to sustain the heritage of Christianity, writing Ireland's ancient oral stories and preserving these writings during the Middle Ages.

Ireland is now a thriving member of the European Union (EU), with a highly developed democracy and a modern economy. While much of its government and history is based on Britain's, today's history is being written by current affairs such as immigration, economic hardship, and terrorism, which color each step toward the future. Ireland remains proud of its recent and ancient history, most notably its emergence as a free state and most recently as an economic powerhouse during the Celtic Tiger years of the 20th century.

© SARAHJANE SWEENEY

History

ANCIENT IRELAND

The early history of Ireland blends fact with myth, resulting in a time of kings and gods, pagan myths, and stories. Few facts exist about ancient Irish history, but what little is known comes from references in Roman writings, poetry and mythical stories, and archaeology. It is theorized that the earliest inhabitants arrived around 6000 B.C., after the polar ice caps retreated and the climate was more hospitable. These early inhabitants were hunters, fishers, and gatherers who settled along the eastern coast of Ireland.

In 4000 B.C. the establishment of farming and agriculture ushered in a Neolithic culture, characterized by stone weapons and tools, pottery, rectangular wooden houses, huge stone monuments, and communal megalithic tombs where they buried their dead, many of which were astronomically aligned, such as Newgrange. The people learned to keep sheep, pigs, and cattle, and to raise crops to sustain themselves.

The Bronze Age in Ireland began around 2000 B.C., when the settlers were taught to alloy copper with tin to produce bronze artifacts. Elaborate gold and bronze ornaments, weapons, and tools were made during this period. The Bronze Age settlers erected stone circles in Ireland, as well as *crannogs* (lake dwellings), which were easily defended.

Around 400 B.C., the Iron Age arrived when the Celts invaded Ireland. Their victory was a result of tempered-iron weapons and their superior skills in battle. During the 5th century the fighting eased and the clans joined to form the ancient kingdoms of Ireland: in Tuisceart, Airgialla, Ulaid, Mide, Laigin, Mumhain, and Cóiced Ol nEchmacht. Within these ancient Irish kingdoms existed a rich culture and a society with a distinct class system separating the royalty, the middle class, and the slaves.

CHRISTIANITY COMES TO IRELAND

In the spiritual history of Ireland, the greatest and most famous name is Patrick, who later became St. Patrick. His arrival in Ireland resulted in major changes and civilizing influences that further shaped the country. Historians now know that Patrick was born to wealthy British parents in the 4th century and was captured by Irish raiders when he was 16 years old. He was sold into slavery in Ireland and remained there, working as a shepherd, for six years. Lonely and scared, Patrick turned to religion and became a devout Christian. He managed to escape back to England when he was 22 but later returned to Ireland as a missionary, beginning a lifelong quest to convert the Irish to Christianity until his death on March 17th, A.D. 461.

St. Patrick is credited with the preservation of the tribal and social patterns of the Irish; the introduction of the Roman alphabet, which enabled Irish monks to preserve Celtic oral literature; and the collapse of the pagan druid tradition. Scholars at the Irish monasteries learned Latin and Christian theology, founded monasteries across Ireland, and made illuminated manuscripts, the most famous of which is the Book of Kells. Irish monks are today credited with keeping Latin learning alive during the Dark Ages.

THE VIKINGS

Irish civilization was curtailed by the invasion of the Scandinavians around A.D. 795. Thanks to navigable rivers and streams, broad pastures, and unorganized inhabitants, Ireland was ripe for attack. The Vikings—an umbrella term for the Danes and the Norsemen—looted and destroyed monasteries, abducted women and children and used them as slaves, and raided and killed entire villages. The Vikings established the city of *Án Dubh Linn* (Dublin), meaning the "black pool," as well as Wexford, Cork, and Limerick. Additionally, the Vikings gave Ireland its name, combining the Gaelic word *Éire* with the Viking word *land*: Éireann (Ireland).

The fighting between the Irish and the Vikings continued for more than two centuries, until the legendary Brian Boru came into the picture. Born around A.D. 940, Brian organized the Irish armies and led them in battle against the Danes. Brian defeated the Danes, recapturing Cashel, and becoming king of Munster. In 1002, Brian became the *Ard Ri* (High King) of the entire island of Ireland. This was the first time there had been just one king who was responsible for the defense of Ireland against the Vikings. Brian set to work rebuilding churches that had been damaged or ruined and building new monasteries, as well as organizing searches overseas to replace lost books and artifacts.

Gradually, however, the disruptive, unruly forces began to stir again. In 1013, the people of Leinster and Dublin revolted. In an effort to curtail the revolt, Brian's armies ravaged much of Leinster and besieged Dublin. After a break for Christmas, on Good Friday 1014 Brian returned again to fight the Battle of Clontarf. By this stage, the Vikings of Dublin had joined forces with troops from Scotland and the Isle of Man. The ensuing Battle of Clontarf resulted in thousands of deaths, from which Brian Boru's armies eventually emerged as the victors. But while Brian Boru's army won the battle, he was killed by a group of Vikings as they retreated.

Ireland soon returned to small, disparate battles; however, the Vikings and the Irish no longer battled for power, with the Irish clearly being the dominant force. The Viking presence remained in Ireland, but they soon began to intermarry, eventually becoming as Irish as the Irish themselves, leading to a lasting peace.

ANGLO-NORMAN INVASION

During the 11th and 12th centuries in Ireland, the Catholic Church prospered, and in the mid-12th century it was reformed. The Church of Rome used a document attributed to the Roman Emperor Constantine entitled *Constitutum domini Constantini imperatoris* to claim ownership of all the land and islands it could. Ireland, the land of saints and scholars, was on the list of donated lands. The island was still rife with paganism, and in the eyes of Rome, a godless and rebellious place. In 1155, Pope Adrian IV gave King Henry II of England an official document that bestowed papal approval to invade and conquer Ireland, so long as he agreed to pay annual revenue to the papal treasury. Many historians, however, believe this document was a forgery.

Despite permission to invade Ireland, King Henry II had his hands full fighting the French and Spanish. It wasn't until 1167, when the deposed king of Ireland, Diarmuid MacMurrough, met King Henry II in France, that anything was done. MacMurrough begged the king's help in regaining his throne. King Henry II pledged his support, and MacMurrough took a letter of recommendation from the king to Richard FitzGilbert de Clare, famously known as Strongbow, in Wales. MacMurrough granted Strongbow his daughter in marriage and promised the right of succession to the kingdom of Leinster in exchange for his help.

MacMurrough returned to Ireland in 1169 with trained foreign mercenaries and succeeded in recovering Leinster and capturing Dublin and the area around it, establishing the Anglo-Norman colony called The Pale. This marks the beginning of foreign rule over Ireland. When MacMurrough died, he passed his kingdom to Richard Strongbow, but when King Henry II landed in Ireland with his armies in 1171, Strongbow and most of the Irish kings submitted fully to him as Lord of Ireland, further cementing Britain's rule over Ireland.

THE TUDOR INVASION

In the late 15th century, King Henry VII began a mission to make Ireland a part of the English kingdom and extended English law over all of Ireland. He passed his mission on to his son, King Henry VIII of England, who used a "surrender and regrant" policy, in which he tried to coerce Irish chiefs into taking secure titles, lands, and a role in government in exchange for replacing their language and customs with English ways. This campaign continued into the rule of his daughter, Queen Elizabeth I, who tried to make English law and local government more palatable by treating the Gaelic chiefs as good subjects.

This policy didn't work like the Tudors wanted it to. The government had a great deal of difficulty controlling self-serving conquistadors like Humphrey Gilbert and Walter Raleigh, who were more interested in making their fortunes rather than teaching the natives the benefits of

Saint Carthage's Cathedral, Lismore, County Waterford

© SARAH-JANE SWEENEY

English rule. The result was a slow escalation of violent battles, culminating in the Nine Years War (1594–1603), in which the minority lords joined forces with support from the Spanish king, Phillip III, to revolt against England.

The English armies crushed the rebellion in 1603, and the lands of the Irish lords were confiscated and given to English lords. At this time, a central government was established for the first time, and Irish culture, law, and the language began to be replaced. Subsequently, James I of England pronounced English law the sole law of the land, closing Catholic schools and opening Protestant institutions. During this era, the distinctions between Irish, Anglo-Irish, and English became realigned with Catholicism (Irish) and Protestantism (English).

CROMWELL AND WILLIAM OF ORANGE

In the ensuing years, England sank into civil war, leaving Ireland largely to its own devices. However, when King Charles I was executed in January 1649, English Parliament commissioned Oliver Cromwell to invade Ireland. Determined to impose Protestantism on Ireland and enforce the authority of the British in Ireland, Cromwell took 10,000 disciplined forces and captured Drogheda in 1649, and Dublin shortly thereafter. He proceeded to confiscate all Catholic holdings and interjected Protestant control over the island. Within two years of his departure from Ireland in 1650, most of Ireland was under English (Protestant) rule.

In 1685 James II, a Catholic, succeeded to the English throne. The Irish had high hopes that he would be more sympathetic to them than previous rulers, and for a short time James II was able to have his Parliament restore all Catholic lands that had been confiscated since 1641. Unfortunately for the Irish, the English Parliament was anxious about his Catholic tendencies and invited the Dutchman William of Orange to take over the monarchy, deposing James II and forcing him to flee to France. William of Orange and his wife, Mary, daughter of James II, became King and Queen of England. William of Orange proceeded to take his armies to Ireland, defeating the Irish forces in the Battle of the Boyne in July 1690.

Triumphant in the aftermath of the Battle of the Boyne, the Protestants took numerous steps to procure lasting victory over the Catholics. They continued confiscations of Catholic property, reducing them from 22 percent to 14 percent, passed an act in 1704 preventing Catholics from buying land, and forced existing estates owned by Catholics to divide the lands between all of the sons of the family, gradually reducing them to small holdings. The passage of the Penal Laws made it illegal for a Catholic to even sit in the Dublin parliament, hold office, or intermarry with a Protestant.

REBELLION AND UNION

Influenced by both the American and French Revolutions, the Irish established the Society of United Irishmen in the 18th century, aiming to gain emancipation for Catholics and unite Irish Protestants and Catholics in one goal: independence from England. In 1798, the revolutionaries launched an armed rebellion against British troops. With help from French reinforcements, the revolutionaries got as far as Sligo but were eventually defeated by the British forces.

Although the rebellion was quashed, it became clear to the government that Republicanism in Ireland could not be ignored. To solve this problem, British prime minister William Pitt induced the Irish Parliament to pass the Act of Union on January 1, 1801, which formally united the Kingdom of Great Britain and the Kingdom of Ireland, creating the United Kingdom of Great Britain and Ireland. All local and regional parliaments were eliminated, and the entire United Kingdom was ruled from a centralized London parliament.

THE POTATO FAMINE

Between 1845 and 1849, a fungus attacked the potato crops of Ireland, a crop that had previously provided 60 percent of the country's food. The Great

© SUSAN LEGG

an abandoned cottage in County Mayo's countryside

Potato Famine of Ireland is credited with killing about a million Irish people from starvation and epidemic disease. Another two million or so emigrated out of Ireland in under a decade. The effects of the famine were worsened by action and inaction on the part of the English government. At the time of the potato famine, the government was in the grips of a fashionable policy called laissez-faire, which argued that the state should not intervene in the economy. By 1900, only about 4.5 million Irish remained living in Ireland, with abandoned and derelict farmland littering the countryside. Today in Mayo and Galway you can still see signs of these derelict farms, crumbling to the ground and nearly obscured by grass.

THE 20TH CENTURY

The inaction on the part of the British during the potato famine left the Irish angry and bitter. Anti-British sentiment began to increase, leading to an intense political reawakening in the early 20th century and the beginning of years of unrest and violence in Ireland.

On Easter Monday, April 24, 1916, the Irish nationalists staged an insurrection. Famously called the Easter Rising, the uprising was organized by the Irish Republican Brotherhood and aimed to establish an Irish Republic and end British rule. The rebels commandeered the Dublin Post Office and various other key sites throughout the city, raising the Irish Flag and declaring themselves the Republic of Ireland. After seven days of fighting, the British quelled the rebellion, court-marshaling and executing 15 members of the rebellion.

Despite what may have initially seemed like a failure, the Easter Rising led

THE WORLD'S FIRST POLICE FORCE

It may be hard to believe, but before the 1800s, there was no such thing as a law-enforcement force in Ireland or, indeed, the world. In 1809 a British man named Sir Robert Peel became a member of parliament (MP) for the Irish seat of Cashel City, County Tipperary. During his term he introduced the Act of Parliament, which brought about the formation of the Irish Peace Preservation Force.

In 1822, Sir Robert Peel introduced the Constabulary Act, which replaced the earlier peacekeepers with the newly formed Constabulary Police of Ireland. The job of the constabulary was to arrest those who broke the laws, as well as to prevent crime. Known as "peelers" or "bobbies," Sir Robert Peel's constabulary (both those established in Great Britain and in Ireland) later became known as the world's first police force.

Robert Peel's Metropolitan Police Act was passed in 1829, permanently appointing paid police constables to patrol the streets of London and enforce order in Ireland. In 1883 special Irish branches were set up to deal with Irish nationalist fighters.

© SARAH-JANE SWEENEY

getting help from an Irish *Garda* (police officer)

In 1923, after the creation of the Irish Free Station, an unarmed Irish police force named *An Garda Síochana* (The Guardians of the Peace) was introduced. The national police service is headquartered in Dublin's Phoenix Park and represents every county in Ireland.

to a change in public opinion. In the 1918 generation election, Sinn Féin, the left-wing party, triumphed, taking numerous seats in the Irish Parliament. The Sinn Féin MPs (members of parliament) refused to sit in the British Parliament and formed their own parliament called the Dáil Éireann (Irish Parliament). This led to the start of Ireland's War of Independence in 1919. The Irish Republican Army fought a primarily guerilla war with the British throughout the year. In 1920, the Government of Ireland Act was passed, giving Ireland two parliaments—one for the Unionists and one for the Nationalists—but keeping both parliaments under the United Kingdom Parliament. Fighting continued, but in July of 1921, a cease-fire between the British and the IRA led to negotiations that eventually culminated in the Anglo-Irish Treaty on

December 6th, 1921. The treaty established the Irish Free State, which was composed of 26 of the country's 32 counties and allowed it to become self-governing under the dominion of the United Kingdom. The treaty allowed the six counties of Northern Ireland to remain part of the United Kingdom.

The Anglo-Irish Treaty divided the Dáil Éireann and resulted in the Irish Civil War. Fighting was rife between pro-treaty and anti-treaty factions, the pro-treaty side feeling the terms were the best the country could possibly hope for, while the anti-treaty side angry that the treaty didn't result in a united, independent Ireland. However, neither side had the resources or the soldiers to win the conflict, and ultimately the fighting ended with a truce (of sorts) in May 1923, and the original treaty stood.

In 1937, the Republic of Ireland wrote and adapted a new constitution that created the independent and democratic state of Éire (Ireland). After World War II, in 1948, Ireland became the Republic of Ireland, officially cutting all ties and leaving the British Commonwealth.

The mid-1950s in Ireland was tainted by continuing emigration, high unemployment, and economic depression. Nearly 60,000 people emigrated in 1958 alone. Various plans went into effect to rebuild the Irish economy, including restoring the agricultural industries and giving subsidies to foreign companies that set up factories in the Republic. By the early 1960s, the Irish economy was growing, and exports continued to rise.

PEACE TALKS

With ongoing economic fluctuations, Ireland joined the European Economic Community (the forerunner to the EU) in 1973. This brought enormous economic benefits to Ireland in both direct aid and investments from foreign companies, transforming Ireland from a predominantly agricultural society into a modern, technologically advanced one. Joining the EEC forced Ireland to develop policies on issues they had not previously had any say over. However, Ireland still faced rising debt and unemployment throughout the 1980s, and severe economic problems were at the forefront of Irish politics.

Throughout the years since the Republic had gained its freedom from the United Kingdom, violence in the North of Ireland had waxed and waned numerous times. In the 1980s, the "Troubles" in Northern Ireland were addressed in the Anglo-Irish Agreement, an agreement between the United Kingdom and the Republic of Ireland that gave the Irish government an advisory role in the governing of Northern Ireland. In December 1993, the English and the Irish signed the Downing Street Declaration, reaffirming that Northern Ireland would be transferred to the Republic only if a majority of people in the

North agreed. Peace talks between the North and South continued and finally culminated in the Good Friday Agreement in 1998, a historic breakthrough that pledged both governments to resolving their differences through peaceful and democratic means. The agreement envisioned a peaceful future based on equality, mutual respect, and acceptance of each other's diversity.

MODERN IRELAND

Throughout the peace talks that occurred near the end of the 20th century, the Republic of Ireland was experiencing an unprecedented economic boom. Ireland proved to be one of the fastest growing economies in the world, growing by 40 percent, and property values tripled between 1995 and 2004, earning Ireland's economy the nickname the Celtic Tiger. Between 1987 and 2003, unemployment dropped from 17 percent to 4 percent, with economic growth averaging at more than 5 percent between 1987 and the end of the century.

But, as with all rapid growth, problems developed in Ireland. Traffic in the big cities became relentless, urban sprawl increased, as did water and air pollution, and the cost of living skyrocketed so high that by 2003 Ireland was tied with Finland as one the most expensive countries in the EU. Ireland became known across the island and abroad as Rip-off Republic, thanks to a popular RTÉ television show that highlighted the high cost of living in Ireland.

In 2008 the Irish economy collapsed when a series of banking scandals rocked Ireland and the unsustainable real estate boom finally began to deteriorate. The real estate boom was perpetuated by government incentives to

© SARAH-JANE SWEENEY

Traffic in the cities can be very congested.

IRELAND'S MAIN POLITICAL PARTIES

Irish politics are dominated by two political parties that evolved from Ireland's civil war: Fianna Fáil and Fine Gael. However, there are 11 total political parties, and coalition governments are common.

Fine Gael is the largest government party in Ireland as of 2011. It is viewed as a center-right wing party but also identifies with the values of social democracy. Fianna Fáil is Fine Gael's main competition, featuring a decidedly Republican outlook. Fianna Fáil was originally founded by Éamon de Valera in 1926 as a party that was radically anti-Treaty.

The Labour Party traditionally participates in coalition governments and sits on the center-left of politics. The infamous Sinn Féin party, meaning "ourselves" in Irish, is the leading left-wing party. It was founded by Arthur Griffin in 1905 and has historically been linked to the Provisional Irish Republican Army (IRA). This party is focused on achieving reunification of Ireland, as well as an expansion of social services in Ireland.

The Socialist Party is a Marxist political party formed in 1996 by extreme left-leaning members of the Labour Party. The People Before Profit Alliance (PBPA) party was formed in 2005. It aligns itself with the left, seeking to eliminate neoliberalism and war. Politicians who align themselves with the Independents do exactly what their name says: They are independent and can align themselves with whichever party they want to. These politicians are sometimes called upon to support minority governments.

The Workers and Unemployed Action Group (WUAG) is a left-wing political party formed in response to unemployment and a declining economic situation in the 1980s. The Green Party advocates ecologically sound and socially liberal policies, and the Workers' Party aligns itself with the international workers and communist parties. The Communist Party of Ireland was historically influential with the trade union movements, but today it is quite small and hasn't stood in any recent elections.

property developers, who borrowed huge amounts from Irish banks, such as the Anglo Irish Bank, which expanded by extending these loans. Then the bubble popped and the economy collapsed. The declining Irish property values, trading difficulty, and lax superiority by the regulatory body of banks caused a rapid deterioration of Ireland's economy, and the island sank into a deep recession. In January 2009, the Anglo Irish Bank became nationalized by the Irish government when it was determined that money alone would not be able to save it. In February 2009, the Bank of Ireland (BOI) and the Allied Irish Bank (AIB) each received €3.5 billion in bailout money, but by September 2010, the cost of bailing out the banks of Ireland had risen to €45 billion.

With unemployment soaring to 11 percent and angry protesters marching in Dublin over the government's handling of the economic crisis, something needed to be done. On November 21, 2010, the Irish government asked for a bailout from the EU, agreeing to an €85 billion rescue package. As part of the package, the government promised to pass an austerity program that would include four years of tax increases and spending cuts.

Shortly after the bailout was announced, Ireland's prime minister, Brian Cowen, called an election, which took place in February 2011. Angry at the government for its role in the recession, the people resoundingly voted Fianna Fáil—Brian Cowen's party—out of power in the worst defeat since the beginning of the Irish state in 1921. Opposition party Fine Gael won a record 76 seats, while Labour became the second-largest party. Fine Gael leader Enda Kenny was announced as prime minister in a coalition government formed with Labour.

Government

The Republic of Ireland is a modern, independent, and sovereign parliamentary democracy. The basic law of Ireland is ruled by the *Bunreacht na hEireann* (Irish Constitution), a fundamental legal document that establishes the government of Ireland and defines the powers of the legislative, executive, and judicial branches. In addition, the Constitution sets out the fundamental rights of its citizens, covering the family, personal rights, education, private property, and religion.

The *Uachtarán na hÉireann* (President of Ireland) is the head of state. This role is mostly a ceremonial one, carrying out certain constitutional powers and functions. The president is directly elected by the people for a seven-year term,

Dublin's Four Courts, Ireland's main court buildings

© SARAH JANE SWEENEY

THE PROPORTIONAL REPRESENTATION SYSTEM

Ireland has a very different electoral system than the United States, using the proportional representation system, with a single transferable vote in multiseat constituencies; for example, at Dáil elections. In this system, the names of all candidates appear in alphabetical order on the ballot, and the voter simply indicates his or her choices in order, placing a 1 next to the first choice, a 2 next to the second choice, and so on for all candidates on the paper.

When all the papers have been counted, the quota is calculated in order to find the smallest number that guarantees the election of a candidate. This formula is calculated by dividing the total valid votes by the amount of seats to be filled plus one. If a candidate receives more than the necessary quota, the additional votes are transferred to the remaining candidates in the order of preference indicated by the voters. In each round of counting, the candidate with the least amount of votes is eliminated, and their votes are redistributed, again according to order of preference. Counting continues until all seats are filled. While this may be a complex, labor-intensive system, the proportional representation system ensures that the political parties win the percent of seats that reflects their public support.

with reelection allowed once. Ireland's *Taoiseach* (Prime Minister) is elected by the *Dáil Éireann* (Lower House of Representatives) as the leader of the political party (or coalition parties) that wins the most seats in the national election. A *Tánaiste* (Deputy Prime Minister) is also appointed by the Dáil.

The dichotomous *Oireachtas* (National Parliament) is composed of the *Dáil Éireann* (House of Representatives) and the *Seanad Éireann* (Senate). The Dáil has 166 members that are elected every five years under the proportional representation system. A member of the Dáil is called a *Teachta Dála,* or TD. The Seanad is composed of 60 members. Eleven members are nominated by the Taoiseach, six are elected by the national universities, and 43 members are elected by established panels.

The workings behind passing a bill are quite complex. The Government begins by presenting a proposed bill to the Oireachtas, at which state the House debates, amends, and votes on the bill. If the bill is passed it goes through five stages in the Dáil before being initiated and sent to the Seanad. The Seanad is allowed to delay legislative proposals and can consider and amend bills for 90 days. Once a bill has been passed by both the Dáil and the Seanad, it is sent to the president for signing into law, at which stage the bill is considered an act. While legislative power is given to the Oireachtas, all laws are subject to the obligations of the EU before they can be passed.

Economy

Ireland has suffered an often oscillating economy, particularly since joining the EU in 1973. While the EU injected billions of euros into the economy, Ireland suffered a severe recession in the 1980s, with high levels of unemployment and emigration. The shift from an agriculturally driven economy to a modern, knowledge economy brought Ireland into the economic boom known as the Celtic Tiger. From the late 1980s through 2000, Ireland became one of the fastest growing economies in the world. The country's high-tech industries, service industries, and trade and investment industries all made it a modern, formidable economy. EU aid increased investments in the country's infrastructure and education system, improved productive capacity, lowered the corporate rate tax, and made Ireland more attractive to foreign businesses.

Unfortunately, the sudden high growth of the Irish economy led to problems. The property market went through the roof and inflation escalated, making Ireland one of the most expensive places in Europe. Irish banks lent money to borrowers at the speed of light, nearly tripling their lending between 2002 and 2007. Four out of every five people were borrowing for inflated mortgages used to pay for homes with skyrocketing prices.

When the property bubble burst and the banks collapsed toward the end of the first decade of the 2000s, the rug was pulled out from under the Irish economy. The household debt was considered the highest in the developed world, and emigration was estimated at 1,000 people every week in 2010. In 2008, Ireland became the first country in the EU to officially enter a recession, only worsened by a string of banking scandals that rocked the country in 2009.

The implosion of Ireland's economy fostered a somber mood and a sense of hurt pride prompted by previous centuries of rule under British power. The people were angry at their predicament and ashamed to have to accept falling under foreign yoke for the next few decades. But despite their tumultuous economic history, the Irish have retained a sense of optimism for their future. The history of hardship—flowing through famines, poverty, mass emigration, colonization, civil war, and a crippling recession—has given them a sense of togetherness and a pragmatic attitude about the future.

PEOPLE AND CULTURE

Ireland has an ancient history that evolved over centuries of myths and legends that gave way to its modern culture. Celts, Vikings, Normans, and the English have settled in Ireland, and their footprints color the heritage of this exquisite island. As such, the people of Ireland are as vibrant as its history, with language, culture, music, folklore, art, sport, and numerous traditions associated with Ireland and the Irish people.

While Ireland is no longer synonymous with weathered old men sitting in their woolly jumpers (sweaters) or tending sheep in their rain-drenched fields, the beauty of the land, the rich heritage of the nation, and the friendliness of the people haven't changed. Castles from the Normans and English still dot the land, interspersed with crumbling farmhouses left from the mass emigration that happened during the potato famine of 1845–1849.

But Ireland is not a homogenous society with blanket terms that can define its people. For such a small country there is a diverse range of lifestyles that exist, from the bustling capital of Dublin to smaller, rural communities such

© SUSAN LEGG

as the *Gaelteacht* (Irish-speaking areas). There are close-knit communities in rural Ireland where the inhabitants still spend Sundays going to church together and then congregating at the local pub for an afternoon roast dinner. Many people in the capital might spend their weekends recovering from a hangover, going to an art exhibit, or possibly living it up at a U2 concert. Whether rural or urban, the Irish subsist in a social climate that was developed over years from a mainly agricultural-based society to what it is in modern time—a rich, diverse, colorful culture that spans age, race, religion, and gender.

Ethnicity and Class

The ethnicity of the Irish is intricately woven with its nationalism, intertwining myth, legend, history, religion, culture, and language to create the fiber of what Ireland is today. The Irish are a diverse, multifaceted group where ethnicity can be divided many different ways, ranging from race to class to nationalism. This partition is compounded by an emerging divide between rural and urban Ireland, between social classes in Ireland, and between young, liberal Irish and older, more conservative Irish.

Historically, the Irish people are descendents of Gaelic Celts, with heritage from the Vikings, Normans, Scots, and the English all contributing to the population. As history marched forward, Ireland as a nation experienced numerous

© SUSAN LEGG

Many homes – including Moore Hall, Ballinrobe in 1923 – were torched for political reasons.

recessions, depressions, and famines, as well as political upheavals, repression, and violence. Because of this, many young people have traditionally emigrated out of Ireland, primarily to western countries. There are an estimated 50–80 million Irish people scattered throughout the world. Historically, those that stayed in Ireland were mostly considered subclass, particularly throughout British rule.

However, the Irish do not have a typical lower, middle, or upper class in the British sense. There are a smattering of lords and ladies who originated from British rule, some well-established families who accumulated wealth before the Irish gained independence from England, and some conventional families who have amassed their wealth through profitable business. But as a whole, Ireland classes are widely divided into the working class, the middle class, and the unemployed. The working class divides into semiskilled and unskilled workers. The dominant middle class can be divided into the upper middle class, consisting of professionals such as doctors and lawyers, and the mobile middle classes, including professions such as teachers and nurses. Finally, the unemployed are those who are on the dole (unemployment benefits).

The one exception to this class system is the Traveller community. The Irish Travellers are a minority community of ethnic Irish origin. They feature their own separate language and set of traditions with distinct rituals, including death and cleansing, early marriage, and a desire to be mobile. Primarily nomadic, the Traveller community has existed on the margins of Irish society for centuries.

This ethnic community has suffered formidable levels of racism throughout mainstream Ireland, including from the media, education system, and government. They are regularly referred to as *tinkers* or *knackers,* terms originally given to them based on what they did—tinkering being the mending of tinware and knackering being the acquisition of old horses to slaughter—and evolving into racist slurs that are now used by many Irish as an insult to friends. Even in modern Ireland, Travellers are sometimes refused services or access to public places such as pubs, hotels, and restaurants.

Immigration

In the late 20th century, the Celtic Tiger brought high-tech jobs and industries to Ireland, pushing the predominantly agricultural-based society into the background and bringing to the foreground a new trade-based society established from an educated workforce. Ireland's job force had to quickly expand, hiring more people, including migrant workers, to fill jobs to sustain the booming economy. While the Celtic Tiger did much for Ireland's economy, it also ushered in a new age of increasing immigration and new ethnicities. The economic boom brought such a huge wave of immigrants that in 2007, one in seven people in Ireland were born outside the country, and the percentage of immigrants in Ireland rose faster in just one decade than it did in Britain over half a century.

The influx of immigrants from around the world changed Ireland's once homogenous society into an emerging multicultural one. Previously, Ireland had been a country more used to seeing people leave than immigrate. In the 1950s about 50,000 Irish emigrated out of Ireland. In the 1980s an average of 35,000 people left Ireland every single year. However, in Ireland in 2006, the Irish national census recorded that 420,000—about 10 percent of the population—were foreign nationals. Of course, this rapid increase brought its own set of tribulations: little or no social or community services for immigrants, a lax infrastructure, and a health-care system not adequately equipped to deal with the sharp population increase.

In 2008, when Ireland was the first country in the European Union (EU) to announce it was in a recession, Irish emigration began again in earnest. In the year leading up to April 2010, Irish emigration increased by 40 percent, and Ireland's Economic and Social Research Institute predicted that 200,000 people would emigrate from Ireland between 2010 and 2015.

Immigration in Ireland continues to be a turbulent topic. Several high-profile cases have dominated the news headlines, including the 2009 case of two Polish men killed in Dublin by a gang of teenagers using a screwdriver, the assault and subsequent death of a Polish man in Dublin in 2010, and the racially motivated murder in 2010 of a 15-year-old Nigerian boy by two Irish men. As the economic boom began dwindling and unemployment reached record levels, some began blaming the immigrants.

The vast majority of people in Ireland, however, are horrified by racist behavior. Various organizations such as the Irish Human Rights Commission and Sport Against Racism Ireland (SARI), an organization that promotes cultural integration and social inclusion through sport, work to eliminate and address racism against immigrants.

The picture is entirely different for expatriates from western Europe and America, with most Irish accepting them with no problems. Rather than immigrating to Ireland for economic success, these people are typically drawn here by the Irish people's reputation for friendliness, a more relaxed lifestyle, the ancient culture, and the stunning beauty of the country. As such, they are welcomed with open arms, treated with the friendliness that the Irish people are famous for, and accepted wholeheartedly.

Customs and Etiquette

Ireland is a land of social people who have turned speaking into an art form. The gift of gab, as the Irish call it, means they tend to be lyrical, poetic, and verbally eloquent. In general, the Irish love teasing and joking, and tend to take the piss (make fun of people) just to entertain themselves. This is rarely meant maliciously, and the best thing to do is go with the flow and return the teasing. Just be sure not to take it seriously.

The Irish hate loud, boisterous behavior. Unfortunately, Americans have gotten quite a reputation for being both loud and boisterous, so remember to tone down your voice and curb your enthusiasm. The key here is to be conservative. Wearing white tennis shoes, baseball hats, T-shirts, shorts, or fanny packs will immediately pinpoint you as an American. (As an aside, never call it a fanny pack in Ireland; *fanny* means vagina in Ireland, and they get endless amusement over this social faux pas. Call it a bum bag.)

MEETING AND GREETING

A traditional handshake with a smile is the standard greeting in Ireland. When at business or social gatherings, you should shake hands with everybody when you arrive, men, women, and older children, and then shake

IRISH SUPERSTITIONS

The Irish are a superstitious lot, brought about by an ancient history rich in folklore and magic. I have never in my life met a group of people with so many superstitions. Indeed, if you do a search online, you will find hundreds of thousands of websites listing the superstitions that the Irish hold, from charms to elixirs, legends to myths. While many people don't pay any attention to superstitions these days, there are some that they still ponder. For example, did you know it is considered bad luck in Ireland to put your shoes on the table, place a bed facing the door, cut your fingernails on a Sunday, or give a knife as a gift? Many Irish still throw spilled salt over their shoulder to ward off seven years of bad luck after breaking a mirror, and of course, if you find a four-leaf clover, you will always have good luck.

These ancient Irish superstitions were compounded by beliefs aligned with important dates on the calendar. For example, on May 1st (May Day) you should never light your pipe from the fire, nor take the embers of you fire outdoors. On January 6th (Epiphany), children had the tail of a herring rubbed across their eyes to ward off disease for the rest of the year. On February 1st (St. Brigid's Day), a single straw from the Christmas nativity scene was placed in the house rafters to ward off evil spirits.

hands again when you leave. Maintain good eye contact during your greeting to establish trust, and use the person's name repeatedly in the conversation in order to establish a relationship. Greetings are warm and friendly in Ireland, but stay away from being physically demonstrative, as this makes them uncomfortable. This rule does not hold true on a night out at the local nightclub, when you may see your friend *snogging* (kissing) a random guy on the dance floor.

GESTURES AND LANGUAGE

One of the biggest differences between Ireland and America in terms of language is the use of the word *feck*. *Feck* is used prolifically as anything from a colorful adjective to a replacement of the "f" word. It is rarely meant to offend and shouldn't *always* be taken as cussing. However, the reverse "V for victory"

IRISH WEDDINGS

Getting married in Ireland is, for some, a dream come true. Perhaps because of its religious background, the Republic of Ireland views marriage as a solemn legal contract, and as such, there are strict guidelines and rules for getting married here. There are two types of ceremonies allowed in Ireland: civil or religious. No matter which type you choose, you must first notify the Registrar of Marriages in the district you intend to marry at least three months prior to marrying.

For a civil ceremony, you should reside in the area you wish to marry for eight days to establish residency. Then 21 days must pass before you are allowed to get married. A civil ceremony can be held in a Registry Office or at an approved venue, such as a fixed structure – no outdoor wedding ceremonies allowed – with a registrar solemnizing the marriage.

For a religious ceremony, the residency requirements that apply to a civil ceremony are null. Actual residency requirements vary for each religion, as do various rules. For ex-ample, the Catholic Church requires "letters of freedom" to be submitted declaring you are free to marry. No matter what religious ceremony you choose, the person solemnizing the marriage should be listed on the "Register of Solemnisers" in order for the marriage to be legal.

Weddings in Ireland tend to be spectacular, formal affairs, with the ceremony and the reception including all traditional aspects, from the Irish blessing, to throwing the flowers, to the bride and groom's first dance. The reception typically includes numerous bottles of wine or champagne, dancing, toasts, and the cutting of a traditional Irish wedding cake – fruit cake soaked in good Irish whiskey, with one tier stored away to be used at the christening of the firstborn. All of this takes anywhere from months to years of planning: I was often surprised to find friends getting married who would set their wedding date up to two years in advance, simply to be able to have time to plan the elaborate affair.

sign—the first two fingers forming a *v* and the palm of the hand facing the signer—means eff off and is used to offend.

Certain topics of conversation should be steered clear of and never brought up in casual conversation: The Troubles in Northern Ireland, religion, abortion, and the war in Iraq, to name a few. Additionally, don't reference Lucky Charms, leprechauns, or pots of gold unless you really want to irritate the Irish.

DINING CUSTOMS

Dining customs in Ireland are similar to North America's. Don't talk with your mouth full or put your elbows on the table, although your hands should remain visible, not lying on your lap. Eating with your hands is considered very bad manners. Everybody in Ireland uses the Continental style of eating—a fork in your left hand and a knife in your right hand—and people are shocked by Americans who only use the fork.

Since the Irish are such a social bunch, business is often conducted in restaurants after business hours, surrounded by good food and lots of alcohol. By the end of the meal, you will have eaten three to five courses and drank anywhere from one glass of wine to a whole bottle of wine. Just make sure you're able to leave the restaurant on steady feet without seeming a drunken fool. These dinners are usually paid for on the company dime, but if you invite your spouse, you should pay for him or her separately.

Religion

Ireland is a country where religion has always been paramount. The Catholic Church has historically ruled the government, controlled the legislature, and wielded influence over Irish society. The religion an Irish person ascribes to is typically what they are born with, and it is often synonymous with nationalism. It is a statement about heritage more than one of religious beliefs. Before independence, aligning yourself with Catholicism meant you were a nationalist, meaning you were in favor of an independent, Irish state. Aligning yourself with Protestantism meant you were a unionist, in favor of staying united with Great Britain. According to the 2006 census, approximately 90 percent of Irish people call themselves Catholic.

Despite these statistics, modern Ireland is not a Catholic state. While there are references to religion in Ireland's constitution, the Catholic Church is not mentioned, and no religious body is given preference over another. In fact, the Irish constitution guarantees that no penalties are to ever be imposed due to

© SUSAN LEGG

Knock Shrine is a famous pilgrimage site.

religious belief. Consequently, this makes Ireland one of the most religiously free countries in the world.

Religion in Ireland is slowly losing its grasp, however. The once unquestioning reverence for the Catholic Church's authority has been rocked by a series of scandals: a well-known Galway bishop using diocesan funds to support his mistress and son, extreme physical and mental punishment, pedophilia in the clergy, and the slave labor endured by unmarried pregnant women in the Magdalene laundries.

RELIGION IN SCHOOLS

Even though the Irish constitution doesn't mention Catholicism, you would be hard-pressed to believe it when looking at Ireland's education system. While students of any religion may attend, Irish schools are governed by boards chaired by the local Catholic bishop, and the teaching of the Catholic religion is central to the curriculum. The state-funded primary schools (called national schools) include religious schools, multidenominational schools, and *Gaelscoileanna* (Irish-speaking schools). Secondary schools, while funded by the state, are also run by religious orders and have a faith-based ethos.

Regardless of the religion that is taught at school, children who do not ascribe to religious beliefs can still be admitted, and parents may withdraw their child from religious classes. However, due to the predominance of Catholicism in Irish schools, more than 92 percent of students who leave school identify with Catholicism as their religion before they go on to complete secondary education. It is interesting to note, however, that of the students who go on to complete a third-level degree (university), only 86 percent list themselves as Catholic.

Gender Roles

In 1975, only about 30 percent of women aged 25–34 participated in Ireland's workforce. By 2004 this had increased to 76 percent. As you can see, much has been done in Ireland to equalize gender roles. Over the past few decades, attitudes have changed, and the Irish government has become involved in gender mainstreaming to promote equal opportunities for men and women. There have been changes to legislation on maternity leave, parental leave, and adoptive leave, as well as the development of a child-care infrastructure, all contributing to a narrowing of the gap between men and women. In 2007, The World Economic Forum published a report ranking Ireland 8th around the world on gender equality. Comparatively, the United States only ranked 31st, and the United Kingdom ranked 15th.

In 1998 the Employment Equality Act was passed to outlaw discrimination in relation to employment, enforce equal pay for work of equal value, and oversee the conditions of employment. In 2000 the Equal Status Act was passed to protect against discrimination outside the workforce. The National Development Plan Gender Equality Unit was established in the Department of Justice, Equality and Law Reform in 2000 to provide support to the government on implementing gender equality.

However, while much has been done to establish gender equality in the workplace, there are still remarkable inequalities in areas such as pay grade, level of esteem in the workplace, and opportunity for professional achievements. Certain jobs are still linked to gender roles; for example, 73 percent of men are employed in the labor workforce, as opposed to just 50 percent of women. In the agricultural industry gender roles are particularly strong, with men often dealing with farm production and women handling agricultural production, such as eggs and honey.

Only about one third of women aged 55–64 have a job. While this is due to social attitudes and traditionalist values among this age group, it is also because their level of education is comparatively poor. Among women aged 25–54 who have two or more children, only 22 percent are employed full time—one of the lowest in the Organisation for Economic Cooperation and Development (OECD). While feminism and gender equality face many obstacles among traditionalists, there is a growing movement in the government to equalize the genders.

GAY AND LESBIAN IRELAND

Homosexuality in Ireland has suffered a complicated history. In fact, being gay was punishable by death until 1861 and was a criminal offense from 1885 until 1993. While lesbianism was never the focus of such laws, both male and female homosexuality was condemned by the powerful Catholic Church. These British laws were inherited by the Republic when it became a free state.

However, by the mid-1970s, the Irish Gay Rights Movement had started fighting for law reform and against discrimination. Since the decriminalization of homosexuality in 1993, the prevailing attitude and outlook on homosexuality in Ireland has changed dramatically. A 2008 survey by the *Irish Times* showed that 63 percent of Irish people supported same-sex marriage. And in 2010 the Civil Partnership and Certain Rights and Obligations of Cohabitants Act was passed in the Dáil and the Seanad, and signed into law by the president. The law came into effect on January 1, 2011, and the first public civil partnership ceremonies took place on April 5, 2011.

Modern Ireland prides itself on being open-minded and nondiscriminatory. Dublin has a vibrant gay scene, with numerous gay and gay-friendly locations. Bars like The George and The Dragon in Dublin are easily identifiable by the rainbow flag placed outside the door. Others are more discreet but definitely still exist. The Gay Community Network is a good source for gay people, and various organizations are available for support, including the Gay and Lesbian Equality Network (GLEN) and the National Lesbian and Gay Federation.

Despite the prevailing attitude of open-mindedness, discrimination against gays and lesbians does exist. Attitudes are particularly bleak outside of urban towns and cities. Even within the larger towns and cities, verbal aggression can occur in almost any context. Physical aggression is much rarer — and generally affects males more than females — but the likelihood of it happening increases when alcohol comes into play, particularly after the close of a nightclub or bar.

© SARAHJANE SWEENEY

Dublin and Cork have gay pride parades every year.

The Arts

Ireland is a nation with a rich culture that is represented through its vibrant collection of arts acquired throughout history: artifacts and ornaments during the Bronze Age; illuminated manuscripts, such as the Book of Kells, during the medieval period; Celtic crosses during the days of the Normans; and the art of modern living artists such as figurative painter Louis le Brocquy and sculptor Dorothy Cross. This nation of scholars has produced numerous famous writers—James Joyce, Oscar Wilde, Samuel Beckett, George Bernard Shaw, and William Butler Yates—as well as actors and performers such as Gabriel Byrne, Saoirse Ronan, U2, and Enya.

LITERATURE

For a relatively small island, Ireland has contributed greatly to world literature. Ireland lays claim to four Nobel Prize winners—William Butler Yeats, George Bernard Shaw, Samuel Beckett, and Seamus Heaney—with three of the four born in Dublin. Irish-language literature has the largest body of written language, both ancient and current, of any Celtic language. Irish poetry dates back to the 6th century, making it the oldest vernacular poetry in Europe.

Ireland has undoubtedly produced some of the western world's most notable literary geniuses. Jonathan Swift's publication of *Gulliver's Travels* in 1726 is widely considered the beginning of Irish literature. This was followed by an explosion of Irish literary geniuses in the 19th century, many of whom

© SARAH-JANE SWEENEY

Irish Museum of Modern Art

a fairy tree in Carrowkeel, Sligo

© SUSAN LEGG

are famous still. Bram Stoker wrote the classic horror novel *Dracula* in 1897. James Joyce wrote *Ulysses* in 1922, which introduced the literary technique called stream of consciousness, which attempted to record the thought process as it happened, ignoring logical or editorial interruptions. The Irish poet and playwright William Butler Yeats is recognized as a writer of inspired poetry. Finally, Oscar Wilde's social comedy *The Importance of Being Earnest* is still performed to delighted audiences today.

Ireland's literature includes many myths, legends, and fairy tales that began thousands of years ago when the Celtic Druids wove folklore as a part of everyday life. Some of the superstitions surrounding good and bad luck exist even today. For example, in 1999 a multimillion-pound highway being built in Latoon, County Clare, was diverted in order to avoid tearing down a solitary hawthorn tree—the fabled dwelling place of fairies. The locals argued that if the tree was torn down, everyone who drove on the new road would suffer bad luck. Many miseries—sickness, death, missing people—are attributed to the bad luck of the fairies. On the flip side, leprechauns are said to bring good luck; the trick is to catch and hold onto one. If you do, legend says the leprechaun will lead you to its pot of gold at the end of a rainbow.

MUSIC AND DANCE

Music and dance represent a favorite pastime in Ireland, with traditional Celtic music playing an important part of Ireland's heritage. The uilleann pipes, bodhrán, tin whistle, concertina, and the Irish harp all contribute to the unique melody that constitutes traditional Irish music. This style of music

TRADITIONAL IRISH MUSICAL INSTRUMENTS

- Uilleann pipes: This is the national bagpipe of Ireland, possessing a sweet tone with a wide range of notes.

- Tin whistle: Also called a penny whistle, the tin whistle is a simple, six-holed woodwind instrument often used in Celtic music.

- Concertina: Originally produced in England and Germany, this free-reed musical instrument looks similar to an accordion, but each button produces a separate note.

- *Bodhrán:* Pronounced bow-rawn, this ancient instrument is a one-sided Irish frame drum that has become increasingly popular throughout the Celtic music world.

- Irish harp: *Clàrsach* in Irish, the Irish harp features brass wire strings and a resonating chamber carved from a single piece of wood, typically willow, producing a high, clear sound.

has influenced numerous varieties of modern music, including country, roots, modern rock, and punk music. Contemporary music has also been successful, with performers such as Clannad, Enya, Van Morrison, Sinéad O'Connor, and U2 achieving worldwide success.

The emigration of the Irish throughout history has brought Irish dancing to the world, influencing modern dance such as tap dancing, flat footing, clogging, and buck dancing. Performances such as *Riverdance* and *Lord of the Dance* have brought international acclaim to Irish music, depicting the Irish culture and its influence on other cultures, as well as celebrating the Celtic heritage. These performances use traditional Irish step dancing, characterized by dancing mostly with the legs and feet while the arms hang stiffly to the side.

PUB CULTURE

No matter what divides the people of Ireland—religion, sexual orientation, social class, age, race—the pub culture pervades across all barriers. The pub is the beating heart of Ireland, the blood flowing through its veins. This is where you can go to not only drink a pint of Guinness or Bulmers (hard cider), but to have a bit of *craic* with good friends, chat with neighbors, listen to traditional music or a poetry reading, have a good dance, or even eat dinner with your family.

The stereotypical view of the Irish is that they drink a lot. Is this accurate? Well, yes. Put it down to the ability to socialize better at pubs, or the love of a taste of some Irish whiskey or a thick, Irish stout beer, or perhaps the incessant

an Irish bar

© CHRISTINA MCDONALD

rain that drives people indoors, but the Irish do drink more than people in most other countries. In fact, Ireland had the second-highest per capita alcohol consumption in the world (after Luxembourg) according to the OECD's Health Data 2009 survey.

A change in pub culture began in Ireland with the introduction of the smoking ban in March 2004. Debate still rages as to whether the smoking ban has resulted in lower sales and whether it has been a good or bad thing. Many pubs have certainly closed down in the last decade. In 2010 there were only 7,616 pub licenses, down from 8,922 in 2005. However, this can also be attributed to ever-increasing prices and a deep recession. I can say from personal experience that my friends—almost all of whom are smokers—viewed the smoking ban as a good thing in terms of socializing, forcing people away from their cozy tabletop conversations outside to a larger group of half-inebriated people ready and willing to socialize.

HOLIDAYS AND FESTIVALS

The Irish calendar is an amalgamation of old pagan customs and Christian traditions inherited from the English. Historically, the Irish people celebrated Midsummer's Day with dancing, singing, and country fairs. The holiday welcomed the sunrise on the longest day of the year and acknowledged the days would become shorter. The ancients celebrated this tradition on June 23rd or 24th (even though the longest day technically lands on June 21st).

On October 31st, the ancient Irish celebrate Samhain (pronounced Sow' en), which literally translates as "end of summer." Today the name and meaning of the holiday has changed to Halloween, but originally, Samhain was the Celtic New Year and celebrated the honor of the sun in order to ensure it would return the next year. Pope Boniface superimposed the Christian festival of All Saints Day over this pagan festival.

December is full of festivities, with the Irish celebrating several local Christmas traditions before celebrating the day itself on December 25th. St. Stephen's Day (December 26th) is traditionally the day for wren hunting—a group of boys would set out to hunt a wren.

The national holiday in Ireland—and probably the most famous worldwide—is St. Patrick's Day on March 17th. This public holiday is celebrated throughout Ireland with parades, street fairs, carnivals, music, festivals, and general partying. While legend attributes this day to St. Patrick, who banished the snakes and correlated the shamrock to the trinity, what is celebrated now is something entirely different. Perhaps because it marks the lifting of Lenten restrictions on drinking alcohol, this is a day that is marked by national drinking and partying. As one of my friends in Ireland proclaimed, this day was an "excuse for a piss-up."

PLANNING YOUR FACT-FINDING TRIP

While you may be anxious to jump ship and start your new life in Ireland, it is always a good idea to consider a visit first in order to learn more about the island, the culture, and the people. Try for an extended vacation—at least two weeks—and take in the sights outside of the touristy areas, making sure you look past the traditional pubs, the ancient stone castles, and the thatched-roof cottages to the reality of life there. Ensure you would be happy with the day-to-day aspects of Ireland: shopping at a weekly market instead of a 24-hour Wal-Mart if you choose a rural area; tangled traffic with angry, aggressive drivers in the urban cities; spending long hours indoors while mist and rain cover the hills; or having to switch the emersion on before you're able to have hot water for a nice, long shower. These are the little things that you'll want to make sure you're happy with before making the move across the pond. It is easier to take a fact-finding trip than it is to move overseas, only to regret it later.

COURTESY OF TOURISM IRELAND

Preparing to Leave

Ireland is a fairly small country, with each major town about 3–4 hours from each other. That being said, life is dramatically different between urban and rural, north and south, or east and west settings. You will most likely never be able to see all of Ireland in depth during your fact-finding trip, so try to just get a good idea of what you're interested in. If you find living in a rural setting appealing, make sure part of your trip includes a stay in a rural town or village. If you are awed by the wild beauty of the west coast, make sure you head that direction.

Consider the amount of time you have for this trip and organize the areas you are most interested in to fit into your time allotment. Dublin is a good starting point, but be sure you do some research to plan your trip from there. Make sure to do research online, in guidebooks, and in travel magazines to see what accommodations, settings, and areas suit your tastes. If you want to take in a concert or one of Ireland's many *fleadhs* (festivals or fairs), be sure to organize your trip around those dates.

DOCUMENTATION AND IMMUNIZATION

While citizens of European Union (EU) member states can travel freely to and from Ireland with just a national ID card, American citizens must possess a valid passport that does not expire for a minimum of six months past the day you plan to enter Ireland. Be sure to check your passport prior to booking your plane tickets, and if your passport is due to expire soon, renew it at your local embassy or U.S. Passport Agency. Certain foreign nationals entering Ireland need a visa prior to arrival—the countries requiring a visa are listed on Ireland's Department of Foreign Affairs website—however, American citizens do not require a visa to enter Ireland if they are staying for less than three months.

The law does not require any health documents or vaccinations to enter Ireland. However, if within 14 days of entering Ireland you have visited a country where a contagious disease was prevalent, you may be required to provide proof of immunization from that disease. It is recommended that you be up-to-date with routine shots such as the MMR vaccine (measles, mumps, and rubella), the DPT vaccine (diphtheria, pertussis, and tetanus), poliovirus, etc.

You should ensure that your health insurance policy covers you while abroad, as the cost of medical care overseas can be quite high for a nonresident. Many credit cards offer limited coverage if you pay for your airline ticket using a credit card. You can also buy traveler's insurance, but make sure you read the fine print and ensure you are covered for emergencies like an unexpected illness or injury, a trip to the hospital, or an evacuation. At a minimum, make sure your policy covers initial medical treatment and an emergency flight home.

If you need to bring medication into Ireland, bring enough for the duration of your trip, a copy of the prescription, and a letter from your U.S. physician stating what the medication is for. This will help you get through both U.S. and Irish customs with less hassle. If you run out of your prescription when in Ireland, you can check with the local pharmacy (called a chemist) and find out if it is available under a European brand name. If so, you can see a general practitioner (GP) who can prescribe the medicine for you. If it isn't available, your doctor in the United States can mail the prescription to you in Ireland, including an explanation letter for customs.

WHEN TO GO

The best times to visit Ireland are undoubtedly in the spring and summer. I always found the months of May and September to be the sunniest months, with June through August the warmest. Ireland's proximity to the Atlantic Ocean gives it an oceanic climate, so you will certainly still see rain even in the spring and summer. However, don't feel let down if you wake up to storm clouds and rain. The weather is very changeable, and it can rain in the morning, then change to bright sunshine in the afternoon. And when the sun comes out, there is no place more stunning than this jewel of an island.

July and August are peak tourist season, so prices are higher, and you have

© SARAH-JANE SWEENEY

When the clouds clear, you can see out to the Atlantic.

a slimmer chance of getting good budget accommodations. Make sure you book your accommodations well in advance of your trip to avoid being without a bed for the night.

Rain falls more frequently on the west coast (up to 270 days a year!) than it does in the rest of the country. Your best bet is to always expect rain. Dress in layers in order to be prepared for warm sun, cold wind, or what the locals call a "soft" day—a warm day with misty rain that falls for hours. Make sure to bring an umbrella and good walking shoes or rain boots, and leave the sandals, shorts, and swimming suits at home. Keep in mind, the rain is what makes Ireland the brilliant emerald color it is famed for.

If the rain doesn't bother you and you want to avoid most of the crowds, booking in the winter is a good plan. It rarely gets below freezing, and accommodations are much easier to find. You may have less daylight and more rain in the winter, but you will get a better grasp of what the country is like outside of the touristy months.

CURRENCY

Ireland is a member of the EU and, as such, uses the euro. The euro was adopted by 12 member states in January 1999 when the Economic and Monetary Union (EMU) was formed. Euro notes and coins were subsequently circulated in January 2002. There are seven euro notes that are uniform throughout the EU. The notes are available in different colors and sizes, and are available as: €500, €200, €100, €50, €20, €10, and €5. They feature designs that are symbolic of Europe's architectural heritage, not actual or existing monuments. Additionally, there are eight euro coins: €2, €1, 50c, 20c, 10c, 5c, 2c, and 1c. Each coin features a common European face on one side and individual motifs on the flip side. Ireland's coin has a harp, the date, and *Éire* on it.

You can order euros from your local bank prior to departure.

© SARAH-JANE SWEENEY

ATMs are readily available in the cities.

VAT AND TAX-FREE SHOPPING

Value Added Tax (VAT) is a sales tax included on all goods in Ireland. The current VAT is 21 percent, although this will rise to 22 percent in 2013, and then to 23 percent in 2014. VAT is one method of taxation used by the Irish government to generate income for services such as education and health care.

Most shops in Ireland operate a tax-back scheme that allows residents from outside of the EU to purchase products and receive the tax back. The process is a bit time-consuming, but it isn't difficult and is definitely worth it if you spend much money while in Ireland. Keep in mind you will need to collect your refund within three months of your purchases. Additionally, shopping at any of the large airports will net you duty-free products, so you won't have to pay taxes here, either.

Here are the steps for getting your tax back after shopping in Ireland:

- Shop at retailers that participate in the VAT refund scheme. You will see a Cashback or Ireland Tax Free sticker displayed on the shop window if they do. Most tourist-oriented stores do, as do many department stores.

- When you pay for your purchases, make sure you have the retailer fill out the refund document, also called a "cheque." You will need to have your passport with you.

- Bring your unused merchandise to the airport prior to leaving. Some retailers will staple and seal the shopping bag for you.

- Process your documents at your last stop in the EU before flying home. Make sure you arrive early at the airport to do this. You will have to go through a separate line at customs in order to get your documents stamped. If you run out of time and leave without the stamp, you will most likely lose your money.

- Once your documents are stamped, you will need to go to a merchant representative at the airport, such as Global Blue or Premier Tax Free. They will charge you about 4 percent as a commission fee, then refund your money.

Alternatively, you can buy euros at an exchange office or set aside some of your local currency to exchange at the airport after you first arrive. If you run out of euros, any of Ireland's banks exchange money at the local currency exchange rate. Always be sure to check the commission rate and exchange rate prior to exchanging cash.

The best option for carrying money throughout Ireland is to use your debit or credit card to withdraw money from an ATM (Automated Teller Machine), often referred to as a cash machine, cash point, or pass machine in Ireland. You will most likely be charged a foreign transaction fee from your bank, and many credit card companies charge a 1–3 percent transaction fee. However, this usually ends up being less expensive than paying the exchange rate plus a commission fee. ATMs are prevalent throughout the urban towns and

- Some retailers handle VAT refunds directly. While this eliminates any intermediary fees, you are responsible for contacting the retailer yourself, mailing them your stamped documents, and then waiting for them to send a refund check.

Keep in mind that even if you think you are doing everything correctly, sometimes you just don't get your VAT refund. Maybe you can't find the official customs booth or you don't have every piece of paperwork. Only you can decide if going through the process to get your VAT refunded is worth the hassle.

© SUSAN LEGG

Duty-free shopping is available at most airports.

villages but are more difficult to find in the rural areas, especially the *Gaeltacht* (Irish-speaking areas) and smaller villages, so make sure you withdraw money before heading out to the countryside.

International transfers are also a practical and convenient way of receiving money. There are two ways to receive money at an Irish bank: the long way or the short way. The long way can take up to eight days. For the long way, your bank sends your money to an Irish bank of your choice, you take your passport to the bank, then the bank pays the money to you in euros (minus a transfer fee and commission fee). Alternatively, if you want the money quicker, you can go to Amex, Thomas Cook, or Western Union, which can transfer your money to you in Ireland (sometimes adding a hefty fee).

When withdrawing money from an ATM, you should always observe the same safety precautions as you would at home. Ireland has become a hot spot for scams in which cardholder details are stolen through skimmers—devices planted in machines that memorize your card number—and the more advanced scams have tiny video cameras that record your movements to identify your PIN number. Cover the keypad when you enter your PIN and be aware of people standing nearby. Travel with a backup credit card, travelers checks, or U.S. dollars in case your card is lost, stolen, or damaged.

Travelers checks are widely accepted at banks but are not accepted for everyday purchases. Make sure you bring your passport when cashing your travelers checks. You will be charged a commission, and the exchange rate is usually pretty poor. On the plus side, travelers checks offer more security if you lose them or if they are stolen. Remember to keep a record of the serial numbers separate from your money. This will help you get a refund faster if they are lost or stolen.

If you travel to Northern Ireland, you will need to exchange your euros for British pounds, as Northern Ireland is still part of Great Britain. The British currency that you will use in Northern Ireland are £100, £50, £20, £10, and £5 notes and £2, £1, 50p, 20p, 10p, 5p, 2p, and 1p coins.

AIRPORTS AND AIRLINES

Ireland has four international airports and eight regional ones. You can purchase tickets from a travel agent or directly from the airline, but the best deals

are often found by doing a bit of research online. Be sure to check the terms and conditions prior to purchasing your tickets.

Irish airlines offer both full-service and no-frills flights. The main Irish airline is Aer Lingus, a full-service airline offering direct flights to Britain, the United States, and continental Europe. Aer Arann is a small, full-service airline that flies regularly between Ireland and Britain. Ryanair is Ireland's no-frills airline, offering inexpensive flights to Britain and continental Europe. While the competition from Ryanair has resulted in a general reduction in fares, there are many hidden fees that you should watch out for. Be aware that you will pay per way, rather than round-trip. Prices are always listed before taxes have been added. Most airlines in Europe charge baggage fees, and Ryanair charges you for priority boarding, using a credit card to pay for your ticket, and to check in online, although you are charged even more if you check in in person.

Arriving in Ireland

Most flights to Ireland from North America fly to Dublin Airport on the east coast or Shannon Airport on the west coast. If you fly into London and transfer, you can get a short, direct flight to one of Ireland's regional airports. Whichever airport you land in, you will be required to go through customs and immigration before being allowed into the country.

CUSTOMS AND IMMIGRATIONS

All non-EU citizens are subject to the laws of immigration control before entering Ireland. While in London this might take up to an hour of waiting in a line, I have rarely had to wait more than a half hour. Dublin Airport is busier than most other airports, but small regional airports such as Galway or Knock only take about 10–20 minutes.

Once you arrive at Immigrations, the immigrations official will flip through your passport and ask why you are in Ireland. As an experienced traveler, this is often my least favorite part of traveling. I can, however, relay that I have honestly never experienced a mean or overtly authoritarian guard at Immigrations Control upon arriving in Ireland. While thorough and efficient, the guards tend to be chatty and welcoming to North Americans. Regardless of how you are treated, however, once the guard has deemed you fit to enter Ireland, he or she will stamp your passport, allowing you to stay in Ireland for up to three months. If you wish to stay longer than three months, you must register with the Garda National Immigration Bureau and apply for permission.

You are not likely to have your luggage searched when going through customs, but customs officers do have the right to stop and search anybody at their discretion. These checks ensure that nobody is carrying illegal, prohibited, or restricted goods into the country. You can bring duty-free goods into Ireland, but bringing bulk items may saddle you with a hefty fine if the customs officials label the items as intended for commercial use.

TRANSPORTATION

Unlike many cities throughout Europe, Ireland does not have any underground subway system or trains that rapidly link travelers to the city center. Your transport options include buses, taxis, or a car. Some of the smaller airports do not have any public transportation available at all. There are five buses linking you with Dublin city center. Airlink and Aircoach are the fastest buses. The Dublin Bus takes a nondirect route, but it takes up to an hour in traffic, stopping at nearly every bus stop along the way. There are nine national bus services departing from Dublin to destinations throughout the country, and three bus services are available from Shannon Airport to various parts of the country.

Taxis are an efficient way of getting to your destination, but the meter can ratchet up the cost pretty fast. You can find taxi ranks outside the exit of any of the main airports, with signs pointing you in the right direction. If you

Bus Éireann, Ireland's national bus

don't see any taxis, ask one of the staff at the airport for the phone number and call a taxi. Be sure to ask the price prior to departure, especially if the taxi isn't metered.

The larger airports have international car rental desks available, but if you intend to drive in Ireland you should possess a full valid national driving license or an international driving permit—not just a U.S. driver's license. You can obtain these types of licenses from your local AAA office. Book car rentals well in advance, especially during peak season. Driving is on the left, and seat belts should be worn at all times. Be aware that driving can be a fairly hairy experience in Ireland. The roads are narrow and windy, and the drivers are overly aggressive. You can purchase a red L (for learner) sign to put on your car window, warning other drivers you are a new driver. Always make sure to purchase the Collision Damage Waiver insurance. Ireland has one of the highest traffic accident rates in western Europe.

Getting Around

There is a good network of trains and buses in Ireland's larger towns. Iarnród Éireann (Irish Rail) offers a convenient and reasonably faster way to travel; however, train services are not available to smaller, more rural areas. In the past, Ireland's public transport options have been a laughingstock. Services

WORDS TO USE

There are many words that, across boundaries, may be mistaken and misconstrued. For example, in Ireland if you ask somebody for a "ride," they will think you mean you want to have sex with them. "Cheers" means thank you, not just a toast to good health. "Craic" does not refer to an illicit drug; it just means good times.

If you want your food to go, especially in fast-food restaurants, you ask for a "takeaway." French fries are called "chips," and potato chips are called "crisps." When looking for the restrooms, ask for the "toilets." Diapers are called "nappies," and a crib is called a "cot." A day care is called a "creche." The place you park your car is called a "car park," and your house doesn't have a yard, it has a "garden" (a yard is an enclosed commercial area). Waiting in a line is called "standing in the queue." If somebody tells you something is located on the first floor, it actually means the second floor to Americans – the Irish start with zero on the ground floor, then first, second, etc.

The elevator is called the "lift," an eggplant is an "aubergine," cookies are "biscuits," and pants are "trousers." You don't walk on the sidewalk, you walk on the "pavement." If you are at the bank, you "lodge" your money rather than deposit it. You pay with "cheques," drive on "tyres," and fly in "aeroplanes."

were ridiculously slow, arriving and leaving at random times, and completely unreliable. Now, however, the frequency and speed of these services has been increased and are more dependable. Bus Éireann (Irish Bus) and numerous private bus companies connect most of the rural towns, but you should hire a car to see the smaller, out-of-the-way villages.

Dublin is the only city in Ireland that offers local transportation options besides city buses. The Luas is Dublin's tram system. It operates two lines: the red line, which originates from Connolly Station in Dublin city centre, and the green line, which runs south to east from St. Stephen's Green at the top of Dublin's Grafton Street. The Luas also links Dublin's Connolly and Heuston train stations. The Dublin Area Rapid Transit train (DART) is a local train that connects 27 stations along Dublin's coast, from Malahide in the north to Bray in the south via Connolly train station.

Practicalities

ACCOMODATIONS

Accommodations in Ireland are some of the most expensive in Europe. However, depending on your budget, your taste, where you go, and how long you will be in Ireland, there are a variety available. You can choose nearly any type of lodging, from a basic shared-room hostel or a self-catering cottage to a room in a grand, luxurious castle.

Hostels and university campus accommodations are typically the least expensive types of accommodations. Both are frequented by backpackers, so expect a young vibe, late-night parties, and a group atmosphere. Hostels typically have 4–16 beds in a room, a shared bathroom, a shared kitchen with cooking facilities, and a common room. College campuses typically offer better quality rooms than hostels. Some are self-catering, but some are not. Prices start around €25 in Dublin's city center and increase if you request a private room or a private bathroom (referred to as en suite), and throughout the high season. Prices are a little less expensive in the smaller towns.

Guesthouses and B&Bs offer more privacy than hostels or campus rooms. They are typically housed in larger family homes that feature a separate area for guest rooms. This option is great if you are sharing with another person. They serve a full Irish breakfast in the morning, but many do not provide TVs, telephones, or Internet access. Prices vary according to how many people are staying. I have stayed in B&Bs for as low as €45 for two people sharing, but they can cost upward of €100 in the high season.

Hotels in Ireland come in all shapes and sizes. You can stay in an ancient, refurbished castle or a stately country house, or even a chain hotel if you want a bit of consistency with American standards. Hotels can be a great place to stay with children as long as you find a hotel carrying the Family Friendly symbol. These hotels offer playgrounds, playroom, and kids' meals.

If you are bringing the whole family on your fact-finding trip, your best options are self-catering accommodations, which are much less expensive for a group of people. Self-catering accommodations can range from modern apartments in the city center to holiday cottages on the outskirts of a charming little village. Either way, you will have to cook and clean on your own, but on the plus side, this allows you to base yourself in a more realistic location for experiencing the real Ireland.

FOOD

Irish cuisine evolved over centuries, taking its influence from the animals farmed and the crops grown here. On my first trip to Ireland I was awestruck by how big the section for pork was in the grocery store: There was every type of pork, sausage, bacon, and ham you can possibly imagine spanning aisles.

Irish food may not be as glamorous as French food or as romantic as Italian food, but it combines good-quality ingredients with simple recipes to make homey, family-oriented dishes designed to keep you full for hours. A poem from the early 19th century praised the traditional Irish stew: "Then hurrah for an Irish Stew / That will stick to your belly like glue."

Most meals in Ireland are prepared with no herbs or spices besides salt and pepper, and the dishes are often served without gravy or sauces. The most well-known Irish dishes are Irish stew and corned beef with cabbage, although corned beef is rarely served in Ireland—it is bacon and cabbage. Other recipes such as boxty, coddle, and colcannon are traditionally Irish, all of which primarily feature the potato, and soda bread is still a popular type of bread. Tea is drank the British way, with milk and sometimes a spoonful or two of sugar.

In the 21st century Irish food has evolved to include foods that are more common to Western culture. Many popular dishes from across continental Europe and America have been introduced here, including pizza, cheeseburgers, and pasta. Indian foods, especially curries, are very popular, as well as Turkish kebabs.

Sample Itineraries

If you know exactly where you want to settle in Ireland, you should go directly there on your fact-finding trip. This will give you more time to get a realistic sense of what the area is like. If you are not sure, start in Ireland's capital, Dublin, head to Galway and Cork, then perhaps to Limerick. Make sure to see some of the rural villages as well as the larger towns and cities.

TWO WEEKS

If you only have two weeks to see Ireland, it's a good idea to see a few places rather than trying to rush all over the place. It isn't nearly enough time to see everything, but you can certainly get an idea for the flavor of the country. Fly into Dublin, as this historic city will give you a good introduction to Ireland. Dublin's compactness means you can walk nearly everywhere, so don't bother renting a car. Traffic is a nightmare in Dublin, and you don't want to waste time.

Stay in Dublin's touristy Temple Bar if you want to be close to the city center, or out in Ballsbridge if you want it a bit quieter. On your first full day in Dublin, wake up early and enjoy a traditional Irish breakfast at one of the

TRIP TIPS

Be careful when crossing the street! The Irish drive on the left side of the road. Most streets have *look right* painted on the streets to help you remember. Also, if you are used to driving an automatic transmission, you will have to learn manual in Ireland (almost all cars are manual here).

When withdrawing money from a cash machine, don't withdraw in multiples of 50; for example, withdraw €120. This will ensure that you have a few smaller bills for paying for the taxi or taking the bus. Don't even bother to take one hundred dollar bills with you; Irish banks typically refuse to exchange them. Thomas Cook on Grafton Street and the currency exchange office at the Bank of Ireland near Trinity College are the only businesses that might exchange them for you. Visa and MasterCard are widely accepted throughout Ireland, but it would be very rare to find American Express or Discover accepted.

Tipping taxis and in restaurants is usually about 10 percent. Make sure to check the bill to see if the service was included. Tips aren't expected in pubs, bars, or clubs.

Most shops are closed on Sunday, so be sure to stockpile food and essentials on Friday or Saturday to get you through the weekend.

Guns are not legal in Ireland. Not even police (except special services) have them. The fact that Americans are allowed to carry concealed weapons is something that shocks and horrifies the Irish.

© SUSAN LEGG

Eyre Square, Galway

many Irish pubs. Begin in Temple Bar, visiting the charming shops and bars, then walk down to the River Liffey, crossing under the romantic arc of the Ha'penny Bridge, and walk up to O'Connell Street. Take in the shopping on Grafton Street before grabbing a sandwich for lunch and enjoying it in St. Stephen's Green.

The next day, start off at Merrion Square, which is Dublin's grandest Georgian square and home to many of Ireland's famous writers such as Oscar Wilde. Cross Upper Merrion Street and visit The National Gallery, which holds the national collection of European and Irish fine art. Grab lunch or afternoon tea at the Lord Mayor's Lounge at the Shelbourne Hotel. After lunch, head to Trinity College's Old Library and witness the 8th-century Book of Kells. Just outside of Trinity College, catch bus 123 from Dame Street to finish your afternoon at the Guinness factory.

On your third day, take the DART (15-minute journey) out to the harbor town of Dún Laoghaire for an idea of what Dublin is like outside the crush of the city center. You can relax in one of the many restaurants or pubs, or stroll along the pier. Fishing, sailing, horse riding, and swimming are readily available. End your day at an Irish pub for dinner, enjoying some traditional music and dancing.

On day four, rent a car and head west to Galway. The drive takes about three hours, but take your time stopping at the sights in the towns and villages along the way: Larchill Arcadian Gardens in picturesque Kilcock, Clonard Abbey, The Kilbeggan Distillery, and Athenry Castle. Buses and trains are available between Dublin and Galway if you don't want to drive.

Stay three nights in Galway's beautiful Eyre Square, a perfect, city center location. Or for something a bit quieter, stay in Salthill, a traditional seaside location with a magnificent promenade near the water. Take in one of Galway's many festivals, as this gives you a good idea of the culture and heritage alive in Ireland. Day five, wander Galway's cobbled, stone streets, stroll down Shop Street, and view the Spanish Arch, before continuing down to stroll along the water.

The next day, drive out to the Gaeltacht to get a real sense of the Irish countryside. Visit the eclectic shops in the picturesque village Spiddal, then continue on to the seaside town of Clifden. On day seven, take a day trip from Galway out to the limestone landscape of the Burren, County Clare. You will see tranquil valleys and imposing mountains encased in limestone, megalithic tombs such as Poulnabrone, and ancient limestone monuments. On your way back to Galway, visit the beaches of the village of Corofin, situated on the edge of the Burren.

The next day, drive south to Doolin, about an hour from Galway. Stay one night here and take a trip out to the coast to visit the stunning Cliffs of Moher. These majestic cliffs tower over the rugged Atlantic coastline, rising up 214 meters (702 feet) from the sea. Make sure to visit an Irish pub and listen to some traditional Irish music, which is what Doolin is famed for.

On day nine, head south to Limerick, the capital of Ireland's midwest region. Stay here for two days to experience the city's historic and cultural relevance. Vibrant Limerick offers a variety of shopping, dining, entertainment, and historical sites. You can visit Foynes Flying Boat Museum, The Hunt Museum, or Lough Gur Neolithic Settlement and Stone Age Centre for a bit of culture. Limerick is the sporting capital of Ireland, so be sure to take in a game of rugby, Gaelic football, or hurling if you can.

On day 10, continue south to Cork. Stop in the town of Kilmallock to see King's Castle, Kilmallock Church, and the remains of the medieval town wall before arriving in Cork. Stay two days in Cork. Visit touristy Blarney Castle to kiss the Blarney stone, but also go to The Old Midleton Distillery or the Beamish and Crawford Brewery for a bit of heritage. Wander the city center and then visit Blackrock Castle, the Cork Public Museum, and St. Finbarr's Cathedral. Take a day trip out to the seaport town Cobh to see the final port of call for the *Titanic*.

On day 12 of your trip, head east to Waterford, the capital of the sunny southeast of Ireland, before returning to Dublin. Waterford hosts a number of festivals throughout the year, including Lawlor's Hotel Jazz Festival, The Guinness Féile Na Ndeise (Traditional Irish Music Festival), and the Waterford

Film Festival. You might also have enough time to visit the famous Waterford Crystal Visitor Center before heading back to Dublin the next day.

ONE MONTH

This is the real way to see Ireland. One month gives you enough time to view all the main tourist attractions, but you get to stay longer, experience more, and take more day trips to places off the beaten path. You can follow the two-week itinerary, adding a few days or weeks to various locations as you see fit.

Begin by adding two or three days to Dublin to visit St. Patrick's Cathedral, the historic General Post Office, Ardgillan Castle, the Dublin Writer's Museum, the James Joyce Museum, and Dublin Castle. Take a day trip from Dublin out to the River Boyne, a river that rises in the Bog of Allen in Kildare, just north of Dublin. The area is dotted with prehistoric monuments such as Newgrange, Dowth, and Knowth.

After Dublin, head to Galway, taking a detour south near Athlone to visit the village and monastery of Clonmacnoise. Add two or three days to your visit to Galway in order to see Connemara, Portumna Castle, the Galway Hooker Boats, and Dunguaire Castle in Kinvara. If you have time, plan to stay in the Gaeltacht or the Aran Islands for a night or two in order to really grasp rural living in Ireland.

After Galway, head north to Sligo and take an extra few days to visit Carrowmore Megalithic Cemetery, one of the four major passage tomb cemeteries in Ireland, then head to Knocknarea and Cúil Irra Peninsula. Then head south and follow the two-week itinerary for Limerick, taking a detour to visit the Rock of Cashel—a stone fortress that was the traditional seat of the kings of Munster—in County Tipperary. Follow the two-week itinerary for Limerick, taking an extra week to see the sights around Limerick. Drive the Ring of Kerry to see spectacular coastline between Kenmare and Killorglin, and then visit the Dingle Peninsula to see a bit of the "auld country." Head to the Beara Peninsula and visit the fishing port of Castletownbere, from which you can take a ferry to Bear Island. Visit the Lakes of Killarney for beautiful castles and a sense of old-world charm.

After Waterford, stay a day or two in the glacial valley of Glendalough. This picturesque valley in County Wicklow sits amid tranquil lakes and offers breathtaking scenery. You can visit St. Kevin's Kitchen, which is actually a church, or the Glendalough Monastic Site before heading back to Dublin.

Practicalities

Here are some reliable, tried-and-true choices for sleeping and eating on your fact-finding trip to Ireland. Do keep in mind, however, that whatever type of accommodations you choose, rooms, bathrooms, and beds are much smaller in Ireland than standard American rooms. En suite refers to a room with a private bathroom attached. Many rooms will have a shared en suite, meaning you share with the room next to you, so be sure to check this when booking. You should always book your accommodations ahead of time, as it is difficult to find last-minute accommodations in the high season. Additionally, prices increase dramatically in the high season. Food is generally more expensive at restaurants than at cafés, and portions are a lot smaller than in America.

DUBLIN

Dublin is a multicultural hodgepodge of things, and food and accommodations are no exception. You can end up staying in a fancy hotel or a grimy one, a charming hostel or a mold-encrusted one, so try to read reviews online to get a more accurate picture of the accommodations you are choosing. No matter where you stay or what your budget is, make sure to book ahead of time.

Accommodations

Abbey Court Hostel (29 Bachelor's Walk, Dublin 1, 353/1-878-0700, fax 353/1-878-0719, www.abbey-court.com, €15.00–39.50) offers beautiful, clean, budget accommodations right on the River Liffey, just a stone's throw from the major attractions of Dublin. For a safe, cookie-cutter option, **Ballsbridge Inn** (Ballsbridge, Dublin 4, 353/01-437-3444, www.d4hotels.ie/ballsbridge-inn. html, €59–149) is available in one of the nicer parts of Dublin. Situated in an imposing Georgian building on a tree-lined street near St. Stephen's Green is **Waterloo House** (8-10 Waterloo Road, Dublin 4, 353/1-660-1888, www. waterloohouse.ie/, €100–150), offering luxury B&B accommodations for the discerning traveler. For relaxed grandeur, stay at the five-star Merrion Hotel (Upper Merrion Street, Dublin 2, 353/1-603-0600, fax 353/1-603-0700, www.merrionhotel.com, €455).

Food

The traditional Irish restaurant **Gallagher's Boxty House** (20-21 Temple Bar, Dublin 2, 353/1-677-2762, fax 353/1-677-9723, www.boxtyhouse.ie/, €30) serves pub-style Irish food, boxty pancakes, and coddles for dinner. For a good pub that serves excellent beer and food amid a cracking environment, head to

The Quays Restaurant (10-12 Temple Bar Square, Dublin 2, 353/1-679-1923, www.quaysrestaurant.com, €30) in the heart of Temple Bar for Irish stew, lamb shank, or just a few pints of beer with live music. To step outside of Irish cuisine, try exotic **Salamanca Tapas Restaurant** (1 St. Andrew's Street, Dublin 2, Dublin City, 353/1-677-4799, www.salamanca.ie/, €40) for the best tapas I have had to date in the world. Open for dinner only, except Sunday serving brunch. **The Italian Corner Restaurant** (23-24, Wellington Quay, Dublin 2, 353/1-671-9114, www.theitaliancorner.ie/, €35) serves fantastic Italian food at a great price for both lunch and dinner. The drawback is it can get quite busy and boisterous; if you're looking for something quiet, stay away.

GALWAY

Galway is perched on the west coast of Ireland, right on the River Corrib, between Lough Corrib and Galway Bay. Surrounded by so much water, it is only fitting that Galway is one of the premier places in Europe to eat fresh seafood. This cosmopolitan city is known for offering a wide choice of cuisines and quality food, and being a top tourist destination, it offers a diverse range of accommodations.

Accommodations

Situated off a corner of Eyre Square, **Kinlay House** (Merchants Road, Eyre Square, Galway, 353/91-565244, fax 353/91-565245, www.kinlaygalway.ie/, €25) offers good, quality, budget accommodations in the heart of Galway.

© SUSAN LEGG

Hostels offer the least expensive form of accommodations.

Inishmore House (109 Fr. Griffin Road, Galway, 353/91-582639, fax 353/91-680021, www.inishmoreguesthouse.com/, €60) offers an excellent B&B set in a picturesque family home just outside the city center. If you want something a little classier, try the **Galway Bay Hotel** (The Promenade, Salthill, Galway, 353/91520520, fax 353/91520530, www.galwaybayhotel.net/, €120). Overlooking the Galway Bay and the Clare Hills, this luxury hotel is located in Salthill and features gourmet award-winning cuisine and a stunning atmosphere. If you are planning to stay in Galway for a week or more, you can book self-catering accommodations at the modern **Arús Grattan Holiday Apartments** (Salthill, Galway, 353/91-525951, fax 353/91-581-837, www.galwayselfcatering.com, €100–700 per week).

Food

Head to **McDonaghs** (22 Quay Street, Galway, 353/91-565001, www.mcdonaghs.net, €10) at the bottom of Shop Street for some spectacular fish-and-chips at the fish-and-chips bar or a variety of fish dishes from the seafood menu. Open for lunch and dinner. For a no-frills restaurant that serves some of the best quesadillas, fajitas, and burritos I have ever tasted, dine at **La Salsa** (6 Mainguard Street, Galway, 353/91-539700, €8) for lunch or dinner. **Ard Bia at Nimmos** (Spanish Arch, Long Walk, Galway, 353/91-561114, www.ardbia.com/, €35) features a beautiful riverside location in a medieval stone customs house that overlooks the Claddagh Basin. Open for lunch and dinner. **Viña Mara Restaurant** (19 Middle Street, Galway, 353/91-561610, www.vinamara.com, €40), tucked away in a little corner off Shop Street, serves consistently fabulous Mediterranean food amid a classy atmosphere for lunch and dinner.

CORK

Cork is the second-largest city in Ireland. In fact, most Corkonians call it the "real" capital of Ireland. The city portrays a cosmopolitan, contemporary vibe that you may not find throughout the rest of Ireland. It offers a variety of diverse accommodations, depending on your mood and your budget. Cork food is usually made from local produce, and traditional dishes include crubeens (boiled pigs feet) and drisheen (a type of black pudding).

Accommodations

For a special treat, stay at **Hayfield Manor** (Perrott Avenue, College Road, Cork, 353/21-484-5900, www.hayfieldmanor.ie/, €200), a luxury manor house set within two acres of mature gardens in Cork city. This opulent hotel offers a spa and leisure facilities. **Garnish Guesthouse** (Western Road, Cork

City, 353/21-427-5111, fax 353/21-427-3872, www.garnish.ie/, €70) is a welcoming, clean, homey little B&B situated in an attractive Georgian house. If you're traveling on a budget and want something simple but clean, head to **Sheila's Hostel** (Belgrave Place, Wellington Road, Cork, 353/21-450-5562, www.sheilashostel.ie, €15).

Food

Although it features a dubious name, **Strasbourg Goose** (17-18 French Church Street, Cork, 353/21-427-9534, www.strasbourggoosecork.com, €20) is a little French bistro–styled gem hidden away in Cork and serving up European cuisine for lunch and dinner. Want a taste of home? Head to **Gourmet Burger Bistro** (8 Bridge Street, Cork City, 353/21-450-5404, www.gourmetburgerbistro.ie, €10) for an organic gourmet cheeseburger slathered in bacon for lunch or dinner. For some first-class vegetarian food, check out **Café Paradiso** (16 Lancaster Quay, Cork 1, 353/21-427-7939, www.cafeparadiso.ie, €35).

LIMERICK

Limerick is a pretty little city situated on several curves and islands of the River Shannon in the southern area of Ireland. The city has been dubbed the European City of Sport as it regularly features numerous sporting events, including rugby, hurling, and soccer. There is an array of sleeping arrangements, but be sure to book ahead of time if a sporting event coincides with your stay. Food reflects a diverse choice of traditional Irish and European dishes.

Accommodations

The luxury boutique townhouse **No. 1 Pery Square Hotel & Spa** (Georgian Quarter, Limerick, 353/61-402-402, fax 353/61-313-060, www.oneperysquare. com, €170) is situated in Limerick's historic Georgian Quarter and offers iconic luxury. For something a little more casual but still supremely chic, head to **The George Hotel** (O'Connell Street, Limerick, 353/61-460-400, fax 353/61-460-410, www.thegeorgeboutiquehotel.com, €90). An always predictable bet, the **Radisson Blu Hotel & Spa** (Ennis Road, Limerick, 353/61-326-666, www.radissonblu.ie/hotel-limerick, €100) offers good, spacious accommodations at reasonable rates.

Food

Arabica (3-4 Cornstore, Shannon Street, Limerick, 353/61-444-497, www.arabica.ie, €10) is undoubtedly one of the best cafés in Limerick, serving coffee that is just a cut above the rest and fresh food for lunch and dinner. **The**

Glasshouse Restaurant (Riverpoint Building, Lower Mallow Street, Limerick, 353/61-469-000, www.glasshouserestaurant.ie, €25) is situated on the banks of the River Shannon, offering a funky atmosphere on the 1st floor and sweeping views of the river on the 2nd floor. Open for dinner daily. To spice it up a bit, head to the **Spice of India** (28 O'Connell Street, Limerick, no phone, www.spiceofindialimerick.com/, €20) for a typical Indian dinner, or order takeout (referred to as "takeaway" here) if you're exhausted from your day of sightseeing. Online orders are accepted.

DAILY LIFE

MAKING THE MOVE

So you've done your homework, you've visited, and you've decided Ireland is still the place for you. Now you're ready for your dreams to come true. You're ready to go—in your mind, at least. Next comes all the paperwork, the planning, the organization, the details: How do you get your visa? Is it legal to set up shop in Ireland? How will you find a house in the right location? Which school should your children go to? Like most Western countries, Ireland is very bureaucratic, and moving there takes a great deal of patience.

Don't get too overwhelmed by all of the work. Do a lot of research to find out what the steps are, then take it from the top and work in steps. It is natural to have a million questions for a move as big as this. This book is a great resource for moving, but you should also browse various websites, particularly blogs and forums, to find out more inside tips for the big move. If you keep your head, remain patient, and plan your move thoroughly, you will be living your dream life in Ireland before too long.

© SARAHJANE SWEENEY

Visas and Immigration

Your first step to moving to Ireland is to find out if you have any entitlement to move there. You may be coming to study, to join a family member, to work, or to retire. You may be looking to seek asylum or protection from persecution, or you may have Irish parents or grandparents and want to try moving to their homeland. Whatever the reason, you need to find out if you are entitled to live in Ireland before you are allowed to arrive. This entitlement largely depends on your nationality and what you plan to do once you get there.

Once you have established if you are entitled to live in Ireland, you should verify if you will need a visa to enter Ireland. U.S. citizens are not required to have a visa to enter Ireland for less than three months. An Irish visa is not entry permission so much as a document giving permission to seek admission from the officials at Immigrations. The immigrations officer may not allow you to enter Ireland if you can't financially support yourself, if you plan to get a job but don't have a work permit, or if you suffer from any number of infectious diseases.

If you are planning on staying in Ireland for more than three months, you must register with the Garda National Immigration Bureau (GNIB). You will have to prove your entitlement to remain in Ireland, as well as submit

IRISH CITIZENSHIP ELIGIBILITY

If You Were:	Then You Are:
A. Born in Ireland on or before December 31, 2004	An Irish citizen.
B. Born in Ireland on or after January 1, 2005	Entitled to Irish citizenship if your parents are Irish and entitled to Irish citizenship if your parents are foreign nationals who were legally resident in Ireland for three out of four years before your birth.
C. Child of A and born outside of Ireland	An Irish citizen.
D. Child of C and a grandchild of A, and born outside of Ireland	Entitled to Irish citizenship, but you must first register in the Foreign Births Register.
E. Child of D and a great grandchild of A, and born outside of Ireland	Entitled to Irish citizenship by having your birth registered in the Foreign Births Register, but only if your parent D had registered by the time of your birth.

documentation that you can support yourself for the entirety of the time you are in Ireland. Your passport will then be stamped with a stamp number indicating why you are allowed to stay. Be aware that the GNIB will not register you beyond the expiry date listed on your passport, so you should ensure you passport is valid for at least 12 months before arriving in Ireland. After registration with an immigrations official, you will receive a GNIB Registration card, also referred to as an Immigration Certificate of Registration.

HOLIDAY VISAS

U.S. citizens holding a valid passport are not required to apply for an entry visa or register with GNIB if staying in Ireland for less than 90 days. Whether you need a visa or not, though, you will have to go through Immigrations in order to get approval to enter Ireland. Upon approval at Immigrations, your passport will be stamped with a holiday visa that is good for up to 90 days.

Your holiday visa allows you to leave Ireland and reenter only once. If you plan to leave and return to Ireland more than this, you should apply for a multiple-journey visa. A multiple-journey visa does not allow you to leave Ireland, then return and restart your 90-day holiday visa period. It simply allows you to leave and reenter Ireland any number of times while your 90-day visa is valid. You cannot renew or extend a holiday visa.

STUDENT VISAS

Whether you want a semester abroad or to get your graduate degree, if you plan to study in Ireland for longer than three months you will have to apply online for a "D study" visa. Ireland is a popular study-abroad location, so be sure to start your application early in order to avoid disappointment. There is no rush service, and government bureaucracy can take a very long time.

In order for your student visa application to be processed, you need to have a letter of acceptance from a recognized Irish school, university, or college, showing that you will be pursuing full-time education. Additionally, you will need to provide evidence that you have the ability to pursue the course through English, evidence that your tuition has been fully paid, proof of medical insurance, and evidence of sufficient funds (€7,000 per year) to support yourself throughout your course of study. You will also have to provide proof that you intend to return to your country of residence when you leave Ireland.

Make sure to bring all of this documentation with you when arriving in Ireland. Remember that even if your student visa is approved, it does not mean you can bring family members with you. You may not receive entry into Ireland if you bring, or intend to bring, your children or other family members with you. The student visa is only for you.

Employment Permits

There are four types of employment permits in Ireland: work permits, green card permits, spousal/dependant work permits, and intra-company transfer permits. Each of these employment permits is entirely dependent on a variety of factors, including your nationality, what your salary will be, and how long you plan to stay in Ireland. As a U.S. citizen, you are not required to have an entry visa before arriving in Ireland, but you should be aware of which permit you are applying for and have all of your documentation in order before you begin the application process.

To get an employment permit, the first thing you have to do is get a company to hire you. Don't get too excited, though. You can't just apply for an employment permit and then show up in Ireland and plan to look around for work. This is an arduous process that takes a lot of time and patience on your part. Employment permits are only issued *after* you have a job offer in hand from a prospective Irish employer who has first tried to recruit an Irish or EU citizen. Then a hefty fee is levied on the employer sponsoring your employment permit.

WORK PERMIT

A work permit is required for all citizens outside of the EU and is issued by the Department of Jobs, Enterprise and Innovation. They are only given to those earning more than €30,000 per year, although in some circumstances occupations earning below this are considered. The work permit is only approved for two years, but you are allowed to renew it for a further three years if you stay working for the same company.

Applications for work permits are made through the Employment Permits Section of the Department of Jobs, Enterprise and Innovation by the prospective employer or employee. You must include two recent passport-size photos, evidence of your certified qualifications, the appropriate fee, copies of all visas, and copies of your GNIB card. Additionally, you should submit evidence that a labor market needs test was conducted, advertising the vacancy locally and nationally so any Irish citizen (and EU citizen) is ensured precedence in the hiring process.

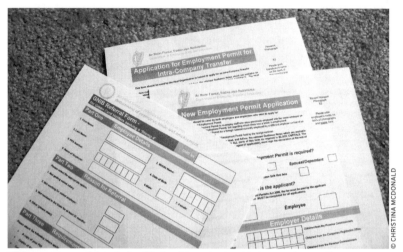

Various paperwork has to be filled out in order to obtain a work permit.

GREEN CARD PERMIT

A green card is an employment permit given to highly skilled workers who earn €60,000 or more annually. This is the best type of employment permit you can hold. It allows your spouse, civil partners, and dependents to join you, and it allows you to gain permanent residency in Ireland after just two years. So if you have the kind of skills that high-end employers dream about, you may have a chance to get the green card.

In order to apply for a green card, you must have a job offer in hand with an employer registered with the Revenue Commissions. Within two weeks of your green card expiring, you can apply to renew your permission to stay with your local immigrations office, providing you are working in the same occupation, for the same employer, and receiving the same salary as listed on your green card permit.

SPOUSAL/DEPENDENT WORK PERMITS

Spousal/dependent work permits are available to those who are married to or in a civil partnership with, or are a dependent of, a person with an employment work permit. This type of work permit can get quite pedantic and may be a bit tricky to negotiate; however, legislation that came into effect in 2007 made it easier for spouses and dependents to become employed by allowing them to apply for work permits without a labor market needs test.

INTRA-COMPANY TRANSFER SCHEME

This scheme is designed to help transfer senior management, trainees, or key personnel from overseas companies to its Irish branch. To be eligible, you must be earning a minimum of €40,000 per year and have been working for the company for at least 12 months before transferring to the Irish branch. Applications are granted for up to 24 months initially but can be extended to a maximum stay of five years. As with all periods of stay that extend past three months, you should register with the GNIB office in the area you will be living. While your spouse and dependents are allowed to join you, they must apply for a spousal/dependent work permit in their own right.

Retiring to Ireland

There is no specific visa allotted for those wishing to retire to Ireland. Again, this is not a situation you can just jump into and expect to be cleared at all angles. While U.S. citizens do not need a visa to enter Ireland, you must have permission to remain for longer than three months. If you are retiring, you must register with the local immigrations office where you plan to move, and you must be able to prove you have enough money to support yourself throughout the duration of your stay. You may also have to provide proof of a private insurance plan.

The United States has special social security agreements with Ireland, which protects your pension rights and social security contributions. The agreement lets you add your social security credits from both the United States and Ireland so you can qualify for benefits. This means you may be entitled to social security taxes, social security retirement, disability, and survivor's insurance benefits if you retire to Ireland. The agreement does not cover benefits of the U.S. Medicare program or the Supplemental Security Income program. Additionally, retirees are eligible to receive free fuel, free TV license, a telephone allowance, and a household benefits package that includes electricity, natural gas, or bottled gas refill allowances.

Irish Citizenship

If you want to avoid all the confusion and runaround necessary for visas and permits, you simply need to prove Irish citizenship. Well, maybe it sounds easy, but this is a complex area with threads that weave in and out of the bureaucracy of the Irish government in an often baffling way. Basically it boils down to this: You can gain Irish citizenship through birth, descent, naturalization, or marriage.

THROUGH BIRTH

Obviously the easiest way to claim citizenship is to be born in Ireland; if you were born in Ireland or have a parent born in Ireland, you are automatically considered an Irish citizen. You don't have to apply for citizenship or register your birth. However, if you were born in Ireland to foreign national parents after January 1, 2005, you are not automatically entitled to Irish citizenship; your parents should be able to show they lived in Ireland for three of the past four years before your birth. If you were born outside of Ireland, but one of your parents is Irish, you are considered an Irish citizen, but you have to register as a foreign-born citizen and apply for citizenship.

Citizenship entitles you to an Irish passport.

© SARAHJANE SWEENEY

THROUGH DESCENT

If you were born abroad, and your parent is an Irish citizen who was also born abroad, you can still claim Irish citizenship. Also, if one of your grandparents is an Irish citizen, even if none of your parents were born in Ireland, you may become an Irish citizen. If you have any of these links, you should register your birth in the Foreign Births Register at the Irish Department of Foreign Affairs before claiming citizenship.

THROUGH NATURALIZATION

You can become a naturalized Irish citizen if you can prove five years of legal residence in Ireland out of the last nine years. Alternatively, if one of your parents was a naturalized Irish citizen, you can become an Irish citizen, providing you were born after your parent was naturalized. The Garda Síochána (the Irish Police) will need to submit a report to the Irish Naturalization and Immigration Service Center about your background, proving you are of good character and haven't been in any trouble. You will have to make a declaration of loyalty to Ireland and assert your intent to reside in Ireland after the naturalization. You can also apply for naturalization if you are married to an Irish citizen.

ADVANTAGES OF CITIZENSHIP

There are a number of advantages for claiming Irish citizenship, including being a citizen of the EU, which makes it easier to live and work in any EU country and allows you to freely travel throughout the EU. Additionally, there are many health and welfare benefits you are eligible for as an Irish citizen, as well as pension rights and unemployment compensation after you start working in Ireland. You are also allowed to purchase property in any country of the EU.

DUAL NATIONALITY

U.S. law can be a bit murky around the waters of dual nationality. The United States does not require you to choose one citizenship over another, and you do not risk losing U.S. citizenship if you are automatically granted citizenship in Ireland (for example, if you are born there). However, if you apply for Irish citizenship, you may lose your U.S. citizenship if you expressly state that you *intend* to give up your U.S. citizenship. So if you show up belligerent, stating you intend to stop being a citizen of the United States, that's exactly what's going to happen. Keep your cool and stay a bit vague, and you'll keep it.

You should be aware that having an Irish passport does not automatically eliminate your social duties as a citizen of America. You are still required to complete your U.S. taxes every year; pay loans, credit cards, or mortgages in the United States; or serve in the military. Basically you have to obey the laws of both countries. Keep in mind that even if you have an Irish passport, U.S. law states you must use your U.S. passport when entering the country.

Moving with Children

If you are planning on making the move to Ireland with children, it is a good idea to include them in your plans. Take them with you on your fact-finding trip so they can get a sense of what the country is about. Talk to them about their new home and school, and help them get excited about meeting new people and learning a new culture. You can show your children pictures of their new home and neighborhood. If they actively participate and assist with choices—from housing to location to schools—they will feel more of a sense of ownership and acclimate better to their new life.

Closer to the day of the move, help your children collect contact details from their friends. Children adjust to new cultures with astonishing ease, but you should be prepared for a longer adjustment time (and possibly some sulking

© SUSAN LEGG

Irish cities are full of young people.

or tears) with adolescents and teenagers. They often suffer from homesickness, missing their old friends, their favorite TV shows, their favorite foods, or their extended family. This may result in anger or depression and end up as a tearful plea to "go home."

Be patient and reassure your children, no matter what their age. Take the time to listen to what they have to say about their new environment, what they like and don't like, and their ideas on how to make it better. If you have very young children, it may help them feel more at ease if you go with them to school the first few times.

Even though your children won't need to learn a new language, there are still various slang words, cultural references, and inside jokes they won't get. Establishing a new routine will help your children adjust, as well as get settled into school. Bring as many of your children's personal belongings as you can so you can offer them a sense of familiarity. If you are moving to a larger city like Dublin, or even Galway, you can find the local expatriate community and help your children get involved with other American children.

IRISH SCHOOLS

While children are not required by law to go to school until age six, most Irish children begin around age four or five. There are three types of schools available for the primary-education sector: state-funded, private, and special schools. State-funded schools include religious schools, multidenominational schools, and Gaelscoileanna (Irish-speaking schools).

TIPS FOR TRAVELING WITH CHILDREN

From the drama of the Cliffs of Moher to the fun of kissing the Blarney stone, or the excitement of watching a live hurling match to the mystery of a stone castle, traveling to Ireland can be an enjoyable adventure with children. However, there are a few tips to make sure this trip is filled with fun, rather than drama.

Make sure you have the names and contact information for your children's pediatrician. Your children should be up-to-date on their routine immunizations to avoid catching anything nasty when traveling. Pack a small medical kit that includes diapers (if your children are small), diaper rash cream, antibiotics if necessary, and a small bottle of ibuprofen or acetaminophen.

If you will be traveling for a long time or your children are very young and may need to go to the bathroom a lot, try to get an aisle seat. After 10 hours on a flight, the person sitting next to you may lose the ability to be polite when you or your children crawl over them for the hundredth time.

Jet lag and the time difference can really mess up your and your children's sleep rhythms. Try to stay awake when the sun is up by getting out for walks or taking your children outdoors. Sunlight is a natural way to regulate sleep. Alternatively, melatonin, a naturally occurring hormone that helps to regulate sleep, is sold as a supplement for insomnia. Consult your pediatrician to see if this is an option for your child and for specific dosage instructions.

DAILY LIFE

Most Irish primary schools are managed by the local Catholic Church, and the teaching of the Catholic religion is central to the curriculum. However, there is a growing choice of multidenominational schools available in Ireland.

Similar to America, state-funded primary schools give priority to children living in the immediate area of the school. However, this can get a bit tricky if the school in your area is full or has a waiting list. Then you have to look outside of your area. Keep in mind when doing this that public bus transportation is not available; you are responsible for taking your children to, and picking them up from, school.

Secondary schools are also funded by the state. Like primary schools, they are managed by religious orders and have a faith-based ethos. Despite religion being prevalent in school, it is perfectly acceptable for a parent to withdraw their children from the religious classes.

Keep copies of your children's school transcripts, their immunization records, and other health information, such as medical prescriptions, eye prescriptions, and dental records. Also, keep copies of your birth and marriage (or divorce) certificates, bank drafts, letters of credit, tax documents, and social security cards handy to present at Immigrations.

Moving with Pets

Funnily enough, moving with a pet is more difficult than moving with your child. The process has become more rigorous in modern years to ensure that diseases such as rabies are not introduced. All dogs and cats that enter Ireland from anywhere other than Britain must spend six months in quarantine unless they have been approved for travel under the Pet Travel Scheme—also called a Pet Passport. The Pet Passport certifies pets traveling between EU member states and certain qualifying non-EU states (including the United States) that have been microchipped and are vaccinated against rabies.

In order to import your dog or cat into Ireland from the United States, you must make sure to apply for the Pet Passport, completing each of the following in order:

- First, get your pet microchipped. This should be done before anything else.

- Second, get your pet vaccinated for rabies. This can be done the same day as the microchipping.

- Six months before you go to Ireland, get your pet's blood tested to ensure there are enough rabies antibodies. Your pet must have a result greater than 0.5 IU/ml.

- Twenty-four to forty-eight hours prior to your departure, have a licensed vet treat your pet for ticks and tapeworms.

- After all of this has been completed, have a Veterinary Certificate (Pet Passport) endorsed by your veterinarian.

- Finally, accompany your pet (or have somebody acting on your behalf) on an approved carrier into Ireland.

If you want to import your cat or dog into Ireland from America but your pet hasn't been fully prepared for the Pet Passport, you can choose to put your pet in an approved public quarantine for six months. There is only one such quarantine location in Ireland, and it is in Dublin. Space is typically available, but you should call and reserve space ahead of time to ensure room for your pet. There is no flexibility on this. Customs officers offer three choices if you aren't prepared with the Pet Passport: shell out the money for quarantine, export your pet back home, or euthanasia.

What to Bring

Moving to Ireland is going to be an entirely different experience than renting a U-Haul and moving across town, or even across the country! You are going to have to seriously weigh whether bringing things will be worth the cost of shipping. Try to find the bottom line and stick with it. Anything you can't bear to part with but can't ship for practical reasons can go in a storage unit. It should also be noted that many rental homes are fully furnished, so you will have all the necessities, including beds, couches, tables, etc.

Where you are in your life will certainly play a large role in deciding what to bring with you. Students, for example, may be able to shove all their personal belongings into their airline baggage allowance and travel unencumbered. Families, however, require much more, shall we say, stuff. Families collect little mementos from their lives together, which, for obvious reasons, are difficult to part with.

Unless you are particularly attached to any of your furniture, this can be the first to go. Furniture weighs the most and can easily be replaced at one of Ireland's many furniture stores—from cookie-cutter IKEA to cheap-and-cheerful Argos to stunning custom-made furniture at Kelco Designs.

Electronics and appliances can also be eliminated with one fell swoop. Electricity in Ireland is not compatible with U.S. voltage. Ireland runs a 220V electrical system, and the United States runs a 120V electrical system with a flat three-pin plug, so you can't just plug your appliances into an electrical

© SUSAN LEGG

Ireland has an entirely different electrical system than the U.S.

DAILY LIFE

SHIPPING CHARGES

If you are moving your family to Ireland permanently, shipping your goods may be a viable option. However, be aware of various charges that you might incur. You will need a survey on-site at your U.S. property in order to get a quote for what costs you might expect. A fee will be charged for hauling the container to your residence, packing it, then returning it to the port. You will have to pay for the services of a removal company in the United States, then to clear customs in the United States. Once your goods leave the United States, you should expect a fee for shipping to Ireland via a shipping line, Terminal Handling Charges in Ireland, then to clear Irish customs. An additional fee is charged to clear the port, ship to your destination, unload at your residence, and return to the port. In addition, documentation fees will be added from both the United States and Ireland.

outlet. You have to buy a converter or transformer, as well as an adaptor for the plug. There are, however, many U.S. travel shops, department stores, and Web vendors such as Amazon that sell kits with converters and adaptors. It really comes down to personal preference and practicality. Would it cost more to ship your home theater system and sort out the converter and adaptor, or just buy a new one in Ireland?

Laptops are often like an extra appendage and are indisputably one of the most important things you'll want to bring. Also, laptops are a lot more expensive in Ireland than they are in the United States, so it's a good idea to bring your own rather than buying a new one there. You'll be happy to know that most laptops these days have a dual voltage charger, so all you need is the three-prong adaptor plug in order to charge your laptop. Ditto most digital cameras, although if you have an older one you should check your owner's manual first. Many hotels, B&Bs, pubs, and cafés offer wireless Internet access for free or a small charge.

You should also note that it is important to change your address with the USPS when moving to Ireland. You cannot do this via the standard website but should fill out the change of address card and hand it in to your local post office. The USPS forwards first-class mail internationally at no extra charge, but they will not forward anything that requires a customs form.

SHIPPING OPTIONS

If you find you simply cannot part with some (or all) of your goods, you can hire a relocation company to ship your items to Ireland. Expats from America will find plenty of companies available for shipping goods to Ireland. Since competition is quite fierce, you should shop around and make sure you get a reliable removals company. One of the largest in Ireland is Careline Moving and Storage (www.careline.ie/), which caters to international relocations. They have offices in Dublin and Limerick. Make sure any relocation company you hire is a member of the British Association of Removals (BAR) and they give you full disclosure to all charges and potential charges. Do your research carefully, but the general rule of thumb is the more expensive, the better service you will get.

Be warned: Shipping goods is not cheap. It costs, on average, €4,000–5,000 from the East Coast and an additional €1,000–1,500 from the West Coast. You can save money by packing your goods yourself and collecting them from the drop-off center, or you can pay the full whack for door-to-door service, in which the relocation company will pack your goods, ship them, clear customs, deliver, and unpack them for you. Large shipments require containers of 20–40 feet, which are shipped through a shipping line, but small shipments are sent in a shared container (150 cubic feet), only leaving for Ireland when the entire container is full. This means you may be waiting a while for your goods to arrive.

When your containers land in Ireland, they must clear customs. You will be responsible for any customs costs levied by the officials. However, if you plan to take up residency in Ireland, you can obtain relief from customs charges if you previously lived outside the EU for 12 months or more, and the items will remain in your possession (you can't sell or lend them) for at least 12 months.

HOUSING CONSIDERATIONS

Finding the perfect place to live may well end up being your biggest task when moving to Ireland. Negotiating the legal and practical logistics of a foreign country can be quite rigorous, not to mention exhausting. Not only do you have to decide what location you should live in (city center, suburbs, town, village, rural), you have to decide what type of housing you want (attached, detached, or semidetached house; cottage; apartment; single room), and you have to decide whether you want to rent or buy. Buying means you have to retain the services of a lawyer, spend months wading through paperwork, and secure a mortgage that will allow you to purchase your dream home. But renting can leave you with a grumpy, inefficient landlord or a sense of "throwing money away."

While you may feel like these decisions are endless, take heart. All of these intricacies will be addressed and attainable answers found to make finding housing in Ireland easier than it may seem at first glance.

The Irish Housing Market

Keeping track of house prices in Ireland right now is a full-time job in its own right. You're best to leave that to the auctioneers (the real estate agents of Ireland). However, there is a lot to be said for research. Ireland's real estate market dramatically increased in the late 1990s through 2008 due to the economic boom they experienced. Prices began to stabilize in 2007, but the property bubble burst in 2008. By 2010, house prices had fallen by 35 percent compared to 2007, and in April 2011, a fire sale of homes in Dublin saw a fall of up to 65 percent from peak selling prices.

Houses are available.

While all of this is bad for Ireland's housing market, it does mean it is a buyer's market. People are desperate to get rid of their properties, often at ridiculously low prices. But you should make sure you are either a cash buyer or that you can secure an international mortgage from a multinational bank. Banks such as HSBC, Lloyds TSB, and Bank of Scotland are capable of financing international mortgages, so you may be able to get a mortgage from one of them. Keep in mind that banks have tightened their lending practices, with the number of home loans approved in Ireland falling by 73 percent in mid-2010.

Renting or Buying

The decision to rent or buy is not only a practical one, it is a personal one. You may be a student only needing a small room or a retiree wanting to invest in property right away. It mostly comes down to your budget, but for most expatriates, starting out renting is your best option. This gives you the time to try out different cities, towns, or neighborhoods, as well as gives you time to decide if Ireland is really the right place for you.

Whether you decide to rent or buy a property, do not sign a lease or put down a deposit until after you have arrived in Ireland and had a chance to see the property yourself. This way you can avoid scams and resulting disappointments, as well as get a feel for the place: hear the sound of the early-morning delivery trucks at the next-door flower shop if you decide to live in the city center, or experience the long morning drive into the city for work each morning if you choose the country. Take your time checking out the property you are interested in, getting a feel for its surroundings (is it next to a noisy pub or in the middle of a leafy neighborhood?) and your neighbors (are they mostly students or families?), and determining the state the property is in (is it newly built or damp and molding?) and how close it is to public transportation (will you have to drive everywhere, or is there a bus stop one block away?). These are the things you will be able to grasp by going in person rather than looking at photos online.

RENTING

Renting a property in Ireland is similar to what you're used to in the United States—you search for the accommodation that suits you, put down a deposit, sign a lease, then move in. Only…things are a lot more laid-back in Ireland, particularly now that owners are desperate to get renters in. Deposits may be required but are often overlooked, leases may be signed but are often not even mentioned, and background or criminal checks? Never done.

One of the biggest shocks to me upon moving to Ireland is that most rented accommodations are already furnished—from the teaspoons in your silverware drawer to the matches for lighting the candles. While you may not like your landlord's Pepto-Bismol pink walls, you won't have to buy furnishings. Needless to say, you shouldn't change anything unless specifically allowed by your landlord first.

Some apartments and larger houses come unfurnished. If you choose an unfurnished property, you will need to set aside some money to furnish your new home. You can speak to your landlord about reimbursement at the end of your lease, but most likely you will just have to sell your furniture if you choose to move to a furnished property after living in an unfurnished one.

Finding the Right Place

Rentals can be found via newspapers, the Internet, or signing up with rental agencies. The best way to find a rental is through word of mouth. Ask any friends or contacts if they know somebody who knows somebody else who is renting out a place that would suit you. Since the Irish rental market tends to be pretty laid-back, landlords are more willing to rent to somebody that

CRACKING THE CLASSIFIEDS' CODES

- NS: no smoking
- All mod cons: all modern conveniences
- Pm: per month
- Pw: per week
- En-suite room: room with bathroom
- Double or single room: double or single bed in the room
- Garden: yard
- To let: for rent
- NTL: television and Internet

- Refuse included: includes garbage
- Bedsit: studio with shared bathroom facilities
- Accommodation to let: generally refers to a room in an apartment or house
- Property to let: refers to the whole house
- WC: bathroom (stands for water closet)
- Ha: hectares
- GFCH: gas fired central heating
- OFCH: oil fired central heating

DAILY LIFE

comes recommended and who will be more likely to pay their rent and not wreck the place.

You can see To Let signs hanging outside of accommodations that are available to rent, or turn to the classifieds in the local newspaper. The best way to look for rentals, however, is to browse listings online. Websites like www.daft.ie, www.let.ie, www.property.ie, and www.houserental.ie offer classifieds to help you find a suitable rental. These ads are updated regularly, and you can sort your search according to what you want or need, whether it is an elevator or a balcony with a view.

You can also register your details with an estate agent in the area you are looking in. The bonus of being registered with an estate agent is they usually manage the properties they show you, which means you have somebody to do the searching for you, you have 24-hour emergency services once you move into the property, and you have help setting up essential utility bills. You will have to provide an employment reference, bank reference, and previous landlord reference, and pay deposits and fees to get set up with an estate agent.

Rental Prices

The recession and property market bust in Ireland have caused rents to drop a bit, but probably not as much as you would expect. In fact, rental prices have recently begun to climb again: The 2009 national average rental rate was €771, and the 2010 national average rental rate was €840. This is because banks are not approving mortgages, so people aren't purchasing homes and are being forced to rent. Additionally, since Ireland's economy has been so tumultuous over the past few years, people are simply choosing to rent rather than buy.

In 2011, rents had dropped a total of 27 percent (with a national average at €830 per month) since the peak of the property boom in 2007. This trend differs dramatically between large and small towns. In Dublin city center, rent costs more than double that of a small town like Castlebar. Some places in Dublin like Rathgar and Ranelagh in the suburbs or Parnell Street or Temple Bar in the city center have been almost totally unaffected by rent drops. People simply want to live in these areas, and prices have stayed static to reflect this. However, if you are okay living in the suburbs, you may be able to save hundreds of euros in rent each month. Additionally, keep in mind that landlords will generally drop the rent if you agree to stay for longer, and it is not unusual to ask for a lower rate and have the landlord accept.

Leases

There are two types of tenancy agreements in Ireland: periodic and fixed term. Periodic tenancy is not for a fixed amount of time and is generally an informal oral agreement. This type of tenancy is by far the most common in Ireland. Fixed-term tenancies cover a specific amount of time—usually six months to a year—and are usually written in a lease. Many city center locations will require a lease, as will letting agents. However, leases in Ireland are not as hard and fast as U.S. leases. If you need to leave, simply give one month's notice first, and you're free.

A lease for rental property in Ireland usually includes property details, monthly rent, deposit paid, the length of the rental, notice period required, and any other costs that will be covered by the tenant (telephone, Internet, garbage, etc.). Landlords cannot charge more than the current market rate for the apartment, so you don't have to worry about being charged way more than you should. Rent can be reviewed annually, but you must be given 28 days written notice before rent can increase.

Before you sign any papers, make sure you check the property for any damage that you could be levied with later. If your property is furnished, you should get an inventory list so you don't have to pay for any furniture when you move out. Check your appliances to make sure they are usable prior moving in. Read your lease thoroughly in order to establish who is responsible for various bills like water, gas, or electricity.

Your landlord is legally obligated to make sure the property meets certain standards, including roofs, windows, tiles, ceilings, and gardens in good condition. If the property needs repair during the course of your lease, the landlord is required to repair it, but this is often informally deducted from your rent if you agree to organize it yourself.

BUYING

Once you are finally feeling comfortable (and confident) enough to buy a property in Ireland, the secret to success is research, research, research. Buying in Ireland can be complex and time-consuming, so don't set yourself ridiculous deadlines, and keep an open mind. It is important to note that, unlike the United States, there are no national property listings in Ireland. This can be exceedingly frustrating and means the entire process often takes a lot longer than is necessary. Rather than choosing one agent who goes out and searches for houses that suit you, you have to endlessly register with different estate agents, who will only show you what is listed with their company. But if you are willing to invest the time and patience, you will eventually see light at the end of the tunnel and own your own little piece of Ireland.

Once you've decided on your ideal location, use the same ideas mentioned under *Renting* in order to find a house to purchase. Keep your eyes peeled for For Sale signs, read the classified sections (particularly in the region you are looking to purchase), and browse websites to find recently listed properties. Most importantly, sign up with the local estate agent offices and find out what homes they have listed for sale.

Next, think about your budget. This may be entirely dependent on your personal situation, but a house is a giant financial commitment, so don't get yourself in over your head. Find something that is within your budget and suits your tastes. A four-bedroom house in Dublin is going to cost you an awful lot more than an ancient cottage in Doolin.

Purchasing Steps

You should make sure to hire a good solicitor to guide you through the necessary legal paperwork. Unlike in the United States, where all of real-estate-related legal matters are wrapped up with the agent, in Ireland a solicitor (lawyer) is hired to do all of this. Solicitors charge 1–1.5 percent of the total house price.

Once you have settled on your ideal property and have your solicitor to do paperwork, you should arrange financing. Unless you have cash to pay outright, this will be the trickiest part of the process—banks can be difficult to extract money from—but not impossible if you have a stable job, a good income, and a good credit record.

Once you have financing, you can put an offer on the property by paying a booking deposit. This deposit ranges from €3,000 to 3 percent of the sale price but is refundable up until contracts are signed. Your offer should be contingent on a property survey, which will detail any problems with the property, such as mold, a leaking roof, or a crumbling infrastructure. A property survey can cost upward of €400 depending on the size of the property, but this is one area you do not want to skimp on. If you are purchasing an older property, paying the extra money for a more detailed survey may save you bucket loads in future repairs.

I should mention that even after you have put a deposit down, another buyer can swoop in and make a higher offer, rendering your offer null and void. Unfortunately, this is quite common. I had a friend who had this happen to her four times when looking for a house in Galway. Each time she thought the house was her dream house and was absolutely crushed when another buyer offered more.

If everything goes according to plan, the estate agent will issue your solicitor contracts. This is where your solicitor earns the money you're paying. The solicitor checks to make sure there are no tricks in the legalese before approving it and letting you sign. You will also need to finalize your mortgage, submit a direct debit order (for funds to automatically be debited from your account), purchase building insurance, and buy life insurance. (Life insurance is dicussed more in *Hidden Fees*.) At this stage you pay about 10 percent of the purchase price as a deposit, although this amount is usually negotiable. Once your contracts are signed and exchanged, you will sign a few more papers, pay the final amount, and the property will be yours.

Hidden Fees

You already know about your legal fees, the surveyor fee, and your deposit, but there are a few more hidden costs associated with purchasing property that you should be aware of. You should make sure to include these costs in your budget.

You will have to pay stamp duty (tax) to the government. This is 1 percent of the total value of your home up to €1 million, and 2 percent on any value above €1 million. Your lender will charge an application fee for applying for a mortgage. You will be required to get building insurance, which is similar to homeowners insurance, and if you are purchasing with a mortgage (rather than paying with cash), you are required to buy life insurance. Finally, don't forget that VAT adds 21 percent to all professional services, such as the solicitor or the surveyor. These fees add up quickly, so be aware of them prior to making an offer on any property.

Renovating

If you're a big fan of DIY, by all means purchase a fixer-upper and sculpt it into the abode of your dreams. But if you aren't a builder or don't know every single detail about fixing up a house (and have the patience of a saint), my advice is DDIY (Don't Do It Yourself). Spending just an extra few thousand euros on your house may represent a much better value than spending the time and money that will be required to fix it up.

First of all, you will need permission from your local planning authority for any major restoration or building works. This takes a minimum of two months before you will receive a "yay" or "nay."

Renovating an old house may be more work than you expect.

If you stumble across renovations you can't complete yourself, you will need to hire a builder. This can be a separate saga of its own. Suffice to say, really research your builders and get loads of references from their previous employers. Irish builders are notorious for skipping necessary work, arriving late and leaving early, and slowly incurring outrageous bills. Obtain quotes with specific details to avoid receiving a huge bill for work that shouldn't have been done at all.

Building a Home

If you have always had your heart set on a particular style house in a particular part of Ireland that can only come to fruition by being built from the ground up, then building your own home may be a choice you should consider. This option is not for the fainthearted. You will need Zen-like patience and the ability to easily switch your brain on and off throughout the entire building process.

Begin by finding your perfect piece of land. Once this is bought, Irish law requires you to get planning permission for nearly every stage of building on the land. Not only do you have to apply for planning permission, but you must also place a notice in the local newspaper notifying the local public of your

DAMP IN HOUSES

In a wet country like Ireland, there are a lot of cases of damp, or what some would call mold. There are three types of damp that can get into a house and cause damage: rising damp, penetrating damp, and poor-ventilation damp. Unfortunately, most houses in Ireland (particularly older ones) lose out on all counts. Combined with the wet weather outside, damp is a serious problem in Ireland.

Rising damp occurs when water or moisture from the ground rises up into the solid walls and floors of your property. Penetrating damp occurs when water from the outside seeps into the building. Damp due to poor ventilation occurs because, unlike most newer homes in the United States, Irish houses don't have an escape route for moist air, such as vents in windowsills. This causes condensation and water vapor to build up on the inside of the walls.

The best way to combat this is to keep your house heated so you are less likely to experience condensation. Make sure your property has loft and wall insulation to help the property hold heat in longer and keep walls warmer. Also, check to see if the windows have double glazing, which will hold warmth in and keep moisture out.

Make sure you check your new property thoroughly for signs of damp. Sometimes it will look like a stain from a spilled drink, spreading across your walls, ceiling, or floors, while other times it will show as black mold crawling across your walls. Sometimes you may only be able to smell it. Whatever the case, check thoroughly. This is cancer for a house and can also lead to sinus infections and a higher incidence of allergies.

intentions. Strange but true. If you are granted permission, you will have five years to complete building before the planning permission expires.

Once you have your land and your planning permission, you will need to hire an architect to help you come up with the blueprints for your dream home and a builder to you build it for you. Architects generally charge a percentage of the total cost of work (usually about 10 percent). Get references for both from friends or neighbors, but steer clear of estate agents, as they often receive a commission for referrals.

Be wary of an architect who has his "own" builder (or vice versa). Make sure your builder is registered with Homebond and a member of the Irish Home Builders' Association (IHBA), which will insure you against the loss of a deposit in case the builder goes belly up, water and smoke damage for two years, and major structural defects for 10 years after completion. You will be expected to pay your builder a deposit (usually 10 percent of the agreed price), but the remainder of the cost varies between builders. Some require it be paid in stages, while others ask for it upon completion. Make sure this is agreed upon before signing any contracts.

Household Expenses

Whether you choose to buy or rent, once you are ready to move in, you are going to need to set up utilities at your property. Some utilities, like telephone or Internet, you can pick and choose according to your personal preference or your budget. Others, like water or electricity, you simply will have to pay for. Most utilities differ widely based on usage and whether your property is located in a rural or urban setting.

DAILY LIFE

WATER

Water is safe, clean, and drinkable in Ireland, although it is slightly "harder" than in America. This means there is more limestone in the water, causing limescale to build up in the dishwasher, tea kettle, and showerhead. It isn't harmful and can easily be remedied by purchasing various counteracting chemicals.

Your monthly water bill will depend on if you live in an urban or rural area. Urban areas receive water through capital water schemes administered by local authorities. Water is charged according to the amount you use. Rural areas are part of a group water scheme, which is administered by trustees elected by the local authority and gets water supplies from public mains, wells, or lakes. With this scheme, you pay a flat rate.

TV LICENSE

No matter whether you are a tenant or an owner, if your household has a television, you are required by law to have a television license (€160). This license is issued for one year and can be transferred if you move. You can apply for a television license at your local post office. Now, all that being said, this law is not enforced as much as it should be. It is hard to police since the enforcers have to actually go knocking door-to-door. But if you are found to not have a license, you will be required to make a court appearance and be issued a fine of up to €1,000. To avoid the hassle, just pay the fee.

GARBAGE

Garbage is collected weekly in Ireland. You have a number of options for eliminating your waste. One option is prepaid bin tags, which are available for purchase at local shops. Each time you want your garbage taken away, you'll put a tag on your trash can (or "bin") and leave it out for collection. This means you only pay for the waste you send to the landfill. Alternatively, you can choose curbside collection, although this is mainly restricted to urban areas. Fees vary according to region, but the service is the same as in the United States: Leave

COST OF LIVING IN IRELAND

In the 2010 Global Cost of Living Survey, Dublin was ranked as the 42nd most-expensive city for expats to live. Despite this, Dublin, and the rest of the country, are fairly manageable. First off, the cost of living is supported by well-paying jobs, and second of all, there are numerous types of stores and shops that allow you to shop cheaply or expensively. Lidl and Aldi offer cheap prices and bulk buying; Dunnes Stores, Tesco, and Supervalu offer regular specials, coupons, and value shopping; and Marks and Spencer offers fresh market produce with higher prices than the main shops. It costs approximately €65 for one week of groceries for one person in Dublin, but this price drops to about €55 when you get to the smaller towns or cities. The following is a chart of general prices you might come across when living in Ireland. Prices drop the farther out of the towns and city centers you go.

Going Out

Sandwich	€5
Pint of beer	€4.50+
Latte or mocha	€3.50
Glass of (house) wine	€4.50+
Fast-food meal	€3.50+
Restaurant meal	€35+

Groceries

Milk	€1.65 (two liters)
Bread	€2.90
Potatoes	€1.00 (per kilo)
Soft drinks	€1.70 (two-liter bottle)
Juice	€0.99 (one-liter bottle)
Tomatoes	€2.00 (per kilo)
Yogurt	€0.79 (each)

Household

Laundry detergent	€3+
Dishwashing liquid	€1.99
Toothpaste	€2.75+
Shampoo	€4.50+
Deodorant	€2.70
Pain reliever	€1.99

Leisure

Movie ticket	€7+
Theater	€20
Cigarettes	€8.45

Bills and Utilities

Petrol (gas)	€1.52 per kilo unleaded, €1.48 per kilo diesel
Electricity	€80 per month
Telephone line rental	€45+

Public Transportation

Bus fare	€1.15+ (single)
DART commuter train	€2.25 (single)

your garbage bin next to the curb on the day of garbage collection, a garbage truck comes along and empties your bin, and then you get a monthly bill for the service. Recycling and composting are also popular options for eliminating domestic waste free of charge.

TELEPHONE AND INTERNET

Having a landline in Ireland isn't as common as in the United States. Generally you have to rent the line, then pay according to how many minutes you use. Since everybody has a cell phone anyway, many people just eliminate the landline. However, if you do decide to have a landline, make sure to shop around and compare the terms and conditions of the different telephone companies.

The main telephone company is Eircom, which charges for your phone line plus your usage. Eircom owns all of the telephone lines in Ireland but rents out these lines to smaller companies. Beware if you sign up with one of these smaller companies; if the telephone line breaks or needs repairs, Eircom will readily repair it if you have rented the line through them, but repairing it gets a bit dicey with smaller companies.

One of the most important household expenses nowadays is the Internet. Fortunately, Ireland has a number of choices for Internet service, although the service you choose will depend largely on how much you use it, your budget, and whether you are in a rural or urban area. Broadband can be set up through one of the five main methods: digital subscriber line (DSL), cable, mobile, satellite, and wireless. The price depends on the package you choose but will generally boil down to when you are browsing (peak or off-peak times), what you are downloading (documents, music, films), and whether there are services in your area. If you don't have service in your area, you can get a USB dongle key, which provides Internet via a cell phone network.

ELECTRICITY

Electricity in Ireland is generated from numerous sources, including gas, coal, oil, and renewable resources. Ireland's electrical voltage is 230V, and the country uses three-pin plugs, which means you need adaptors and converters if you plan to bring anything electrical to Ireland. Your electricity will need to be set up through ESB Electric Ireland. ESB uses meters to measure the electricity you use, and every two months you receive a bill based on your usage. To set up a new connection, contact the ESB Network (1-850-372-757, www.esb.ie) and give your name and contact details; your Meter Point Reference Number (MPRN), available from the builder or landlord; and your property address.

HEATING

There are two types of heating in Ireland: immersion heating for the hot water tank and central heating for the rooms. Both are different from what you may be used to. In the United States we generally have our hot water heater on all day, with the water heated to a consistent temperature. In Ireland they have the immersion heater, which is an electrical element installed in a hot water tank. It is connected to a switch located somewhere in the house (typically the hallway closet). The only way to get hot water, then, is to flick this immersion switch on and wait for it to heat the water. Most immersion heaters are now fitted with a timer, so you can set the water to be heated at specific times – for example, before you go to work in the mornings.

Central heating is the main type of heating system in Ireland. In America, we generally have forced air, which blows out warm air until the house reaches the desired temperature. With central heating, water is heated in your hot water tank, then circulated through pipes and radiators in order to warm your house. Since most homes don't possess a dryer, only a washing machine (a big shock to me), radiators work as a great location for hanging wet clothes to help them dry quicker.

© SUSAN LEGG

Radiators keep Irish houses warm.

GAS (PETROL)

Everybody in America moans about gas prices, but in reality, America has it easy compared to the rest of the world. Government taxes on gas in Ireland, England, and the rest of the EU raise prices so high they are nearly unfathomable to Americans. Many cars run on diesel, which gets better gas mileage and is slightly cheaper, but this is still pricey. For example, in Ireland gas costs about €1.52 per liter of unleaded fuel (in April 2011), which works out to about €7 per gallon (approximately US$10). This quickly adds up. So it would behoove you to buy a small car or use public transportation as much as possible.

LANGUAGE AND EDUCATION

Despite efforts from the government, and the fact that *Gaeilge* (the Irish language) is listed as its first official language in the constitution, English is in fact the primary language spoken in Ireland. But while you won't need to know any Irish, the Irish do have a curious habit of peppering their speech with Irish words, often called *cúpla focal* (couple of words). They sprinkle these words in during everyday conversations, during work meetings, in news broadcasts, or when conducting business. Additionally, there is a whole new set of meanings for words you already know; for example, *lift* rather than *elevator* or *first floor* rather than *ground floor*.

Learning the intricacies of the cultural differences may take a little time, but they are not difficult. You can often infer the meaning from the context the words or phrases are used in, or, failing that, simply ask. The Irish love

© SARAHJANE SWEENEY

explaining where their words come from and regaling foreigners with stories of their heritage.

The Irish Language

Irish is a Celtic language dating back hundreds of centuries, arriving with the Celtic tribes around 500 B.C. The earliest known form was found in *Ogham* (the early medieval alphabet) inscriptions from the 3rd or 4th century. After Ireland became a mostly Christian island, Old Irish became prevalent and can be found in Latin manuscripts from the 6th century. In the 10th century, Old Irish evolved into Middle Irish, from which sprang Early Modern or Classical Irish, a literary language that was used in the 13th–17th centuries.

The Irish language began to disappear in the 19th century, after centuries of colonization, repression, and emigration began to take its toll on the population. By the time Irish Independence occurred in 1922, there was a severely depleted population of Irish speakers in Ireland. After independence, the Irish language was isolated to remote pockets in rural areas of the country, and the language was often associated with poverty.

In 1926, just a few short years after the Irish gained their independence from England, the Gaeltacht Commission made recommendations to the newly formed Irish government to restore the Irish language. Many of the recommendations were ignored, and others, such as a requirement by state and civil service workers to speak Irish, were implemented but not enforced.

Even in modern Ireland, a qualification for Irish is required to apply for civil service positions, but a high degree of fluency isn't necessary. In my previous job in Ireland I was required to have some degree of fluency in Irish. I took Irish classes for a year but was never forced to sit the exam or prove that I knew Irish. At work, Irish isn't required in the everyday course of work, but perfect command of English is. If an Irish speaker wants to apply for a grant, complain to the government about procedures, or even organize a utility bill, they need to use English, not Irish. All of this has helped enforce the use of English rather than Irish as a primary language in Ireland.

However, since the Celtic Tiger boom in the mid-1990s, the Irish language has experienced a resurgence of sorts, with about 10 percent of the population now being fluent or near fluent in Irish. Students are taught to speak,

USEFUL IRISH PHRASES

While you certainly won't need them, the following phrases (with pronunciation) will be useful to know and will impress any Irish person if you sprinkle them into your everyday conversation.

Irish Phrase	Pronunciation	English Translation
Dia duit.	dia-GWITCH	Hello. (Literally means "God be with you.")
Sláinte.	SLAHN-chuh	Cheers. (Mainly used when drinking.)
Go raibh maith agat.	GORE-uh MAH uh-GUT	Thank you.
Tá fáilte romhat.	TA-falt-cha ROOTS	You're welcome.
Cad es ainm duit?	CED es anim-GWITCH	What is your name?
. . . is ainm dom.	is-ANUM-dum	. . . is my name.
Slán go fóill.	SLAHN-g'FOLE	See you later. (Shorten to slán: goodbye.)
Conas atá tu?	KUH-nish uh TAH-too	How are you?
Tá me go maith.	TAH may guh MAH	I'm good.
Cá bhfuil an leithreas?	kah will an LEH-riss	Where are the toilets?

DAILY LIFE

read, and write in both Irish and English, and in the *Gaeltacht* (Irish-speaking areas), Irish is the designated first language, with even road signs listed in Irish. However, English is still the dominant language and is used in all social, economic, and cultural contexts.

To date, Ireland has had some modern success with preserving and promoting the Irish language, particularly through the Gaelscoileanna and various media outlets produced solely through the Irish language. Additionally, Irish was registered as an official language of the EU in 2005, and many modern software companies now offer software applications for the Irish language.

Gaelscoileanna is the name for schools in Ireland that are taught entirely in the Irish language, with students learning Irish through language immersion. This education movement is one the fastest growing fields of education in Ireland, with approximately 40,000 children being educated through the Irish language outside of the Gaeltacht. These schools provide a much higher success rate in producing competent Irish-language speakers. In contrast, the traditional Irish schools that teach through the English language, offering just classes for the Irish language, produce very few fluent Irish speakers.

Various media outlets have also helped preserve the Irish language. Some of the larger ones are TG Ceathair (TG4), the television channel for the Irish language; RTÉ Raidió na Gaeltachta (RnaG), the radio station for Irish speakers; RTÉ One, a television channel that broadcasts programs in Irish; and *Foinse* (Source), the main Irish-language newspaper. There are a handful of newspapers, magazines, websites, and publishers that print solely in Irish, and most English-language newspapers have an Irish-language column. Additionally, most of the national, regional, and local English radio stations play Irish-language programs regularly.

THE GAELTACHT

The Gaeltacht are designated Irish-speaking areas in Ireland, covering parts of the counties of Donegal, Mayo, Galway, and Kerry along the west coast, as well as parts of counties Cork, Meath, and Waterford. There are less than 100,000 people living in the Gaeltachta, with less than 75 percent of these people fluent in Irish.

The Gaeltacht was established in 1926, after a report by the first *Coimisiún na Gaeltachta* (the Gaeltacht Commission) recommended its formation in order to help restore the Irish language. In the early 1950s another Coimisiún na Gaeltachta recommended an updated definition of the Gaeltacht boundaries, defining Gaeltacht areas in seven of Ireland's 26 counties.

The largest Gaeltacht in Ireland is situated on the west coast in County Galway. The Galway Gaeltacht represents 47 percent of the Gaeltacht population and 26 percent of Gaeltacht land. Galway is a key location for many multinational software and medical industries, as well as the home of the National University of Ireland, Galway, the most important educational and research university in the west of Ireland.

Also on the west coast, just north of the Galway Gaeltacht, is the Mayo Gaeltacht. This Gaeltacht is divided into three distinct areas: Iorrais, Achaill, and Tuar Mhic

© CHRISTINA MCDONALD

The Gaeltacht is the Irish-speaking area of Ireland.

IRISH-LANGUAGE DIALECTS

As with any language, the Irish language has a number of distinct dialects, and these roughly coincide with the provinces of Munster (south), Connacht (west), and Ulster (north). It is interesting to note that Newfoundland (eastern Canada) also has a minor dialect of Irish that resembles the Irish spoken in the 16th and 17th centuries.

Munster Irish is spoken in the Kerry Gaeltacht, western county Cork, Cape Clear, Muskerry, and Dungarvan. Decies Irish is a dialect of Munster Irish spoken in Waterford. Munster Irish uses personal endings instead of pronouns with verbs; for example, "I must" in Munster Irish is *caithfead,* while in other dialects it is *caithfidh mé* (*mé* means I).

Connemara and the Aran Islands feature the strongest Connacht Irish dialect. A different subdialect of Connacht Irish is spoken in Tour-makeady in southern Mayo and yet another dialect in Erris and Achill in northern Mayo. These dialects are similar in vocabulary to Ulster Irish. Connemara Irish lengthens the vowel sounds, making it a very distinct dialect.

The most prominent of the Ulster dialects is the Rosses of Donegal, often used in Irish literature. Ulster Irish is similar to Scottish Gaelic, sharing many typical words and meanings. This type of Irish uses the negative participle *cha(n)* in place of the Munster and Connacht version *ní,* which generally confirms a negative statement.

This diversity between dialects has led to difficulties in defining standard Irish. For example, the simple phrase "How are you?" in Irish will show startling variations in each dialect: Ulster: *cad é mar atá tú?* Connacht: *cén chaoi a bhfuil tú?* Munster: *conas taoí?*

Éadaigh. The main town in the Gaeltacht, Béal an Mhuirthead, is situated outside of Castlebar, the largest town in County Mayo. Mayo has a strong industrial base of homegrown businesses, as well as significant multinational companies.

The Donegal Gaeltacht is situated at the west of the country, along the coastline. This is Ireland's second-largest Gaeltacht—25 percent of Gaeltacht population and 26 percent of total Gaeltacht land—and is considered the most rurally populated area in Europe. The three main parishes in the Donegal Gaeltacht are Na Rosa, Gaoth Dobhair, and Cloich Cheann Fhaola, which hold Irish-language courses for Irish and foreign students.

The smallest Gaeltacht is Meath, consisting of the two villages of Rath Cairn and Baile Ghib. These two villages are actually resettled communities. In the 1930s, the Irish government redistributed land from absentee landlords to poor farmers from other Gaeltacht areas. These Irish farmers came to the Meath villages, bringing their native dialects and customs that are today part of the Meath Gaeltacht heritage.

ENGLISH WORDS ORIGINATING FROM IRISH

Although we may like to think of English as its own unique language, it actually evolved over hundreds of years, picking up various words from multiple languages. Here are a few common English words that were taken from the Irish language.

English	Irish	Meaning
Bother	bodhar	literally means "deaf" (if you are deaf, you won't be bothered)
Banshee	bean sí	woman of the fairy
Bog	bog	soft
Boycott	boycott	from Charles Boycott, who was ostracized in Ireland
Clan	clan	children, lineage
Colleen	cailín	girl
Down	á dún	down
Galore	go leor	plenty, enough
Leprechaun	leipreachán	leprechaun
Pet	peata	tame animal
Shamrock	seamróg	shamrock
Slob	slaba	slovenly person
Smithereens	smidrín	small fragments
Trouser	triubhas	pants
Whiskey	uisce (beatha)	water (of life)

The Cork Gaeltacht is composed of two main areas: The Múscraí Gaeltacht and the Oileán Chleiré Gaeltacht. The largest settlement areas are in the Múscraí Gaeltacht, with the villages of Baile Mhic Íre, Baile Bhuirne, and Béal Átha an Ghaorthaidh being the most populated.

There are two main areas in the Kerry Gaeltacht: Corca Dhuibhne on the Dingle Peninsula and Uíbh Ráthach on the Iveragh Peninsula. The Dingle Peninsula and the Ring of Kerry are two of the most popular tourist routes in Ireland, attracting visitors to this Gaeltacht throughout the year.

The smallest Gaeltacht in Ireland is the Waterford Gaeltacht, representing only 1 percent of Gaeltacht land to the west of Dungarvan. The Waterford Gaeltacht has a population of less than 1,500 people, representing just 2 percent of the Gaeltacht population.

LEARNING THE IRISH LANGUAGE

The Irish language plays an important role in the culture and the heritage of Ireland's people, including the millions of people worldwide who claim Irish heritage. Learning the Irish language is one of the best ways for expats to get a cultural sense of Ireland and identify with the ancient heritage of the Irish people. For those wanting to learn Irish, there are a number of avenues to pursue. Summer courses are regularly offered in the Gaeltacht, cultural centers run Irish-language courses as well as evening courses, and various computer programs such as Rosetta Stone sell applications for learning Irish.

There are three main centers that teach Irish in Ireland: Áras Mháirtín Uí Chadhain in Galway, Oideas Gael in Donegal, and Oidhreacht Chorca Dhuibhne in Kerry. More than 3,000 adults from around the world arrive every year to learn Irish. Áras Mháirtín Uí Chadhain (www.gaeilge.oegaillimh.ie/aras_chadhain.html), the Irish Language Acquisition and Maintenance Centre for NUI, Galway, teaches traditional and cultural activities, holds workshops on Irish singing and dancing, and organizes outings to local places of interest, in addition to teaching the Irish language. Situated in the village of Carraroe in the Connemara Gaeltacht (just outside of Galway), the program offers certificates and higher diploma TEFL (Teaching English as a Foreign Language) courses, an International writers' course, and summer courses for credit in Irish studies and the Irish language.

Oideas Gael (www.oideas-gael.com) also holds annual Irish-language courses to promote the learning of the Irish language and foster Irish culture within the Gaeltacht. Oideas Gael is based in Gleann Cholm Cille in County Donegal and holds courses throughout the year for Irish and non-Irish people, from beginner to advanced speakers.

Oidhreacht Chorca Dhuibhne (www.corca-dhuibhne.com) helps preserve the Irish language in Baile an Fheirtéaraigh (Ballyferriter) on the Dingle Peninsula in County Kerry. Founded in 1980, Oidhreacht Chorca Dhuibhne combines the learning of Irish with preserving Ireland's heritage, history, geology, and biology.

Irish-language evening classes are offered in 15 locations across Ireland by Gaelchultúr, which was established to promote the Irish language and culture. If you want something a bit more intense, Comhchoiste na gColáistí Samhraidh (CONCOS) is a combination of 47 Irish summer colleges throughout Ireland that teach the Irish languages. Approved by the Department of Education and Science and the Department of Community, Rural and Gaeltacht Affairs, these summer colleges immerse students in the language so they can become more fluent.

DAILY LIFE

Education

Ireland has one of the best education systems in Europe and has a reputation worldwide for excellent, high-quality education. Eighty-one percent of Irish students complete secondary school, and about 60 percent of students continue on to higher education—one of the highest participation rates in the world. Full-time education is compulsory for ages 6–15; however, 65 percent of four-year-olds and almost all five-year-olds are enrolled in infant classes. Education is considered a fundamental right under the Irish constitution; therefore, education is free in almost all schools, including higher education in universities.

The Irish Education System is divided into three levels: primary (6–8 years), secondary (5–6 years) and higher education (university). Additionally, preschools, adult education, and further education have been encompassed as part of the education system.

PRIMARY EDUCATION

Primary school operates an eight-year program, including two infant classes (junior and senior infants) that are not required. This is followed by classes one through six, which are composed of languages (including Irish); mathematics; social, environmental, and scientific classes; arts; physical education; and social, personal, and health classes.

The primary-education sector includes state-funded schools—religious, nondenominational, multidenominational and Gaelscoileanna (Irish-language schools)—and preparatory schools, which are fee-paying schools. When the public school system was established in 1831, schools were meant to be mixed

BREAKDOWN OF IRISH AGES AND GRADES

Primary School Grade	Age	Secondary School Grade	Age
Junior Infant School	4	1st	12
Senior Infant School	5	2nd	13
1st	6	3rd (Junior Certificate)	14/15
2nd	7	4th (Transitional Year)	16
3rd	8	5th	17
4th	9	6th (Leaving Certificate)	18
5th	10		
6th	11		

religion. However, this did not end up happening, and today almost all primary schools are managed by the local Catholic church.

Public schools give priority to children living in the immediate area of the school, but if the school is full and they have a waiting list, you have to continue checking with schools until you find one that is open to new students. Each school has their own admissions policy, which students must adhere to before being admitted.

SECONDARY EDUCATION

Secondary education accounts for the subsequent six years after primary school and is comprised of secondary, vocational, comprehensive (combining academic and vocational subjects), and community (combining practical and academic subjects) schools. Like primary schools, secondary-level schools are managed by religious communities and churches. The majority of students attend secondary schools (54 percent), with a smaller amount attending vocational schools (33 percent). Second-level education consists of two cycles: a three-year junior cycle and a two- or three-year senior cycle.

In the junior cycle, students take 10–12 subjects over the course of three years. This course work culminates in the Junior Certificate Examination, an exam combining written, practical, project, oral, and aural testing. Students sit this exam around age 14 or 15. Upon passing, students have the option to take a transitional year, which focuses more on practical work rather than academia. Students engage in independent learning, participate in group projects, undergo work experience, and take sample courses they may be interested in pursuing during the senior cycle. Alternatively, students can opt to skip the transitional year and go straight to the senior cycle.

The senior cycle encompasses years four, five, and six, culminating in the Leaving Certificate Examination. The results of the leaving cert, as Irish students call it, are then used to gain access to universities and colleges.

HIGHER EDUCATION

Higher education encompasses seven universities, 14 institutes of technology, and a number of private colleges. The universities and institutes of technology are all self-governing but state funded. Education incorporates undergraduate studies, vocational and technical training, postgraduate studies, and adult and further education concepts.

Academic degrees break down similar to U.S. universities: a higher certificate (similar to our AA degree) for a two-year full-time course, a bachelor's degree for a three-year full-time course, an honors bachelor's degree for a three- or four-year course, a graduate diploma for a one-year vocational course,

DAILY LIFE

a master's degree (research or taught) for one to two years, and a doctorate (PhD) for three years or more of original research. Grades are slightly different than ours and are broken down into first honors, upper second honors, lower second honors, third, pass, or fail.

STUDY ABROAD

Whether you are considering studying abroad for a summer, a semester, a full academic year, or getting a postgraduate degree in Ireland, you will not only get one of the best educations in the world, but you will also encounter a rich cultural experience that is sure to change your life. Each university in Ireland has a Study Abroad Office, which coordinates all aspects of studying abroad for overseas students.

There are four universities in Ireland: Trinity College, the University of Limerick, Dublin City University, and the National University of Ireland (NUI), which has four constituent colleges, NUI Dublin, NUI Cork, NUI Galway, and NUI Maynooth. Additionally, there are 12 institutes of technology scattered across Ireland, the largest being the Dublin Institute of Technology. The study abroad programs available offer a wide range of courses but involve a full-time course load. Students interested in studying abroad in Ireland should visit the website of the university or institution they are interested and apply directly for their study abroad programs. Alternatively, information is available for students wishing to study abroad at the Irish Council for International Students website: www.icosirl.ie/.

Trinity College is one of the primary colleges in Ireland.

PRIVATE OR PUBLIC

Many parents worry about whether to send their children to private or public schools. Public schools are entirely funded by the Irish government, whereas private schools are subsidized by the government and also receive fees from enrolled students. For example, teachers' salaries at private schools are paid by the government, but if the school wants to hire extra teachers or staff, this is paid for by school fees. Because private schools are government subsidized, the fees tend to be relatively low compared with private schools in the United States. Since private schools financially support themselves (at least partially), they are allowed to select the students they enroll.

Boarding schools became popular just before independence as a way to provide Protestant education to non-Catholic students. Today boarding schools aren't as rigorous in their religious beliefs, and many students attend Mass on Sunday. Some boarding schools in Ireland offer accommodations on-site, while others use local families who are overseen by the school. Some are all-boy or all-girl schools. Some ascribe to a particular religion, while others don't. Most of them, however, are located in the Dublin area, so you will be hard-pressed to find one in the rural areas.

Irish private schools do see a higher percentage of students continuing on to university, but whether they do because of a better education or because the students that attend are typically in a higher socioeconomic bracket is widely debated. All students, no matter whether they attend public or private school, must still work toward their Junior and Leaving Certificate exams, so the curriculum and structure of the classes are relatively similar.

In addition to private primary and secondary schools, private colleges and universities are also available to students, mostly in the region of business and professional educational training. Training includes courses such as accountancy and business studies, law, hotel and catering, and tourism studies. Private colleges and universities are fee generated but still typically receive education grants from the government.

HOMESCHOOLS

Homeschooling your child is a viable education option in Ireland. There is no teaching qualification or university degree required, and you don't have to follow a formal lesson plan or curriculum. No structured, recurrent exams are required until the Leaving Certificate, which can be organized through adult education classes, distance learning programs, or the Dublin Tutorial Center. Additionally, Junior and Leaving Certificate exams can be taken by registering your child in any school in early January of the year your child will complete the exam. The Leaving Certificate is typically required for entering university, but some institutions allow just an interview and portfolio for students who were homeschooled and didn't take the Leaving Certificate exam. Parents interested in educating their children at home must register with the National Educational Welfare Board (NEWB) in order to ensure the level of education is up to state standards.

While homeschooling is certainly legal, it is not a popular choice and is still viewed with a little bit of trepidation by most parents in Ireland. There are only about 1,500 children estimated to be educated at home throughout Ireland, and these are clustered at about 300 homes. A group called The Home Education Network was established in 1998 to support and lobby for home educators. This nondenominational group gives parents support, as well as offers annual conferences on homeschooling.

HEALTH

Ireland has a modern, comprehensive, and reasonably efficient health care system that offers both public and private options, as well as social welfare for those below a certain income bracket. Health care is heavily subsidized by the government, so fees are reasonably low, especially when compared to health care costs in the United States.

While all of this sounds good on paper, Ireland is certainly not at the top of the World Health Organization's ranking of the world's health systems—that honor goes to France—but it isn't below the United States' ranking (37th). Ireland ranks at number 19 out of 190 countries, making it a solid health care system, but not one of the best. All residents of Ireland are entitled to receive health care through the public health care system, but waiting periods can be long, emergency facilities overcrowded, and doctors rushed.

However, the rise in life expectancy in Ireland over the past decade has been unmatched by any other country in the EU. Ten years ago Ireland had

© SARAHJANE SWEENEY

a life expectancy lower than the average EU life expectancy, and now it has exceeded the average rate, with a life expectancy of 79.5 years. Much of these gains have been achieved in the older age groups, showing a decrease in death from major diseases such as cancer, heart failure, and diabetes.

Insurance

There are two types of insurance in Ireland, and entitlement is primarily based on residence and financial means. To prove residence you have to show evidence of renting (such as a lease) or property purchase, a bank account in your name, and a residence permit or visa. All Irish citizens, as well as citizens of the EU who reside in Ireland, are entitled to health care. Those who are not from Ireland or are not normally resident there have to pay the full cost of the service, whether it is public or private, although the hospital may waive some or all of the costs if your income is below a certain income bracket.

PUBLIC HEALTH CARE

The public health care service in Ireland is managed by the Health Service Executive (HSE) and offers two categories of care: Category One and Category Two. Category One is a medical card that covers pretty much any medical expense you can think of—primary care; hospital costs; dental, ophthalmic, and aural services; maternity and infant care (including pre- and postnatal); prescriptions; and appliances like glasses or hearing aids. Eligibility is based on your total family income, age, and number of dependents. Everyone who doesn't qualify for Category One health care qualifies for Category Two. This is a subsidized health care system, whereby the government pays for most of the costs and you pay the rest.

Unfortunately, while the public health care system is free—or nearly so—you can think of it as "free to wait." You will have to wait for a doctor's appointment, wait for a referral, wait to be put on the waiting list to see a consultant, and wait to be seen at the emergency room or for a critical surgery. While you are waiting, people with private health insurance are allowed to jump to the top of the waiting list, making your wait even longer.

Here is how it breaks down: You are sick, so you make an appointment with your local general practitioner (GP). The GP refers you to a consultant who puts you on a waiting list for an appointment (some weeks or months

DAILY LIFE

UNIVERSAL HEALTH CARE BY 2016

There is a unanimous agreement among experts that the two-tiered, public-private health care system in Ireland is vastly unequal and unfair. It leaves people who don't have money waiting on gurneys in the hospital or held on long waiting lists, while people with money to buy private health insurance can skip the waiting list. In order to equalize this health care system, Health Minister James Reilly announced in March 2011 that Ireland's health care system is going to switch to a universal health care insurance by 2016. Universal health insurance is what the UK currently has and what U.S. president Obama envisioned for America during the U.S.'s health care shake-up in 2008-2009.

The new program will implement free GP care for everybody. Insurance will be compulsory, with either a public or private insurance company. The government will then pay the insurance premiums for low-income families and subsidize the rest. This health insurance policy will change hospitals that are for-profit into not-for-profit trusts, with the intent to make health care focus on the patient rather than the profit.

down the line). Once your appointment date is finally set, it can be for months in the future, so you have to sit tight and wait your turn. This is where private insurance comes in handy, essentially giving you a free pass to skip the line.

The overwhelming problems with the health care system in Ireland are the waiting lists and overcrowding in the emergency rooms. In the winter when cases of the flu and colds rise, there are nearly weekly stories of patients lying on gurneys in the halls of the hospital, waiting to be seen for 2–3 days. Part of the problem is simply a lack of enough beds, but another problem is that many beds are being used by elderly patients because there is a lack of local elderly homes. However, when you do see a doctor, they are competent and professional, as well as kind and understanding.

There have been positive strides in making the wait time less for health care operations and procedures. In 2002 the government set up the National Treatment Purchase Fund, which was specifically established to help patients who had been waiting for more than three months. This fund allows the free treatment of public patients in private hospitals in order to reduce waiting times. So far it has helped, with the average treatment time in 2009 being 2.4 months, compared to 2–5 years in 2002.

But the bottom line is...buy private health insurance. It isn't as costly as in America and is definitely worth it. Public health care is overbooked with untenable waiting lists, even for urgent operations. And once you are seen, public health care is not entirely free, except to those with the medical card, so you might as well pay the premium for private health care.

PRIVATE HEALTH CARE

Despite subsidized health care available to Irish residents through the public health care options, many citizens and most expats choose private health insurance. Private health insurance gives you a "skip the line free" card. Rather than being put on the bottom of the waiting list (like the public health care option), you are allowed to jump straight to the top of the list. If you are in a lot of pain or need urgent care, having private health insurance to skip the line is certainly worthwhile.

Private health insurance does not change the structure of health care services; it simply allows you to skip the long waiting period. You (or your insurance company) must pay the full costs of any treatment if opting for this. The good news is the premiums for private health insurance are very reasonable when compared to U.S. health insurance prices.

The major private insurance companies in Ireland are Vhi, QUINN-healthcare, and Hibernian Aviva. The premiums are much less expensive than in America, and to make the deal even sweeter, a 20 percent tax relief is deducted by the health insurance provider on your insurance premiums. Keep in mind that many employers provide private health insurance packages, so you may not need to purchase private health insurance if you are working in Ireland.

St. James's Hospital, Dublin

Your U.S. Health Plan

If you are already covered by a U.S. health insurance plan, do not assume it will cover you when you are in Ireland. Make sure to check with your insurance company *before* you leave and ask them if your policy applies when you are outside the United States and if it will cover emergencies such as a trip to a hospital. You cannot simply go to a doctor, hand over your insurance card, and expect your health costs to be covered. Many doctors and hospitals in Ireland expect payment in cash when you receive the service, especially if you don't have an Irish address. If your insurance company does not cover you while you are in Ireland, you can purchase Travel Medical Insurance, which covers the costs of medical attention needed when you are in Ireland. This type of insurance is usually purchased annually or per trip. This should not be confused with Travel Insurance, which typically recoups any financial losses from your trip, such as lost baggage, cancelled flights, etc. Sometimes this type of policy will cover medical costs, but you should ensure this prior to purchasing. Also note that the Social Security Medicare Program does not pay for medical costs outside the United States.

Children's Health Care

In Ireland, children receive the same health services as their parents. However, there are numerous free services specifically for children even if their parents do not have a medical card. For example, children receive new eyeglasses every two years, free dental care, and free teeth straightening (orthodontist care) if the child's teeth are crooked enough to justify the care based on medical grounds (cosmetic straightening is not free).

There is no particular age that a child is no longer considered a child for health purposes; however, 16 is generally the cut-off point. At this age, children are included on their parents' health insurance, whether it is public or private health insurance. Children are typically charged a reduced premium up to the age of 18 (21 if in full-time education) on their parents' private health insurance.

It is important to note that children who are receiving public health care suffer the same waiting lists as adults, even for the free services. If your children need braces, they could end up waiting several years before being seen by the orthodontist. Figures released in April 2011 by the HSE show that the number of children waiting over one year for treatment at Our Lady's Hospital in Crumlin, Dublin (Ireland's largest children's hospital), has doubled over the past year despite service improvements. Again, the moral of the story is to get private health insurance.

Pharmacies

Pharmacies in Ireland are typically called "chemists," and you will recognize them by a green cross under the sign outside. Don't call it a "drugstore"; the Irish think this term refers to something illicit and are either shocked by the term or find it hilarious. Either way, you will need to refer to it as a chemist, although they will know what you mean if you say *pharmacy*.

There are approximately 1,700 pharmacies in Ireland, so it isn't difficult to find one, particularly in the more populated cities and towns. In addition to dispensing prescriptions, chemists provide information about your medication, help you manage any disease or chronic illness, and some even provide basic health checkups, such as testing your blood pressure and cholesterol levels.

Most minor health concerns, from strep throat to back pain, can be addressed by consulting a chemist, who can give advice on what medicine to take. Drugs that contain codeine, such as Nurofen Plus (ibuprofen with codeine) and Solpadeine Plus (paracetamol with codeine) can be obtained by asking your chemist rather than seeing a GP.

© SARAH-JANE SWEENEY

Boots is one of the main pharmacies in Ireland.

There are no 24-hour chemists available in Ireland, although there are a few late-night ones. Most chemists operate typical business hours (9 A.M.– 6 P.M.), but bigger chain drugstores that have chemists inside, such as Boots or Superdrug, often stay open a bit later in the city centers (closing anytime between 7 P.M. and 9 P.M.).

The bigger chain chemists also sell nondrug items like what you might find in an American drugstore, including health and beauty products like body soap, lotion, or shampoo, as well as various items such as perfume, diapers, or condoms. Sometimes you can even find sandwiches, drinks, and chips (called crisps in Ireland). The smaller drugstores offer essential health and beauty products in addition to medication, but often at a higher price than the chain drugstores.

PRESCRIPTIONS

All residents of Ireland are able to get prescription drugs and medical appliances for free or at a reduced cost. The Drugs Payment Scheme sets a maximum cap for monthly costs of all regular prescribed medicines. Anyone who has a long-term condition and will incur more than the maximum cost can join the Drugs Payment Scheme. All local chemists carry the necessary forms, so if you find you need to avail of the scheme, get a form from the chemist and apply.

If you find you need medications from the United States, it is important to note that you cannot simply transfer them. Irish law prevents chemists from dispensing drugs without a prescription from an Irish doctor. Irish chemists may be a bit flexible about this—if you need a medication right away for, say, diabetes, you can show your previous prescription, and the chemist may dispense a few days' supply—but this does not always hold true. The proper route to follow is to make an appointment with your local GP, show the GP your prescription, and have a new prescription written by the Irish GP to take to the chemist.

DIFFERENT NAMES FOR MEDICATIONS

While you may think of the pharmaceutical industry as a global conglomerate encroaching on all spaces of the world, often the same medicines are sold under different names. In Ireland, aspirin, which contains the active ingredient acetylsalicylic acid, is called Disprin; Tylenol, which contains acetaminophen, is called paracetamol; and ibuprofen is called Nurofen. You should check the ingredients list whenever you are buying medications, or ask the chemist to assist you with finding a similar medication to one you are used to taking.

Preventive Measures and Diseases

VACCINATIONS AND DISEASES

In the mid-1940s in Ireland about 500 children died every year from vaccine-preventable diseases, such as whooping cough, tuberculosis, and polio. Today the death rate is zero. Ireland has eliminated these diseases due to national immunization schemes that brought a higher level of health to the country.

There are no vaccinations required for you to enter Ireland, although the standard U.S. ones are recommended—MMR vaccine (measles, mumps, and rubella), the DPT vaccine (diphtheria, pertussis, and tetanus), poliovirus—so you should be up-to-date on your vaccinations. However, if you have been to a country in the past 14 days where a contagious disease is prevalent, you will be required to provide proof of being vaccinated against that disease. You can view posts for medical concerns and notices on the CDCs website, wwwnc.cdc.gov/travel/.

If you have a child while in Ireland, your pediatrician will recommend the usual array of vaccines, starting with the tuberculosis vaccine at birth. Vaccination is not compulsory in Ireland but is strongly advised by the Department of Health and Children. These services are free to children and young people, and are provided in GP offices, hospitals, health clinics, and schools.

Sexually Transmitted Diseases

Despite various national awareness campaigns launched by the Department of Health, Ireland has seen a huge increase in STDs over the past decade. This is related in part to the economic boom but also to the fact that Ireland has a very young, active population. In fact, 60 percent of reported cases of STDs are among 20- to 29-year-olds. Most young people have very little sex education due to the religious policy of the Catholic Church, and awareness of STDs is not that high. Most young people are very blasé about unprotected sex, and condoms aren't used as much as they should be.

In 2010 nearly two out of every five adults in Ireland had to be tested for STDs at some stage in their life. Just like in the United States, there are many ways to reduce the risk of STDs: practice safe sex by using a condom, avoid bodily fluids, and get tested regularly. Various STD clinics offer free testing throughout Ireland from local community centers and hospitals.

According to AVERT, an international HIV and AIDs charity, there were 6,900 cases of people living with HIV or AIDs in Ireland in 2009. In 2009 there were 395 new cases of HIV, and in 2008 there were 405 new cases of HIV. The bottom line here is that HIV and AIDs are still a big problem in

Ireland. If you suspect you have been infected with HIV, you should immediately get to your nearest STD clinic, which does free testing. The clinic can treat you with a Post Exposure Prophylaxis (PEP), which works to prevent the virus from establishing itself in your bloodstream, but this must be done within 72 hours of exposure.

Environmental Factors

Overall Ireland has a good level of environmental quality. This is due to its proximity to the Atlantic Ocean, its moderate temperatures, and modern EU regulations that help keep all member states "clean."

AIR AND WATER QUALITY

Traffic is the primary source of air pollution in Ireland. Despite cleaner vehicle emissions technology, there are now more cars on the roads, which increases pollution. Power stations, industry, and domestic fuel burning also contribute to air pollution. Even still, you will only really see smog in Dublin, and even then only when it hasn't rained in a few days. Overall the air quality is quite good, with steady winds (and rain) sweeping off the Atlantic Ocean constantly refreshing and cleansing the air. Real-time air quality information is available from the Environmental Protection Agency's website: www.epa.ie/whatwedo/monitoring/air/data/.

Every member country of the EU is obligated to maintain certain water quality regulations, and Ireland is no different. Water is monitored and regularly tested by the local authorities and health boards to make sure it is safe to drink. So you are quite safe to drink water directly from the tap. That being said, bottled water is often favored by expats, especially those with children.

During my time in Ireland I noticed a substantial amount of limescale in the water. Limescale is the off-white, chalky mineral you might find in your tea kettle, hot water tank, or on the surface of your dishes. Although not harmful, limescale lends a slightly bitter taste to water when it hasn't been filtered. It also makes it difficult to clean surfaces, leaving a slight scum on counters, taps, and other hard surfaces. This scum solidifies into a hard mineral as it dries and can be difficult, if not impossible, to remove.

Water softening or conditioning systems can be installed to treat water as it enters your house. For eliminating limescale from your kettle, counter surfaces, or even from your hair, you can add a few teaspoons of malt vinegar or lemon juice, which will dissolve the mineral deposits. You can also purchase limescale-removing chemicals from almost any shop.

SMOKING

In March 2004, Ireland did what the world never thought it would—it became the first country to introduce a full indoor smoking ban. The smoking ban included all work areas and enclosed public spaces, from taxis to shopping centers, restaurants to pubs. The reason for the law was to protect employees and the public from the harmful effects of tobacco smoke and to reduce the incidence of heart and lung disease caused by smoking.

This ban was initially approached with trepidation by smokers throughout Ireland. Publicans worried it would deter people from going out and thus shut the bars down. Employers worried they would see production drop as their workers took more smoking breaks to go outside. However, what happened was that outdoor smoking just became more popular. In fact, most pubs and clubs (and some restaurants) have designated outdoor smoking areas that are more crowded than indoors. These areas are packed wall-to-wall with people socializing, drinking, flirting, and meeting new people. It has introduced an entirely new level of entertainment on a night out.

There are, of course, exceptions to this rule, including prisons and mental hospitals, as well as building sites. Additionally, hotels generally offer smoking rooms if asked beforehand. The smoking ban obviously doesn't apply, for example, to people smoking outside at a bus stop or waiting in a taxi rank. If you're a nonsmoker and come into contact with a smoker outside, you're just going to have to deal with it. It won't help your quest to become entrenched in the Irish culture if you snap at an Irish person to put their cigarette out or theatrically wave the smoke from your face. Tolerate it or just walk away.

Safety

Overall, Ireland is a very safe country. The U.S. State Department reports that Ireland has a low rate of violent crime, and tourists reported only 361 cases of crime and traumatic incidents in 2010, according to the Irish Tourist Assistance Service (ITAS). There are, however, pockets of dangerous zones in the larger cities (Dublin North Central and Dublin South Central being the worst), but most violence is a result of the occasional gang-related or drug-turf fight and is rarely directed at tourists.

Also, there are some incidences of violence fueled by alcohol. You know the

The Irish police maintain the safety in Ireland.

way it rolls. The nightclubs and bars let out, scores of drunken young people are let free onto the streets, and fights break out. Come out of a nightclub 15 minutes after it has closed, and you may encounter two or three fights on the street, but this is rarely directed at tourists or foreigners. The general rule of thumb is, if you're not looking for trouble, you probably won't find it. While Ireland is no crime-free paradise, I never once felt unsafe, even at night.

Petty crime, pickpocketing, and theft have increased in recent years, especially in tourist areas such as along the banks of the Liffey River in Dublin, which is rife with pickpocketers. About 200 Americans report their passport stolen or lost in Dublin every year, according to the Embassy of the United States in Dublin.

Common sense is your best friend. Guard your passport and other official documents carefully, and keep a copy of the data page from your passport in a separate location as your purse or luggage. If you are a victim of a crime, you should contact a *Garda* (police officer) or call 999 or 112, the nationwide emergency phone numbers. The ITAS offers support and assistance to tourists who are victims of crime while visiting Irleand (www.itas.ie/).

DRUGS

Possession of any controlled substance in Ireland is illegal and can land you in jail or kicked out of the country. Even still, recreational drug use in Ireland is on the rise; one in two 18–29-year-olds have tried illegal drugs in the past. Ecstasy, cannabis, and magic mushrooms are easy to come by but are illegal, unregulated, and dangerous.

SAFETY TIPS

Living in Ireland is safe, but there are still incidences of petty crime and assault. Here are a few tips to help keep you safe from crime in Ireland.

Carry light. Carry a minimal amount of cash and perhaps one credit card when walking around. Women should keep their purses over their shoulder with their arm guarding the opening, and men should keep their wallets in their front pockets.

Lock up. Make sure to lock valuables in your house or car when you leave, even if it's just a rental car. Most car theft is opportunistic, so don't leave a visible purse, camera, or even maps that will act as a red flag to a criminal.

Dress down. Don't wear or display any expensive or flashy jewelry or watches. This could make you a target to criminals and peg you as easy prey.

Keep your eyes open. Be aware of where your belongings are – if you are in an Internet café and your backpack is on the floor next to you, for example. Don't just get up to use the bathroom and leave your belongings. Keep your purse secured on your lap, your arm through the strap, and be aware of your surroundings, particularly when talking on your cell phone.

Look confident. Try to seem like you are confident and know what you are doing as you make your way through the country. Appearing lost or unsure can make you a prime target to scammers.

Be careful at night. While the rural areas of Ireland are quite safe, you should always exercise caution when walking around at night, particularly in the city centers. Take a taxi if you can, or walk with a buddy if there are no taxis around. If you feel uncomfortable at any time, carry your phone so you have quick access to call the police. Your keys make a great weapon in a tight situation, so keep them in your hand if you feel unsafe.

SCAMS

Scams involving ATMs have become more prevalent in recent years, particularly with "skimmers"—a small electronic device attached to the outside of an ATM that records your card details. Most ATMs have signs warning you to beware and look for evidence of tampering. You should make sure to protect your PIN, covering it with you hand to ensure it is hidden. Also beware of people offering to "help" you with your transaction, as another recent scam has involved slowing down the ATM, then sending a scammer in to help you, while they really just watch you put your PIN in.

EMPLOYMENT

I've found Americans to be some of the most positive, optimistic people in the world. However, it will take more than your sunny disposition and cheerful smile to get a job in Ireland. If you're not an Irish or EU citizen, getting a job here can be a bit tricky, fraught with difficulties and new legislation that make it downright problematic.

Ireland, like the rest of the world, is in a recession. What's more, economists think the recession will last longer (and deeper) in Ireland than anywhere else. To counteract this, the Irish government have tightened their belts and are limiting work permits and green cards. To give you an idea of the breadth of the work permit issue, the Department of Jobs, Enterprise and Innovation reports that in 2005 there were a total of 7,354 work permits issued, with 600 of these issued to Americans. However, in 2010 there were just 3,394 new work permits issued, only 281 of these to Americans.

Here's a sum-up of what you might encounter when trying to get employment in Ireland: (1) Employers won't hire you until you have a Personal Public

Service (PPS) number. (2) Social Welfare (who issues PPS numbers) won't issue one until you have an Immigration Card. (3) An Garda Síochána won't issue an Immigration Card until you have a permit for Work Authorization. (4) The Department of Jobs, Enterprise and Innovation won't issue a permit for Work Authorization until you have a job offer. (5) See number 1 and repeat.

As you can see, the process for employment is confusing and plagued with bureaucracy. The bottom line is you need to have a very specific skill that is difficult to find in Ireland so that employers are forced to look outside the country. Then you need to have a prospective employer offer you a job before you can get a work permit, and that prospective employer has to be willing to pay a pretty steep fee to sponsor you to work in Ireland.

But while the process (and the prospect) may be daunting, take heart! If you want employment enough, and you have a skill and are qualified, you may just be able to get it. Throughout 2010 and the first half of 2011 there has been a steady growth rate across many job sectors. Even though unemployment has reached nearly 15 percent, HR and recruitment, marketing, science, pharmaceutical, IT, accountancy and finance, and customer service and call center job sectors are all increasing steadily. And, the really good news is that salary expectations have increased by an average of €3,000.

So it's not all doom and gloom. While the economy is rocky and finding work is difficult, it is not impossible. Being hired by a U.S. firm or being transferred by a multinational firm to Ireland is a possibility. There are 600 U.S. firms in Ireland thanks to the low corporation tax rate, including IBM, Intel, and Pfizer, and some of the world's largest businesses have their EU headquarters there, including Google, Intel, Microsoft, and Facebook.

Another option is to freelance for U.S.-based clients or, if you have a business, set up your company in Ireland. Keep in mind you have to register with Immigrations and get permission if you plan to stay more than three months.

The Job Hunt

While having a job sorted before you go to Ireland is obviously the ideal scenario, it is not always a practical one. The main goal is to make sure you have your permits and immigration sorted out. From there the steps to finding a job are pretty much the same as in America.

Ireland has many great employment websites. Do a quick Internet search, and you will see what I mean. Some of the best are www.jobs.ie, www.myjobs.ie, www.iol.ie, www.irishjobs.ie, and www.monster.ie. The main training and employment

PART TIME BAR STAFF
POSITION AVAILABLE

FLUENT ENGLISH &
EXPERIENCE ESSENTIAL

APPLY WITHIN

© SARAH-JANE SWEENEY

Many businesses post Now Hiring signs in their windows.

website you will come across in Ireland is FÁS, but this is an organization specifically for Irish and EU citizens, so Americans don't quality.

Don't forget to utilize the major national newspapers, which will have employment sections in the classifieds: *The Irish Times, The Irish Independent, Sunday Times* (Irish edition), *The Examiner, The Sunday Post,* and *The Herald.* Send your resume (called a CV—curriculum vitae—in Ireland) to any and all businesses you would be interested in working for. Stop in at shops, cafés, or restaurants that have a Now Hiring sign in the window.

There are also various recruitment agencies available, including Adecco, Careers Register, Eden Recruitment, and Step One Staffing Solutions. Like in the United States, most recruitment agencies cater to specific skill sets, so you are ensured job opportunities that match your job history and skills. You can also upload your CV to various job websites to increase your chances of getting headhunted by a prospective employer.

Make sure the entire time you are searching for a job you are networking. Tell anybody and everybody you meet you are looking for a job. Compared to the United States, Ireland is just a village. There are only a little over four million people here, so it's entirely reasonable to think that if you tell a friend, who tells their uncle, who tells his wife, who tells her manager at the local hotel that there is an American looking for a job, you just might be invited to interview. Many businesses in Ireland prefer to hire by word of mouth rather than through the classifieds. It happened to me more times than I care to count, and in more areas than just getting a job! I found a home, concert tickets, a bicycle, and a bed just by networking.

Many U.S. citizens can work in Ireland because of family, some because of a spouse, while others because of a previous employer. Whatever your reason, don't assume your potential employer knows what category you fall under. You don't want to start your interview by saying, "I need a work permit." Whether

WHAT IS A CV?

In Ireland a resume is called a CV, short for curriculum vitae. The main difference is that while a resume focuses on what your skills are, a CV focuses on who you are. A CV has some distinct differences you may encounter, including different content and formats. Here is a good comparison so you know what sort of CV to put together when job hunting in Ireland.

	CV	Resume
Meaning:	Abbreviation for curriculum vitae, meaning "course of life" in Latin	French word for "summary"
Length:	Two pages minimum	1-2 pages maximum
Content:	A historical overview rather than just a work history, including entire academic professional history, plus extracurricular activities	Brief summary of relevant work experience and skills targeted specifically to position
Where used:	Europe, Africa, the Middle East, and Asia; also the United States and Canada for academic fellowships, grants, and medical positions	The United States for most jobs
Employment dates:	Chronological order	Reverse chronological order
Style:	Formal, wordy, leaving no gaps in your history	Professional, succinct marketing tool that makes the reader want to interview you and find out more

If you have a resume, it is easy to convert it to a CV. The employment website www.monster.ie offers free CV templates. Your header should include more personal information than your resume would; for example, your date of birth, your marital status, your driver's license information, etc. Sometimes a header even contains a small head shot.

Write a summary of your skills and experience as an introduction, then split your "professional experiences" section into three parts: career summary, achievements, and career overview. Explain your employment details, specific projects, and job description, giving the potential employer a sense of your overall work experience. It is also perfectly acceptable to include a section on special skills, interests, and hobbies, especially if they are relevant to the position.

Update the format, listing your earliest employment history, and then working down to your most recent experience (opposite from the United States' reverse chronological order). Make sure your CV gives an accurate description of who you are as a person, as well as your skills, including certificates, special recognition, published articles, speeches, organizations you belong to, and contact details for several references.

you start by telling the truth on your CV or once you've gotten an interview, get this information out there right away.

In my experience, Irish businesses hire mostly based on personality and potential more than your actual skills. Of course, you will need a certain skill set in order to get to the interview stage, but if you can secure an interview, are confident and self-assured, and can convince your prospective employer that you are by far the best person for the job, you may just get that job. Be positive and knowledgeable, and, more importantly, research, research, research that company so they know that you know what they're all about.

BENEFITS AND CONTRACTS

If you are looking for a job in Ireland based on its benefits package, you may be looking for a while. Irish jobs do not have benefits packages the way American jobs do. This is because the government offers comprehensive public health care, pensions, and other benefits, so you don't need to rely on your job for these.

Most people in Ireland are on full-time contracts, through which you are employed for an unspecified amount of time, receiving a fixed annual salary and certain employment rights. These contracts may also include private health insurance benefits or other bonuses, such as rights to a company car or share options.

Full-time contract employees pay their taxes through a system called Pay As You Earn (PAYE), which automatically deducts tax from their wages. When starting a new job, you should give your PPS number to your employer. Your employer will give it to the local tax office when registering you as an employee, and then you will automatically have your tax deducted from your pay. There are no annual tax returns to worry about. At the end of the tax year your employer will issue you a P60, which details your taxable income and deductions made by PAYE.

You may also get a fixed-term contract. This is temporary employment, in which your work is terminated on a specified date. This type of contract is valid for up to four years of continuous employment, after which you are considered to have a permanent contract.

When you begin working at a new job, you immediately begin accruing annual leave. This is also set out in your employment contract, whether it is full-time or fixed-term. As an employee you are entitled to four working weeks of annual leave plus nine public holidays. If you have a baby, you get 26 weeks (that's six months!) of paid maternity leave, plus an additional 16 weeks of unpaid leave. If you're the dad? You can take paternity leave, although payment is at the discretion of the employer. If you adopt a baby, you can take 24 weeks of paid leave.

You will notice all of this is much more, ahem…generous, than you could expect in the United States. You will also notice a huge difference in the work atmosphere here. The Irish have an insouciant, carefree attitude about jobs, employment, and work. "Sure, it'll be grand" is common to hear, as is "no worries." They really feel there are no worries. I worked in newspaper offices for years, and it was a rare occasion when I saw somebody stressed out. The Irish just take things one step at a time. And yet they are some of the most diligent, hardworking people I have met, and they will work 12-hour days until the job is done.

Self-Employment

Modern technology has made sitting in an office pointless for many jobs. With just a laptop and an Internet connection, borders are practically invisible, and you can be free to fly where you wish. Last winter I spent six months with my husband and son living in different European cities. We each carried our laptop with us and made sure our accommodations included Internet. While not all jobs are as portable, there are ways to work for yourself while in Ireland.

FREELANCING

Since the advent of the Internet, working at home as an independent contractor has made telecommuting fashionable. Blogging, writing, editing, Internet marketing, medical billing, answering service, desktop publishing, or just about any job you can do at home as an independent contract are great freelance roles that you can do in Ireland.

If you are an established freelancer in the United States and can continue working from home with the ability to bill your clients virtually, you can freelance almost anywhere in the world, subject to visa and immigration laws, of course. You will need to maintain your U.S. bank account in order to get paid, and your salary will be paid in U.S. dollars, which is constantly fluctuating and generally not worth as much as the euro. And then there are taxes, one of the constants of life. Not only are you liable to pay taxes to the Irish government, you are also required to pay taxes to the U.S. government. (See *Tax and PRSI* for more information about paying taxes to the U.S. government.)

While freelancing is a great (and portable) job, you do still have to keep in mind your immigration status when in Ireland. If you plan to stay for longer than three months, you will have to register with the Garda National Immigration Bureau (GNIB) to get permission to stay.

That said, there are scores of Americans roaming around Ireland who simply stay under the radar. If you don't get into trouble with the law, you could probably happily live here for quite some time working as a freelancer. There are no dramatic exportations of foreigners from Irish soil, and nobody goes around checking your papers to make sure you are legal. However, if you plan to stay long-term, it would be a good idea to get your papers sorted out so you can receive health care, pensions, etc. And be prepared to suffer the backlash if you do end up getting caught, which could result in fines, paying back taxes, or deportation.

If you want to work in a field that requires a professional license, you will have to sign up at a local college or university to get the Irish version of that same license. Most degrees, licenses, and certificates do not automatically transfer and allow you to practice in Ireland. While you may get hired based on a general bachelor's or master's degree, something more specific, like a medical degree, will not get you the same job in Ireland as it would in the United States.

STARTING YOUR OWN BUSINESS

Starting a business in Ireland is a wonderful idea—if you have the money. Right now corporation tax is at 12.5 percent, lower than anybody else in the EU and about half that of the United States, so it is a great place to set up a business. Additionally, new companies that set up shop in 2011 may be eligible to receive tax relief on the corporation tax for the first three years.

Despite these definite benefits, starting up a business in Ireland is definitely geared toward the big corporations. As an American starting a business, you will need to begin by first applying for permission from the Minister for Justice and Law Reform. To do this, you need to show that you have €300,000 or more to invest in the country and that you will be creating employment to better the economy of Ireland. If you are successful in your request, you will initially receive permission to start a business for one year. Refugees, dependents of EEA (European Economic Area) nationals, and spouses of Irish nationals are exempt from this rule, so if you fall into this category, you can skip straight to applying for a work permit.

When you apply for permission to start your business, you will need to submit a copy of your passport, a business plan, proof of your skills and qualifications, references from past employers, and reports from the police authorities of each country you have lived in for over six months throughout the last 10 years. Once permission has been granted, you have a few options for what type of business to set up. You will need to talk to a solicitor or an accountant in order to find out if your business should be set up as a sole trader, a partnership, or a limited company. The City and County Enterprise Boards, which provide support to small business, can offer grants, financial support, and training for local businesses that are just starting out.

TAX AND PRSI

How your business is taxed depends on if it is incorporated or not. If your business is incorporated and classed as a company, you have to pay corporation tax. If your business is not incorporated, you are classed as a sole trader. As a sole trader you must register as self-employed with the Revenue Commissioners and pay Class S PRSI tax under the self-assessment system. When you pay self-employment taxes you are required to file a tax return by October 31 following the end of the tax year, which operates according to the calendar-year basis (January–December).

Your self-employment taxes allow you to avail of a limited number of social insurance payments, including Guardian's Payment, Adoptive Benefit, Maternity Benefit, and Widow's, Widower's, or Surviving Civil Partner's Contributory Pension. It should be noted that if you are self-employed and you create new jobs in 2010 and 2011, the Pay Related Social Insurance (PRSI), a tax for social insurance and health contributions, may be exempt for the jobs you create. This is to generate incentive for companies to create jobs to help the Irish economy.

Keep in mind that as a U.S. citizen you will also have to turn in your annual tax return to the IRS. While this seems to be a little-known fact among many expats, it is illegal to skip your U.S. tax return, even when living abroad, although expats are allowed a two-month extension to file taxes (until June 15). The bad news: You can be taxed on your worldwide income, which means you may have to pay tax in Ireland *and* in the United States. The good news, however, is if you earn less than $92,900 (in 2011) you may qualify to not pay tax in the United States. This rate changes each year, so keep an eye on the IRS website for current information. Even if you are eligible to not pay double taxes, you are still required to submit your tax return. Numerous accountants who can prepare U.S. tax returns are available throughout Ireland.

US Working Holiday Authorization

If you are in college or are a recent graduate, you can avail of the US Working Holiday Authorization Agreement, which allows U.S. citizens to work and travel in Ireland for up to 12 months. In order to avail of this agreement, you should complete an application to the Embassy of Ireland in Washington DC, or the Irish Consulates General in Boston, Chicago, New York, or San Francisco. You will have to include your valid U.S. passport, two recent passport photos, a resume with references, an original bank statement showing you have access to €1,500, a return airplane ticket, certificate of medical or travel insurance, proof of qualifications from your school or university, and a fee of €250.

J-1 VISA

A more limited version of the US Working Holiday Authorization is available as the J-1 visa, which is an exchange visitor visa in which students; trainees getting on-the-job training; teachers of primary, secondary, and specialized schools; research scholars; and professional trainees from the United States and Ireland can interchange knowledge and skills in the fields of education, the arts, and sciences. Every summer hundreds of students from Ireland fly to America while American students fly to Ireland. This program allows American students temporary residency status in Ireland (and vice versa) to live and work before restarting college courses.

Labor Laws

Employment laws in Ireland provide strong protection for employees. Complaints and disputes are heard by a Rights Commissioner, who listens to both sides, investigates the complaints, and makes recommendations for resolving the complaints. The Labour Relations Commission offers free services to mediate disputes between employees and employers.

Labor laws protect employee contracts, annual pay and holiday time, working conditions, and equality. Even part-time and seasonal workers are protected under these laws. However, not all workers are protected. If you are working illegally or "under the table," you are not protected by any employment laws and may even receive substandard treatment at work. Irish employers gained a bad reputation abroad during the Celtic Tiger economy of the early 1990s for making illegal immigrants work long hours with inferior pay, no breaks, and no holiday or sick pay.

DAILY LIFE

EMPLOYMENT LAWS

Legislation for workers' rights provide employment protection for individuals. The most important of these are:

- Employment Equality Act 1998-2008
- Maternity Protection Act 1994
- Minimum Notice and Terms of Employment Act 1973
- Organisation of Working Time Act 1997

- Parental Leave Act 1998
- Payment of Wages Act 1991
- Protection of Young Persons (Employment) Act 1996
- Redundancy Payments Acts 1967-1991
- Unfair Dismissals Acts 1977-1993
- Worker Protection (Regular Part-Time Employees) Act 1991

WORKERS' RIGHTS

The average work week in Ireland is 39 hours, with normal working hours falling somewhere between 9 A.M. and 6 P.M. Employees are entitled to a 15-minute break twice a day and one hour for lunch. These times and hours are merely a benchmark, as work can be quite flexible in Ireland. Generally, if you work more than your normal nine hours in a day, you can take those hours off from another day. As long as the work gets done, employers aren't obsessed with the time slots. You are not, by law, allowed to work more than 48 hours in any one week, but the average is calculated over a period of four months.

Discrimination based on gender, sexual orientation, religion, age, race, disability, family status, or social status is illegal under the Employment Equality Acts 1998–2008 and the Equal Status Acts 2000–2008. The Equality Authority ensures that all people in Ireland are treated equally and that discrimination does not happen. If you do ever feel discriminated against, the Equality Tribunal investigates and mediates reports of discrimination.

The Protection of Young Persons (Employment) Act 1996 sets out rules, work hours, and rest intervals for children under 18 who work. Children under 16 are not allowed to work in regular full-time jobs and have restricted hours when working part-time. Children aged 14 and 15 are allowed to do light work during school holidays. No child under 18 is allowed to participate in late-night work.

MINIMUM WAGE

Ireland's minimum wage is acceptable (by U.S. standards) at €8.65 per hour. It was reduced due to the recession but the revised EU/IMF Programme

© CHRISTINA MCDONALD

Workers are entitled to various breaks throughout the day.

of Financial Support for Ireland restored the minimum wage as of July 2011.

While this may seem like a reasonable rate, it is offset by the high cost of living in the city centers. Many people offset the cost of living by staying with their parents. In fact, a lot of people I met (particularly men) lived with their parents well into their late 20s. And if they weren't living with their parents, they would make sure to go "home" for dinner at least a few times a week and take their washing with them. Additionally, their parents quite often paid for various household items. This obviously isn't going to happen for expats, so if you plan on living in one of Ireland's bigger city centers, make sure you get a job that can support you or have a large savings account that will subsidize you.

DAILY LIFE

FINANCE

Ireland's financial history reflects its political development over the last 1,000 years, marking social, economic, and political changes. Ireland's first coins were introduced by the Vikings in the 10th century and initially were equivalent to England's pound sterling. These Irish coins were later debased and a separate Irish pound came into existence, but in 1826 the Irish pound was eliminated entirely and replaced by British currency.

Following Irish Independence and the nation's separation from the UK, the Irish Free State introduced the Saorstát pound (Irish pound). The Irish pound had a fixed link to the British pound sterling until the 1970s, when Ireland joined the European Monetary System (EMS), an agreement that linked the exchange rates of the EU countries. The implementation of a single currency across the EU in 1999 (the physical implementation was in 2002) was huge news for Ireland, the EU, and the world. For Ireland, this facilitated the country's move away from an agricultural-based economy to one driven by global

© SARAHJANE SWEENEY

exports and a high-tech industry. For the EU it meant people, business, and money could move freely between member countries.

While some EU member countries experienced backlash from introducing the euro, Irish consumers and its economy mostly benefited. Thanks to the euro Ireland has experienced a reduction in inflation, foreign exchange transaction costs are reduced, euro notes and coins can be used throughout the eurozone, there is continued price stability, and there are lower interest rates than if Ireland were outside the eurozone. Despite a recession and financial troubles experienced by numerous member countries throughout the EU, the euro is still a strong currency: It's the second most traded currency in the world after the U.S. dollar and has the most bank notes and coins in circulation in the world.

So what does this mean for you? American expats living in Ireland while earning U.S. dollars are hard hit by the exchange rate between the U.S. dollar and the euro. While the U.S. dollar continues to decline, the euro continues to get stronger. In 2008 the euro peaked in comparison to the dollar at €1 to US$1.60. In May 2011 the exchange rate had dropped a bit and was €1 to US$1.45. So if you spend €100, you're actually spending about US$145. In a country with a cost of living as high as Ireland, this surely spells trouble for Americans. If you spend €65 for one week of groceries for one person in Dublin, you are actually spending nearly US$95. That's just for one week of food! Petrol, which is hugely taxed by the Irish government, costs about €7 per gallon, which is about US$10 a gallon. The result: a painful crimping of style on American expats living abroad.

Cost of Living

The World Cost of Living Survey 2010 ranked Dublin as the 42nd most-expensive city for an expatriate to live. In 2010–2011 Trinity College Dublin averaged the cost of living for one academic year (nine months) at €10,400 per year, including €4,900 for rent and electricity, €3,200 for food, and €2,300 for miscellaneous items. However, this estimate is for one person between September and May. So you can expect to spend an awful lot more than that if you aren't a student, you have a family to provide for, you have to buy health insurance, or include the entire year in your cost-of-living estimate.

The average price for a two-bedroom apartment is €950–3,000, a two-bedroom house is €999–2,300, and a room in a shared apartment is €400–1,000. Your electric bill will cost approximately €500 per quarter in the winter, significantly less in the summer. A cell phone costs about €60–100 per month, and a home phone package with Internet and TV costs about €150 per month. If you own a flat or an apartment, you'll have to add service charge, which can be about €2,000 per year for insurance, garbage collection, etc. Despite these outrageous prices in Dublin, the cost of accommodations (as well as everything else) drops considerably once you get out to the suburbs or the smaller towns and villages around Ireland. A weekly grocery shop is on average 14 percent cheaper outside of Dublin, according to the Central Statistics Office. In County Roscommon, a new property will cost you about €154,000, while in Dublin it is €306,000. Child care costs about €144 per week outside of Dublin compared to €192 in Dublin.

What all of this number fracas means is that where you live, how you live, and who you share your costs with will all play a role in deciding your daily costs while living in Ireland. Whether it will add up to be more than what you are paid in America depends on where you are coming from. If you are moving from New York, which ranks 27th on the most expensive cities to live list, you may come out thinking you're getting off cheap. If you are moving from Los Angeles or Chicago, you will probably just about break even. But if you are coming from small town, USA, you may need a high-figure salary or an established savings account to supplement you.

As a whole, almost everything is more expensive in Ireland than it is in the United States. After 2002, when Ireland's economy began to skyrocket and tourists began flooding to the Emerald Isle, Irish businesses saw an opportunity to mark up prices. This eventually earned Ireland the nickname Rip-Off Republic. Due to the current recession, prices have stabilized a bit,

PLASTIC BAG LEVY

In a concerted effort to deal with rising litter problems, Ireland introduced a tax on plastic bags in 2002. If you choose to purchase a plastic bag at the grocery store, a 22 cent fee is added to your bill when paying at the checkout line. The fee is added for each bag, so if you are doing a big shop, it would really benefit you to bring your own bags.

Prior to the plastic bag tax, you could see stray plastic bags littering parking lots, flying around on the streets, and tangling in the gutters. Within weeks of passing the tax, Ireland saw a 94 percent drop in plastic bag purchases, and within a year, nearly everyone had converted to reusable cloth bags. The levy has been so successful that plastic bags are now socially unacceptable – on par with wearing a fur coat or belching in public. Beware the evil looks you might receive if you ignore this social faux pas and buy plastic bags when you live here.

but it is still more expensive to live in or visit than the United States. Things like food and drink, clothes, cars, accommodations, household furnishings, and utility bills are all more expensive here.

On the plus side, there are some things you will find to be cheaper in Ireland than in America. Private health insurance is a prime example. This necessary little expense can cost you thousands annually in fees, co-pays, premiums, deductibles, etc. in the United States. Residents of Ireland, however, receive certain free medical services—maternity coverage is free for up to six weeks after birth, Accident and Emergency is free with a doctor's note, or €100 per visit, €75 per night for hospital accommodations—before even needing private health insurance. And if you do need private health insurance, it will only cost an average of €1,000 (US$1,435) per year to cover a family of five.

Education is also cheaper in Ireland. A bachelor's degree is free to Irish citizens and costs €12,500 per year for non-EU students (about US$17,944) at the National University of Ireland, Galway. Public U.S. universities cost on average US$7,605 per year for undergraduate, in-state student tuition. That's US$30,420 total for a bachelor's degree. Out-of-state students are charged about US$12,000 per year (US$48,000 for a bachelor's degree). This fee goes up to, on average, US$27,000 per year for private universities ($108,000 for a bachelor's degree). So even non-EU students are better off going to Ireland for education, which is exactly why I went there, receiving my master's in journalism after just one year of intensive study.

So it basically boils down to this: If you are an American expat living in Ireland, you may struggle a bit if you are earning the U.S. dollar. Overall, the cost of living is higher, but fortunately, the average Irish salary is a bit higher as well. However, the strong euro and the high cost of living will certainly hit your pocketbook hard if you move to Ireland without a bit of preparation, some extra money, and a good budget.

BALANCING YOUR BUDGET

Balancing your budget means keeping tabs on all of your income and expenses. I know what you're thinking: That's so much work! But the good news is there are many ways you can do this. There are various software products available to track your expenses, you can save your piles of receipts and enter them into an Excel spreadsheet each month, or you can download your bank account statements each month so you can keep an eye on what you spend. You can also keep your costs down by knowing where to shop and buying the cheapest products.

Even city centers have their cheap stores where you can regularly get a deal.

Lidl and Aldi are German discount supermarkets that offer bulk buying at cheap prices. These are dotted through the larger city centers but may be more difficult to find if you're out in the suburbs. Dunnes Stores, Tesco, and Supervalu all sell groceries at fairly standard prices but regularly offer discounted specials and coupons. The larger Dunnes and Tesco stores are also department stores, selling cheap clothing, household items, CDs, DVDs, and personal hygiene products. These stores are in any main town or city. Superquinn, a small supermarket chain prevalent in smaller villages, is a bit pricier than normal grocery shops. Spar and Centra are typically small corner shops, but they have significantly higher prices, so beware when shopping there.

If you're looking for some ridiculously cheap clothes, head to Penneys department store in any city center. Dublin's Henry Street offers good bargain clothes shopping, or for the more upmarket clothing shops, head to Grafton Street. Deals abound at the end of the season, but you won't find those juicy 50–75 percent off sale prices you get in America.

If you stick to shopping at Lidl and Aldi, you will definitely save a lot of money, but you may be compromising some quality. If you're looking for better quality—and a much higher bill—head to Marks and Spencer (fondly referred to as Marks and Sparks). For really fresh quality produce, head to one of the many markets held on the weekends. Dublin, Galway, and Cork all have weekend markets offering fresh produce and food. It may cost a bit more money, but you'll certainly taste the difference.

The cost of eating out has finally begun to fall in recent years. You can now get a sandwich and a coffee or a kebab and a soft drink for a fiver (€5). Although this doesn't compare to the cheapness of a sandwich and a drink in America, it's certainly a good deal for Ireland. You can get an Irish breakfast for around €5 as well, which includes eggs, bacon, black and white pudding, tea, and toast. Whatever way you look at it, it's a reasonable amount of food for a reasonable amount of money.

A significant amount of your money may be spent on socializing (i.e., alcohol). Since much of Ireland's social atmosphere revolves around the pub, it's only natural that you may spend a lot of your time drinking. Statistically, Irish people drink an average of just over 11 liters (3 gallons) of alcohol per year. This equals 458 pints, 119 bottles of wine, or 43 bottles of vodka. If you're not much of a drinker, or perhaps not a drinker at all, this won't be a problem for your finances. But if you do enjoy the occasional drink, be prepared. One drink somehow turns into two, which turns into five, and by the end of the night that has turned into 10. Compound this with the fact that the Irish really don't buy single drinks, they buy rounds, so you're sort of grandfathered in to your drink allocation when you first get to the pub. This means you may end up spending a lot more money on alcohol than you think you will—especially if you're a social butterfly.

Gas (petrol) is another obligation that will ratchet up your monthly expenses. Government taxes on gas in Ireland, England, and the rest of the EU raise prices so high they are unfathomable to Americans. While everybody at home freaks out when the pumps show US$4 a gallon, in Ireland the prices are regularly at €7 a gallon (approximately US$10). This will quickly drain your bank account if you're not careful. Use public transportation or buy a small car that is good on gas mileage.

Banking

You will find it not only convenient, but also necessary to open an Irish bank account once you move here. Not only will you need to have regular access to your money, but most bills are deducted automatically from your account via direct debit. And most landlords will require your bank details in order to deduct your rent each month. While this procedure seems to be something that many Americans shy away from, having your rent, phone, or heating bills paid through direct debit is the standard procedure in Ireland. Your bank account will issue a debit card, which makes it more convenient for shopping at clothing stores, restaurants, or online.

Banks are open Monday through Friday 9 A.M.–4 P.M., with late closing until 5 P.M. on Thursday. The smaller, rural branches close between 12:30 and 1:30 P.M. for lunch. If you need to exchange money, post offices and exchange offices have longer hours than banks, and of course there are many ATMs to withdraw money from. But if you want to do any in-branch banking, you will have to work with the limited hours banks have here.

CURRENCY

Ireland uses the euro, and, as such, your bank account will be in euros. One hundred cents equals one euro, and the coins and notes are easily identifiable. There are seven euro bills in denominations of €5, €10, €20, €50, €100, €200, and €500, and the bills are uniform, without any country-specific emblems. There are eight coins in denominations of 1, 2, 5, 10, 20, and 50 cents, and €1 and €2. The euro coins all have one side in common, while the other side shows the 12 stars of the EU flag, the year, and a national emblem; Ireland's euro coins show the harp and the word *Eire*.

You will probably never receive a bill larger than a 50 from an ATM machine. If you try to use a bill larger than a 100 at a corner shop, taxi, or restaurant—especially if you're only buying something small—you will most likely be given the evil eye and refused service. Carry smaller bills for these services and use your debit card for the rest.

One note about numbers: The Irish don't add a period and double zeros to the end of even dollar amounts, like Americans generally do. So while in the United States you might write €25.00, in Ireland it is just €25. Beware not to type in the additional zeroes after €25 at an ATM, as this will get you €2,500 or, more likely, an error message.

The euro is Ireland's currency.

© SUSAN LEGG

Exchange Rates

An exchange rate is the rate that two currencies can be exchanged at, showing the value of one country's currency compared to another. The most important thing to know about exchange rates is they are capricious, fickle little numbers that will change at the drop of a hat. It is difficult to predict an exchange rate from one day to the next, let alone one week or one month in advance!

If you plan to transfer U.S. dollars from your account back home into an Irish account, you should realize that they will be transferred into euros based on that day's exchange rate. Be aware of what the exchange rate is and how many euros you should expect, as well as what fees will be added on. Keep an eye on the exchange rate and try to transfer your money when the dollar is stronger, otherwise you could lose a fair amount of money in just one transaction. You can check rate calculators online to see the exchange rate on any given day. In the past few years, the euro has stayed much stronger than the U.S. dollar, so you should expect to lose money when transferring to the euro.

If you are bringing U.S. dollars with you and plan to exchange them in Ireland, take them to a bank. A bank will give you the current exchange rate, plus charge you a small fee. Foreign exchange offices are available all throughout Ireland, but they will charge you higher commission fees than a bank will. You can also withdraw money from your U.S. bank account at any Irish ATM, which offers you the best exchange rate. You may, however, be charged fees from both banks, so check this before you leave the United States. One tip: Withdraw the largest amount possible each time so you can avoid multiple withdrawal fees.

OPENING AN ACCOUNT

There are several banks you have to choose from when deciding on where to open a bank account in Ireland, the main ones being Allied Irish Banks, Ulster Bank, Permanent TSB, and Bank of Ireland. Opening a bank account is the same whether you are a resident or not a resident in Ireland; however, nonresidents are entitled to earn interest on deposits without being subjected to Irish taxes.

To open a bank account, you are required to show proof of your identity with your photograph, such as a valid passport or Irish driving license, as well as proof of your address, such as a recent household bill. In addition, you will need to fill out the bank's application form, which is available online or in bank branches.

Most banks require you to apply in the branch, in person. However, I did call around and found out that Permanent TSB has a deposit and a demand deposit account (savings accounts) that can be opened over the phone or online. The demand deposit account issues a card, but you are only able to use it to withdraw money from Permanent TSB branches. To open an account this way, you will need to get the application online or call a Permanent TSB. You will need to include a certified copy of your passport or driver's license, as well as two bills for proof of address. The good thing about this is it creates a perfect means for transferring money from the United States to Ireland so you don't have to carry cash around. Once you are a resident in Ireland, you can change your deposit account into a current account. Alternatively, you can also check if any Irish bank operates a foreign branch near your U.S. address and open an account there.

There are several types of accounts available, depending on your marriage status, your age, and what you want from your account. Any interest you receive is subject to a tax called Deposit Interest Retention Tax (DIRT). This rate is fixed at 27 percent and is automatically deducted by your bank before any interest is paid to you. If you are not considered a resident of Ireland, you may get this tax refunded to you by applying at your bank. Additionally, an annual stamp duty

DAILY LIFE

tax is charged by the Irish government on *each* card you have issued from your bank, not the overall account. This tax is €30 for credit cards, €2.50 for ATM and debit (Laser) cards, and €5 for combined ATM and Laser cards. This tax is directly withdrawn from your bank account each year.

A current account is similar to a standard U.S. checking account. If you're a student, you can open a student current account, which means you can eliminate various fees, such as quarterly fees, foreign exchange charges, and ATM withdrawal fees. Some current accounts offer interest, while others only offer interest over a certain balance. Most of these accounts incur fees, but some allow no fees if you keep a certain balance in your account—usually around €3,000. If you are earning a salary, this is typically directly deposited into your bank account. Most of your bills will be direct debited from this account.

A savings account will usually add interest, although you should shop around, as banks offer widely different rates. A regular saver account has a standing order that regularly deposits money into your savings account, usually from your current account. If you have children, you can open a children's savings account, which typically offers higher interest rates and no fees. Savings accounts usually aren't issued with a debit card; you may receive a card, but it is only for use at ATMs to withdraw money, rather than for use with merchants. There are also accounts for business owners, the self-employed, teens, and graduates. You can also apply for a mortgage, invest money, open a line of credit, or request a credit card at your local bank.

If you receive a debit card with your account, you can use it anywhere throughout Ireland, the eurozone, and the world. You won't be charged a fee within Ireland and the eurozone, but outside of these areas you will. The great news is you don't have to worry about which bank you go to in order to withdraw money. If you have a debit card from Bank of Ireland, you can withdraw money from an AIB or Permanent TSB ATM, no fees added. If you are outside the eurozone, you will be charged a handling fee (about 1.75 percent) on all transactions. Cash withdrawals are charged at a flat fee (about 1.5 percent).

Taxes

Like most citizens in the rest of the world, the Irish dread paying taxes. However, tax evasion is not as endemic as it historically has been in Ireland. This is due to their Pay As You Earn (PAYE) tax system, which directly withdraws taxes from every legal worker's income, as well as harsh penalties that have been imposed for tax evasion.

TOP TAX RELIEFS

There are a number of tax reliefs available in Ireland that most people don't even claim. In fact, according to the Revenue Commissioners, more than one million PAYE workers do not claim all the tax relief they can. If you have lived in Ireland awhile and this is your first time claiming a tax refund, you can go back as far as four years to claim your tax reliefs, including the following:

- **Bin charges:** Everybody in Ireland is entitled to receive relief at the standard tax rate (20 percent) on bin charges, up to €400 (giving you a tax credit of €80). If you are claiming this relief for the past four years, you could receive up to €320.

- **Rent relief:** Rent on private rented accommodations also offers tax relief. In 2009 a single person under age 55 could claim up to €400, and a married person under age 55 could claim up to €800. These amounts double if you are over 55 years old.

- **Medical expenses:** You can claim tax relief at a rate of 20 percent on all qualifying health care expenses, including GP visits, doctors' bills, hospital treatments, maternity care, laser eye surgery, prescriptions, and much more.

- **Dental expenses:** While nowhere near as expensive as in America, dental care in Ireland is certainly not cheap. Certain special procedures such as root canals, crowns, and veneers are all eligible to be claimed as tax relief at the standard 20 percent rate. Regular procedures, such as fillings, do not qualify.

- **Trade union subscriptions:** Union fees can also be claimed back at 20 percent. In 2009 the maximum relief was €350, giving a €70 tax credit.

- **Tuition Fees:** If you pay for tuition at a qualifying course in Ireland, you can claim up to €5,000 tax relief.

- **Flat rate expenses:** Certain industries allow professionals to claim expenses related to their work. For example, in 2009, nurses were allowed to claim €733, journalists were allowed to claim €381, and pharmacists were allowed to claim €450.

- **Marital status change:** Getting married may make you eligible for a significant tax refund. The larger the gap is between you and your spouse's salaries, the larger the refund.

- **Single parents:** Single parents with dependent children can also claim tax reliefs. In 2009 this was €1,830.

- **Unemployed, leaving the country, or haven't worked for a full tax year:** If you have been made redundant or are unemployed during the tax year, if you leave Ireland, or if you haven't worked in a full tax year, you may be eligible to receive tax relief.

DAILY LIFE

Tax laws and regulations are constantly changing, so you should familiarize yourself with the tax laws of Ireland, especially if you own your own business. The best way to understand Irish tax laws is to consult an accountant who will help you stay within the guidelines.

IRISH TAXES

Residents of Ireland pay taxes on their worldwide income. If you are not ordinarily a resident of Ireland, you are charged tax on only your Irish income. You are classed as an Irish resident if you spend 183 days or more in Ireland during a tax year or if you spend 280 days or more spaced over two consecutive tax years. Central government tax revenue mostly goes to pay for expenditure programs, such as universal education, taxpayer-funded health care, social welfare payments, and unemployment benefits.

Unlike in the United States, the average Irish citizen does not have to file an annual tax return. Most people pay taxes through the PAYE system, which means your employer deducts the tax you owe directly from your wages and pays this to the Revenue Commissioners (the Irish version of the IRS).

As soon as you accept a job offer, you give your employer your Personal Public Service (PPS) Number. Your employer will let the tax office know you will be employed by them. Then you complete an application form for tax credits (called Form 12A Application for a Certificate of Tax Credits and Standard Rate Cut-Off Point) and send it to your local Revenue Office. If you employer doesn't receive either your certificate for tax credits from the tax office or a P45 (given to you by your previous employer when you leave), you will be charged emergency tax. The emergency tax means that after four weeks of employment without your tax documents you receive no tax credits, and after nine weeks you start paying the highest tax rate possible. You don't get a refund for any of this tax deducted, so make sure to keep your P45 and PPS number handy.

Your income tax bracket will be determined by your annual salary. In 2011, a single person pays 20 percent on income up to €32,800 and 41 percent on any balance. You will also shell out for Pay Related Social Insurance (PRSI) and the Universal Social Charge on your income. PRSI is a social insurance contribution paid into the national Social Insurance Fund (SIF), and the Universal Social Charge is another health contribution that you pay if your gross income is more than €4,004 per year.

If you are self-employed, you have to register to pay Class S PRSI income tax with the Revenue Commissioners and file an annual tax return. Ireland operates their tax year on a calendar-year basis (i.e., January 1–December 31). Tax returns should be filed by October 31 following the end of the tax year.

The various other taxes in Ireland will surely boggle your mind. I can think of 13 taxes off the top of my head, including excise taxes on alcohol and tobacco; Value Added Tax (VAT) at 21 percent, added to all goods and services; a motor tax if you drive; a plastic bag levy every time you buy a plastic bag (rather than reusing one); and a corporation tax (although Ireland's corporation tax is the lowest in the world at 12.5 percent). I guess it really is true, even in Ireland—nothing is certain but death and taxes.

U.S. TAXES

According to the IRS, all U.S. citizens are required to file their annual tax returns regardless of where in the world they live. This means you. Even if you are a resident in Ireland paying tax to the Irish government, if you are a U.S. citizen you are not absolved from filing your annual taxes and paying Uncle Sam. However, the good news is you may qualify for the Foreign Earned Income Exclusion if you earn less than US$92,900 (in 2011). If you earn more than that and are concerned about being double taxed, don't worry. Ireland and the United States have a treaty to help you avoid double taxation on certain things, most notably income. The legal details of this treaty are quite complex, so you should hire a good accountant who understands international taxes to help you with this. Alternatively, take a trip to Paris. A full-time IRS assistant for Americans living abroad is available at the U.S. embassy there (http://france.usembassy.gov/irs.html), or your can get more details about taxes you might face while living abroad on the IRS website (www.irs.gov).

DAILY LIFE

COMMUNICATIONS

Just one decade ago, Ireland was a totally different place. Nowhere is this more apparent than in the area of communications and telecommunications. We have left the days of cassette tapes, Walkmans, pay phones, VCRs, and calling our friends on a landline to set up a meeting time; now we are in an age of mobile phones the size of our palms, iPods the size of our thumbs, wireless Internet access, Google search engines, Skype calling, mobile broadband, iPads, Twitter, and Facebook. Communication is available from anywhere, with almost anything, at lightning speed.

In 2000, just 21 percent of Ireland's population were Internet users, according to Internet World Statistics. In 2010, that number had jumped to 66 percent. Additionally, 92 percent of all businesses have a computer that is connected to the Internet. Ireland has changed from a rural, agricultural-based nation to one that is focused on global trade and emerging communications technologies. With just a mobile phone or a computer with Internet access, you can talk to your friends and family, and a quick

© SARAHJANE SWEENEY

stop at your local newsagent will keep you in touch with local, national, and global media.

Telephone Services

Ireland's country code is 353. This number precedes any Irish number when dialing from abroad to Ireland. To call Ireland from the United States, dial 011 + 353 + area code + number. Ireland's area codes are organized according to geography and include a prefix 0, followed by the area code. If you are calling from within Ireland, you should include the prefix 0, but if you are calling from outside of Ireland you drop the 0. For example, a full Irish phone number in Dublin would be written as 011 + 353 + (0)1 + number. The 0 is dropped when dialing from abroad but should be included if you are dialing from within Ireland. If you are calling another country from within Ireland, you must add 00 before the country code and number. For example, to call the United States, dial 001 + area code + number. 1800 numbers are toll free from within Ireland, and 0800 are international free phone numbers. 1890 numbers charge a local rate, 0818 numbers are charged at a national rate, and 1850 numbers share the costs with whomever you are calling.

TELEPHONE COMPANIES

There are several companies in Ireland that offer telecommunications services, but the main one is Eircom. Eircom was originally called Telecom Éireann, the state-run telecommunications company. In 1999 the telecommunications market was liberalized and Telecom Éireann was privatized, opening the market up to more competition. Despite this, Eircom still owns much of the phone infrastructure in Ireland. Eircom's main competitors are UPC Ireland (which operates its own cable network), Vodafone Ireland (which is accessed through

© SARAH-JANE SWEENEY

a public telephone box

both Eircom's network and BT Ireland's fiber optics), Imagine Communications, Magnet Networks, and Smart Telecom.

The type of service you receive from your telephone company is based on a consumer contract. Before signing a contract, make sure you shop around for the best price and compare terms and conditions. These terms and conditions may include line rental prices and the cost of calls during peak and off-peak times. A good idea is to ask each operator you are shopping around with to provide you with a printed price list so you can check and compare prices. Once you do sign a new contract, you get what is called a "cooling off" period, during which time you may legally withdraw from your contract without receiving a penalty fee. This is typically seven working days from the day you signed the contract.

The Commission for Communications Regulation (ComReg) offers a website that helps compare the costs of fixed line telephone charges, as well as personal mobile phone and broadband plans (www.callcosts.ie). The site helps you select the phone package that suits your individual needs and usage.

Landlines

Ireland's landline telephone service is still dominated by Eircom, although Digiweb, Magnet Networks, and Vodafone Ireland offer some competition, and there are some fiber optic networks available from BT. Landline companies now offer deals with no connection fees and free installation, so be sure to shop around before signing up.

IRELAND AREA CODES

- 01: Dublin area, certain parts of Wicklow, Meath, and Kildare
- 021-029: Most of County Cork; Cork City, Bantry, Bandon, and Fermoy
- 0402: Arklow
- 0404: Wicklow
- 041-047, 049: Northeast Midlands and parts of Wicklow
- 051-059: Midlands and southeast areas
- 061-069: Southwest and midwest areas
- 071, 074: Northwest area
- 090-099: Midlands and western areas

MOBILE PHONE CODES

- 086 (but also 087, 085, or 083): O2
- 087 (but also 083, 085, or 086): Vodafone Ireland
- 085: Meteor

You do not need to be a resident of Ireland in order to set up a landline. All you need is your address and your bank account details so the company can direct debit your bill from your account each month. There are three ways to set up your new landline: go into the store, call the customer service number, or online. Whichever way you choose, you may end up waiting about two weeks if your location requires a technician to come out to you. (Which is likely if you plug a phone into the socket and it doesn't do anything. If the line is working, you will hear a recording telling you to contact your preferred telecommunications provider.) If you don't need a technician, setting up a landline generally takes about 2–3 working days.

LANDLINE RATES

Your monthly bill will range from about €30 per month for talking off-peak, to about €50 for anytime-talk packages. These prices are generally cheaper during the first six months of your contract, then skyrocket after this, so be sure to check what the price will be after your introductory six months is up. You should be aware that most plans are based on a monthly fee plus per-minute-used rate. Those per-minute calls are charged more for peak times (daytime and weekdays) and less for off-peak times (evenings and weekends). You can get packages with Internet service and television included, often at a lower price than just buying landline service on its own.

Calls from your landline to an Irish mobile are generally charged at a flat rate of 20 cents per minute, but this price depends on which provider you use and the time of day you are calling at. For example, calls between 8 A.M.– 6 P.M.may be charged at an increased rate. International call rates vary from a few cents to a few euros per minute, depending on which provider you use. To save money calling internationally, use Ireland's various cheap call numbers. These services are local numbers you call at the local rate, which then connect you to your intended number.

Cell Phones

The first thing you will want to do when you arrive in Ireland is to get yourself a cell phone (called a mobile phone here). The main mobile operators in Ireland are Meteor, Vodafone, O2, and Three. Tesco (the grocery store chain) also operates a mobile phone service using the O2 network, usually at a greatly reduced price. Before you choose your mobile operator, though, you need to decide if you want a bill phone or a pay-as-you-go phone. With bill phones you receive a bill at the end of the month for all calls (and texts) you have made. With pay-as-you-go phones, you buy credit for your phone from shops or bank machines, use the credit, then top up again when the credit has run out. Pay-as-you-go phones are a good option for expats first arriving in Ireland, as you don't have to sign a contract, you can establish what sort of calling patterns you have, and you don't have to give proof of your address. It is easy enough to switch from a pay-as-you-go phone to a bill phone once you have established residence and can provide proof of your address.

Multimedia 3G coverage for video, Internet surfing, and video conferencing is extremely good in Dublin, but it can get a bit dubious outside the city centers and into the rural areas. However, mobile phone providers offer coverage maps on their websites, detailing where their service is slack and where it is strong. The maps are just a little bit optimistic, but at least they give you a good idea of where you are covered.

MOBILE PHONE RATES

Every provider offers an array of rates and packages to suit a variety of people and businesses. You can choose from texting, talking, surfing the Internet, international calling, and much more. Make sure you check out the various options to find out what will suit you best.

When using your mobile, make sure you pay attention to "peak" and "off-peak" times, as the rates will vary depending on when you use your phone. Peak times occur during the day, when most people (and businesses) make their calls. Calls cost the most during peak times. Off-peak times occur in the evenings, nights, and weekends. These calls cost a lot less. Also, calling another mobile phone that is outside of your network will be more expensive than calling a landline. Some networks offer free talk or texts between mobile phones on the same network. The rates vary widely, depending on which mobile phone provider you choose, whether you have a pay-as-you-go or bill phone, and what package you choose. One bonus is you never have to pay for incoming calls, unlike American cell phones.

Every phone company offers you a free or discounted mobile phone when you sign up for service with them, even if you just opt for a pay-as-you-go phone. You will often receive a certain amount of credit included when you buy a pay-as-you-go phone, sometimes as much as €100.

If your American mobile is a tri-band or quad-band phone, you can bring it to Ireland, get it unlocked, purchase a new SIM card, and use it here. Most phone shops know how to unlock phones, but you will be charged a fee. You may be able to find the code to unlock your phone yourself by doing a simple

Internet search and typing in your make and model details. Once your phone is unlocked you will need to purchase an Irish SIM card, available at any of the cell phone carrier shops. You can often get a cheap (or free) SIM card when you purchase a phone, so it may be best just to get a whole new phone rather than bring your tri-band phone with you.

Internet Service

Odds are that Internet service will be one of the first things you organize when you arrive in Ireland. Besides having a mobile phone, this is the main way of communicating and keeping in touch with friends and family at home. You can choose to subscribe to a different service provider for Internet and telephone coverage, although you usually receive cheaper rates if you bundle them together.

The type of Internet access you will be able to get in Ireland depends on where you are located and if it is available in your area. ADSL broadband coverage is available to most of the Irish population and is delivered through an existing Eircom telephone line using a modem or router. Broadband cable Internet is a good option if you already have cable TV or live in an area served by a cable operator. This type of Internet connection requires a special modem to connect your computer to the Internet. Wireless Internet access is growing in popularity in Ireland, although the coverage is only really good in the main cities. You don't need a telephone line of any kind to have wireless Internet access. SDSL Internet is similar to ADSL, but it requires an extra telephone line separate from the one used for voice calls. It should be noted that rural areas do not offer very good Internet service. While you will have to pay the full price, you will receive very slow service, and sometimes no service at all. If you live in a remote location, you

Internet cafés are easy to find.

© SARAHJANE SWEENEY

would be better off purchasing a USB modem (dongle), which I talk about more in the next section.

Most telephone and mobile phone carriers offer Internet service, and some offer Internet service bundled into packages with telephone or TV service for cheaper than on its own. Compare packages and prices before making a choice. You will often be required to sign a six-month to one-year contract, and if you break the contract, you will have to pay a hefty termination fee, typically a percentage of the remainder of your contract.

Irish Broadband offers wireless Internet service without the need to rent a phone line. Vodafone Ireland offers broadband Internet with free telephone calls (starting at €40 per month). Eircom offers wireless Internet or Internet and talk packages.

Similar to getting your landline set up, getting your Internet service up and running can take weeks. If you are situated in a smaller town or rural area, it takes longer for a technician to get to you than it does if you are in a main city. While you are waiting for your service, there is always the option to go to an Internet café. All of the larger cities and towns have Internet café, as do many smaller towns, but you won't find them in rural locations or smaller villages. You will be charged according to how long you use the Internet, usually per hour. Be aware of cyberthieves and identity theft, and be extra vigilant with your personal belongings. Many cafés, coffee shops, restaurants, and hotels now have free or cheap Internet access available.

USB MODEMS

In the last few years mobile broadband service through USB modems, or "dongles," has revolutionized access to the Internet. This relatively new technology allows you to take your Internet with you wherever you go. Dongles are super convenient, particularly if you live in a rural area. They work like a USB stick—you can pop it into your computer port whenever you need to use the Internet, then take it out when you are finished.

Vodafone, Meteor, O2, and Three all offer mobile broadband service dongles. Similar to mobile phones, dongles can be purchased as pay-as-you-go or bill pay. For a pay-as-you-go dongle, you buy the dongle, then purchase credit in order to use it. For a bill pay, you typically pay for the dongle (although you may get it free if you sign a contract), then pay a monthly price depending on the amount of Internet you intend to use. The providers have data caps, so you aren't allowed to use more than a certain amount in a month. Since mobile broadband is so new, it is relatively expensive, starting at around €20 per month for about a 5GB download limit. The biggest cap is a 20GB download limit with Three Ireland for €35.

Post Offices and Couriers

An Post is Ireland's government-operated postal service. Post offices are open Monday through Friday 9 A.M.–5:30 P.M. and Saturday 9 A.M.–1 P.M. The main post offices don't close for lunch, but smaller, more rural post offices close from 1 to 2 P.M., although sometimes the lunch break stretches a bit longer. Locations and exact hours are available at www.anpost.ie.

Standard letters and postcards cost €0.55 to send within Ireland and typically take 2–3 working days, although this fluctuates widely. That same letter will cost €0.82 to send to the United States and will take 5–7 working days to get there. Again, the delivery times are just approximates, and in my experience post in Ireland tends to be like a river: flowing and meandering at its own pace. Letters, parcels, and packages can be sent throughout the world via Standard Post, Registered Post, Express Post, and Courier Post.

Stamps are available from post offices or from local shops that are licensed to sell stamps (common in rural areas). You can also buy stamps online at www.anpost.ie/AnPost/IrishStamps/Home/. Deposit your mail into any of the green post boxes. Often there are two separate post boxes: a local box and a box for everywhere else.

An Post has branched out in recent years, and you can now take care of an assortment of business by just stopping into your local post office. Besides just sending mail, you can also pay your bills, top up phone credit, get a passport, pay your TV license, get a dog license, exchange money (commission free), and even rent DVDs online and have them delivered to you with An Post Movies by Mail.

Mail in Ireland is delivered through a letter box situated in the front door of your house. This is fine for receiving letters but not so good for receiving packages. If you are not home when a package is delivered to you, you will receive

Drop your mail into any green post box.

NO POST CODES?

Unlike much of the rest of the world, Ireland does not currently use zip codes (called post codes). The exception to this is Dublin and Cork city centers, where a one- or two-digit postal district number is used; for example, Abbey Street, Dublin 1, or Clare Street, Dublin 14. Rural addresses are established by the house name, the nearest post town, the townland, and the county. Urban addresses are established by the house or apartment name or number, the street name, city or town name, and the county (plus the district if in Dublin or Cork).

The Department of Communications, Energy and Natural Resources has been discussing and anticipating the implementation of a national post code system since 2005, when a Working Group recommended the introduction of post codes. This has been consistently put off, although the department is currently targeting the end of 2011 for the implementation of the National Postcode System (NPS).

a slip of paper telling you where you can retrieve it. This is not necessarily the closest post office but may be the nearest routing center, which could be miles away. The first time this happened to me I had to take a very expensive taxi ride out to the Galway suburbs in order to retrieve my package. (It was chocolates for Valentine's Day, in case you were wondering.) So be sure you are there when the package is delivered or that you are able to drive to collect it. The post office will keep your package for five working days, after which it is returned to the sender. Make sure to bring your ID to collect the package.

If you need courier services, An Post ships nationally and internationally. For courier service within Ireland, you are guaranteed arrival the next working day before noon. For courier service to the United States, delivery is guaranteed within 2–3 days, depending on the location. FedEx (http://fedex.com/ie/) and DHL (www.dhl.ie/en.html) offer same-day and next-day delivery. Naturally, you will pay through the teeth for it, but delivery is guaranteed. Irish-owned couriers include Coda Couriers (www.codacouriers.com/), which overnights deliveries throughout Ireland and the UK, and Cyclone International (www.cyclone.ie), which specializes in same-day and next-day courier service to the United States.

Sometimes Irish customs will levy a tax on your package. If the package is new goods, you will be charged VAT at 21 percent, plus a 12 percent duty tax. Sometimes tax is added to used goods as well, from cameras to shoes, both of which I had to pay customs taxes for. One tip: If the package is marked as a gift and the value is less than $50, the chances of you having to pay customs taxes are much slimmer.

Media

For such a small country, Ireland has a host of newspapers, television channels, radio broadcasts, and magazines. In addition to national information, the Irish like to stay tuned in to global media and current affairs. Freedom of the press is enshrined in Ireland's constitution, although libel laws are constantly being challenged.

NEWSPAPERS AND MAGAZINES

Take a walk to any local newsagent, and you will see over a hundred newspapers just focusing on Irish news, from local to regional to national. According to the National Newspapers of Ireland and Joint National Readership Survey, 91 percent of adults in Ireland regularly read the newspapers. The *Irish Times* (www.irish-times.com) and the *Irish Independent* (www.independent.ie) are Ireland's main national newspapers, and, like the United States, they are strongly associated with political leanings. The *Irish Times* is considered Ireland's most liberal newspaper on social issues, and the *Irish Independent* is viewed as more conservative.

The leading Sunday newspaper is the *Sunday Independent,* followed by *The Sunday Tribune* and *Ireland on Sunday.* There is a trend in Irish newspapers to publish Irish editions of UK newspapers, including *The Sun, Mirror, Irish News of the World, Irish Daily Star,* and *The Sunday Times* (the only broadsheet of the group).

Most counties and towns have at least two newspapers; for example, Galway has the *Galway City Tribune,* the *Connacht Tribune,* the *Galway Advertiser,* and the *Galway Independent.* There are two free newspapers published daily in Dublin, *Metro Herald* and *Herald AM.*

Additionally, there are numerous newspapers printed in the Irish language. The most notable of these is the weekly newspaper *Foinse,* which prints Irish-language-related news and Gaeltacht affairs, as well as current affairs and national and international events. It is included in the *Irish Independent* every Wednesday. *Saol* (life) is an Irish-language newspaper published once a month, and *Gaelscéal* is a full-color tabloid published in the Irish language every week.

Popular Irish magazines include *RTÉ Guide, Hot Press, Phoenix,* and *Ireland's Own.* Hundreds of international magazines are available, including *The Economist, Hello!,* and *Reader's Digest.*

TELEVISION

Like much of the rest of the world, television plays a big part in social life in Ireland. From gossip shows to reality television, news shows to made-for-TV movies, there is much to choose from.

There are currently four national channels in Ireland: RTÉ One, RTÉ Two (both operated by RTÉ), TG4 (operated by Telifís na Gaeilge), and TV3 Ireland, operated by TV3 Television Network Limited. Additionally, there are three city television channels: City Channel Dublin, City Channel Galway, and City South (for Counties Clare, Cork, Kerry, Limerick, Tipperary, and Waterford). Setanta Ireland and Setanta Sports 1 broadcast sports games and matches.

If you feel all of this isn't enough for you, you're in luck. Various popular television channels broadcast specialized channels for Ireland, including MTV, Nickelodeon, Comedy Central, E!, and Discovery Channel Ireland. The UK offers various television channels broadcast in Ireland, including BBC News, ITV 1–4, Sky 2, and ESPN.

RADIO

Radio, especially news talk shows, is especially popular in Ireland. Even regular programming and music broadcasts stop regularly to have news updates. There are five national radio stations. RTÉ Radio operates RTÉ Radio 1, RTÉ 2fm, RTÉ lyric fm, and RTÉ Raidió na Gaeltachta. Today FM is operated by Denis O'Brien Group Communicorp. Dublin radio station Newstalk 106 operates on a seminational broadcast status, reaching most of the country, but not all of it. The Independent Local Radio network operates 18 commercial stations licensed for local areas.

RTÉ Radio 1 is the most listened to radio station in Ireland. It broadcasts a mixed radio network of music and speech programming. RTÉ 2fm (called 2 FM) is aimed at a younger generation and broadcasts mostly hit music. This station is recognized around the world as the first radio station to be allowed to play any new singles released by U2, thanks to the long friendship the band has with Dave Fanning, host of *The 11th Hour* on 2 FM. The main Irish-language radio station is RTÉ Raidió na Gaeltachta.

WEBSITES

Numerous expats that have moved to Ireland have set up websites to help newbies move with more ease than they did. You can browse them to help you with anything from questions about immigration to finding a new house. The ExpatExchange website, www.expatexchange.com, offers numerous forums where new and old expats can offer and receive advice about the big move and living in Ireland. Transitions Abroad, www.transitionsabroad.com, features informative articles that help during and after the move. It also lists other helpful expatriate websites, as well as resources for government and international organizations, embassies, consulates, and immigration to Ireland. One of the most useful sites I found was at www.movetoireland.com, which details the experiences of an American man who moved with his wife to Ireland. He gives open, honest information about the move and what to expect once you get to Ireland.

You will find Americans blogging and posting about everything, from their experiences with mold in their new home to where to go get a haircut. Use this advice in your own move and when setting up your life in Ireland. You can avoid many of their mistakes by simply perusing the forums and blogs prior to your move! The websites www.expat-blog.com/en/directory/europe/ireland and www.lonelyplanet.com/ireland/travelblogs both offer insiders' perceptions of living in Ireland.

TRAVEL AND TRANSPORTATION

Ireland, like most major cities throughout Europe, has an extensive network of buses and trains that make navigating the country fairly easy. The island is compact, and most cities in the Republic are located within just three hours of each other. However, while Ireland's trains are superior to America's, they are still not on par with many other European cities. Train travel is more comfortable than bus, but it can be expensive and crowded. And, unlike Europe, there is no subway linking the main metropolitan areas.

The country is crisscrossed by rural roads, national roads, and motorways that connect the cities, towns, and villages. Cars are commonplace, perhaps too much so, since cities like Dublin deal with daily congestion that clogs and obstructs the city center, making travel by car a pain in the neck. In the city and town centers there are good bus services, but bus stops in rural areas are

COURTESY OF TOURISM IRELAND

rare, and you are better off renting a car rather than navigating the bus system if you have to transfer in more than one place.

By Air

Ireland has four international airports: Dublin Airport, Cork Airport, Shannon Airport, and Knock Airport. There are numerous regional airports, including Galway Airport, Donegal Airport, Sligo Airport, Kerry Airport, and Waterford Airport. Even with all these options, you will most likely fly in and out of Dublin Airport, especially if flying to the United States.

Ireland's national airline, **Aer Lingus,** operates regular flights between Dublin International Airport and Boston, Chicago, Los Angeles, Washington DC, San Francisco, and New York's JFK. If you want to fly farther afield, Aer Lingus also schedules flights throughout the UK and Europe. **Delta Airlines** flies from Atlanta and New York to Dublin, **American Airlines** flies from Chicago to Dublin, **Continental** flies from Newark to Dublin and Shannon, and **US Airways** flies from Charlotte to Dublin. You can also fly from the United States to London and catch a connecting flight to Dublin or to most regional airports in Ireland. **RyanAir,** Ireland's low-cost, no-frills airline, offers regular flights between Dublin and the UK, as well as to many places throughout Europe. However, beware of hidden fees, long lines, and even longer delays.

Knock Airport is one of Ireland's international airports.

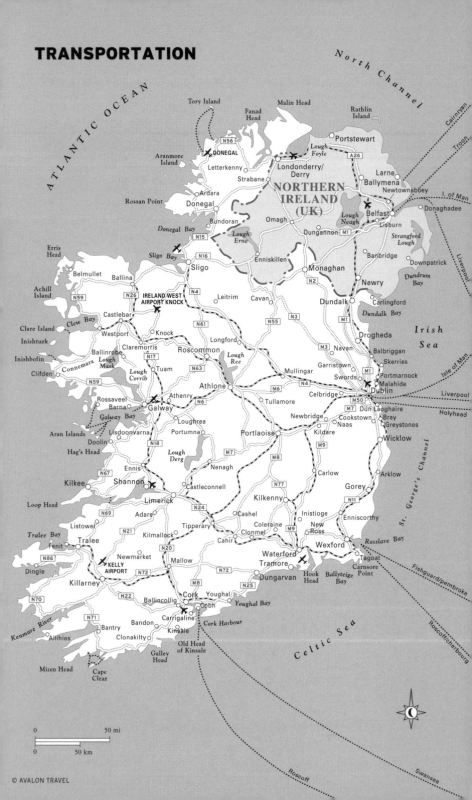

TRANSPORTATION

North Channel

ATLANTIC OCEAN

Tory Island
Fanad Head
Malin Head
Rathlin Island
Cairnryan
Troon
I. of Man

N56
DONEGAL
Aranmore Island
Letterkenny
Lough Foyle
Londonderry/Derry
Strabane
A26
Larne
Ballymena
Newtownabbey
Portstewart

Erris Head
Rossan Point
Ardara
Donegal
NORTHERN IRELAND (UK)
Belfast
Lisburn
Donaghadee
Liverpool

Belmullet
Achill Island
Ballina
Bundoran
Donegal Bay
N15
Lough Erne
Omagh
Dungannon
Lough Neagh
M1
Banbridge
Strangford Lough
Downpatrick
Dundrum Bay

Clew Bay
N59
N26
Sligo Bay
N16
Sligo
Enniskillen
Monaghan
N2
Newry
Carlingford

Clare Island
Inishturk
Castlebar
IRELAND WEST AIRPORT KNOCK
Leitrim
Cavan
Dundalk
Dundalk Bay

Inishbofin
Westport
Knock
N4
N55
N3
Drogheda
Irish Sea

Clifden
Connemara
N59
Ballinrobe
Lough Mask
Claremorris
N17
Roscommon
Longford
M3
Navan
Balbriggan
Skerries
Isle of Man

Rossaveel
Barna
Lisdoonvarna
Tuam
Lough Corrib
N63
Lough Ree
Mullingar
Garristown
Swords
M1
Portmarnock
Liverpool

Aran Islands
Doolin
Hag's Head
Galway
Galway Bay
Athenry
N6
Athlone
M6
N4
Celbridge
Dublin
Malahide
Holyhead

N18
Loughrea
Tullamore
M50
Dun Laoghaire
Bray
Greystones

Kilkee
N67
Ennis
Portumna
Lough Derg
N7
Portlaoise
Newbridge
Cookstown
Naas
M7
Kildare
Wicklow

Loop Head
Shannon
Castleconnell
Nenagh
M8
Carlow
M9
Arklow

N69
Limerick
N24
Castleconnell
N77
Kilkenny
Gorey
N11

Tralee Bay
Fenit
Listowel
Adare
Tipperary
Cashel
Inistioge
Enniscorthy
St. George's Channel

Dingle
N86
Tralee
N21
Kilmallock
N20
Cahir
Clonmel
Coleraine
M9
New Ross
Rosslare Bay
Fishguard/pembroke

KELLY AIRPORT
Newmarket
Mallow
N72
Waterford
Tramore
Wexford
Tagoat
Carnsore Point
Roscoff/cherbourg

Killarney
N22
N72
M8
Cork
Youghal
Dungarvan
Hook Head
Ballyteige Bay

N70
N71
Ballincollig
Carrigaline
Cobh
Youghal Bay
Cork Harbour

Kenmare River
Bantry
Bandon
Kinsale
Old Head of Kinsale
Celtic Sea

Allihies
Clonakilty
Galley Head
Roscoff
Swansea

Mizen Head
Cape Clear

| 0 | 50 mi |
| 0 | 50 km |

© AVALON TRAVEL

When traveling from coast to coast or between the larger cities of Ireland, it is easy and convenient to take hopper flights between the regional airports. **Aer Arann** offers flights to and from Dublin, Derry, Donegal, Sligo, Ireland West Knock, Galway, Kerry, Waterford, Cork, and Shannon. Aer Arann also flies to various cities throughout the UK and to two locations in France. Make sure to book well in advance for good rates.

You will face the same restrictions on traveling to Ireland as you do in the United States, including restrictions on flying with liquids. Most airlines will charge you to check your baggage and will not allow baggage over a certain weight limit. Once you are checked in and your bags safely sent to the plane—or on your person if you are carrying on—you will have to go through security before you are allowed to enter the boarding area. And just so there are no surprises, the security personnel are just as rigorous in Ireland as they are in the United States.

By Train

Iarnród Éireann (Irish Rail) is the state-owned train service in Ireland. Irish trains have a reputation for being late, unreliable, overcrowded, and just plain uncomfortable. However, that reputation is not always as accurate as it was in the past. While Irish rail service may not run with German accuracy, trains generally leave and arrive within a few minutes of their scheduled times. Trains departing from Dublin to anywhere in the country on Friday evenings are packed to capacity, as are Sunday evening trains carrying passengers back in to Dublin. However, midday trains and Saturday trains are usually open and accessible.

One thing you should know about the rail network in Ireland is that it is not very extensive. The trains only link the larger cities and major towns, not the small towns or villages. If you live in or are traveling to remote parts of Ireland, you will have to take a train to the nearest city, then transfer to a local bus service.

Most train lines radiate from Dublin, traveling to Galway (three hours), Killarney (four hours), Cork (three hours), Belfast (two hours), Sligo (three and a half hours), and Waterford (about three hours). Services run every hour or two on the main lines, but you should purchase your tickets and reserve your seats in advance so you are ensured a seat during your journey. You can book seats online at www.irishrail.ie.

If you live near a train station and plan to commute to work using the rail network, you may want to buy one of Iarnród Éireann's seasonal tickets, which are issued as weekly, monthly, or annual passes. You can purchase a single, day return, five-day return, monthly return, student return, family one-day, or family monthly ticket. The longer you extend the return, the more expensive the ticket is. For example, a day return from Dublin to Cork costs €51–71, but a monthly return costs €78.50. However, it's worth it to buy the monthly return if you don't know when you will be returning.

Explorer tickets allow you various travel options, such as day and monthly saver fares, kid and family fares, and student fares. Students with an ISIC card can purchase a Travelsave stamp and receive up to 50 percent off train fares. People under age 26 can purchase Faircards, which also gives 50 percent discounts. InterRail passes are available for travel through the Republic (only allowing discounted fares in Northern Ireland). The Irish Explorer Pass allows unlimited travel in the Republic of Ireland for either five or eight days.

You can get cheaper fares if you book online or call ahead of time. Sometimes fares are as low as €10 for a single ticket, although this refers to select service times and destinations. Expect a baffling array of prices based on time of travel, where you travel, and day you travel. For example, a ticket from Athlone to Dublin will cost €22 during peak times (before 9:30 a.m.) Monday–Friday, and €12 during off-peak times Monday–Friday. On Friday that same ticket will cost you €32.50 during peak times and €12 during off-peak times. Saturday and Sunday cost €15 all day. The average ticket costs around €35–45. The most expensive fare is a single ticket from Dublin Heuston to Millstreet in County Cork, costing €66.

Seat classes include premier (a first-class reserved ticket), standard (a standard-class ticket with a reserved seat), or ticket-only (a ticket without a reserved seat). If you are traveling during peak times, at least purchase a standard ticket so you have a seat reserved, as trains can get very overcrowded during rush hour. Intercity trains offer a bar car where you can purchase drinks and snacks. There are also bathrooms, although I should mention they are dirty and smelly.

Adults over age 66 who permanently live in Ireland are eligible for free train travel. This includes all state-run transportation, such as bus, rail, and Dublin's Luas (tram). Free travel on Iarnród Éireann services was available to tourists in Ireland over age 66 throughout 2010, but this scheme is currently being reconsidered, and no definite plans have been made for its future. If you qualify for the free travel pass, you should carry it with you whenever using public transportation. Children under five years of age are eligible for free train travel, and children under the age of 16 receive half-price tickets up to a maximum fare of €26.

By Bus

Bus Éireann (www.buseireann.ie) is Ireland's national bus service, operating a network of inter-city coach services, commuter services from all major cities and towns, and local bus services throughout Ireland. Bus Éireann's intercity bus service offers more than 50 routes linking the cities and towns in Ireland. City bus services operate in Galway, Limerick, Cork, and Waterford, and town services operate in Sligo, Navan, Athlone, Drogheda, and Dundalk. Bus Éireann also operates local services in rural areas, stopping on request for passengers to get on and off.

The exception to Bus Éireann's local bus service is in Dublin, where **Bus Átha Cliath (Dublin Bus)** operates local services within the city center, in the outer suburbs of Dublin, and in North Wicklow, Kildare, and Meath. Dublin Bus also offers the Nitelink service, operating to the suburbs of the city late into the night. This service operates Monday–Saturday, and departures usually take place between 12:30 A.M. and 4:30 A.M., although some routes offer more limited times. You can purchase tickets on the bus from the driver. A journey at 2 A.M. on a Dublin Bus is a very entertaining experience indeed. You will see everyone from tired night workers to drunken pub crawlers, all chatting away to each other in the Irish people's inimitable way. It's like boarding a party bus.

Just like in the United States, long-distance bus journeys are no fun. The traffic is congested in the cities, the roads are narrow and windy on the rural roads, and it is uncomfortable. However, buses are cheaper—and sometimes a lot faster—than trains, and, in Ireland, sometimes they are the only option. There are a range of long-distance bus services available in Ireland, both private and state owned, offering services on a range of routes. Buses are generally clean, and the long-distance buses have toilets at the back. There is usually no air-conditioning, although you would rarely need it in Ireland.

Ticket prices are based mostly on the distance you are traveling. Most buses are operated by Bus Éireann, so prices can be high, but if you are traveling on a popular route—Dublin to Galway, for example—there will be private companies acting as competition, which drives the price down. **City Link** (www.citylink.ie) offers regular bus services from Galway to Dublin and Cork Airport via Limerick and Cork city. **GoBus** (www.gobus.ie) also operates nonstop services from Dublin to Galway.

You don't need to buy your tickets in advance for any of these services, although you will want to arrive early—particularly on holidays, Fridays, and Sundays—to ensure you get a seat. It will always cost less to buy a return ticket (round-trip) than two singles, although if you won't be returning the next day, check when your ticket expires to make sure your ticket is valid for your return date.

AIRPORT BUSES

Ireland's international airports all operate airport shuttle buses into the city centers and throughout Ireland, although you may be hard-pressed to find any public transportation at the regional airports. In Dublin, **Aircoach** (www. aircoach.ie) departs the airport every 15 minutes, 24 hours a day. The bus line runs directly into Dublin city center, stopping at O'Connell Street, St. Stephen's Green, Fitzwilliam Square, Merrion Square, Ballsbridge, and Donnybrook. Tickets cost €7 one-way and €12 round-trip. Alternatively, the **Airline Express Coach** (www.dublinbus.ie) takes you from Dublin Airport to the Irish bus or train stations in the city center. The 747 and 748 buses go to Bus Áras and to Connolly station, and the 748 bus also goes to Heuston train station. Tickets cost €6 for one-way. Bus Éireann provides regular coach services between Cork Airport, Shannon Airport, Knock Airport, and the surrounding areas.

By Car

Driving a car in Ireland is totally unlike driving a car in the United States. Not only do the Irish drive on the left side of the road, the roads outside of the city centers are narrow, windy, and confusing. All of this is compounded by most cars being manual transmission (rather than automatic); large, multi-laned roundabouts; and angry, aggressive drivers. In fact, Ireland is tied with Portugal for the most traffic accidents in western Europe.

If you don't have nerves of steel, drop by a gas station or an auto shop and buy a red L sign—new learner drivers are required to put this on their car. This sign might just buy you a bit of slack on the road, although it might also warrant you a few glares and honks of the horn.

There is an extensive network of roads throughout Ireland. The speed limit is 50 kilometers per hour (about 30 mph) in towns, 80 kilometers per hour (about 50 mph) on rural roads, 100 kilometers per hour (about 60 mph) on national roads, and 120 kilometers per hour (about 75 mph) on motorways. Some sections of motorways are toll roads, which can be paid electronically ahead of time or at a toll booth.

Just like in the United States, seat belts are required by law. Road surveillance cameras enforce speed limits through machines that photograph your car and send you a ticket in the mail. The cameras are contained inside large gray boxes, and you will see signs warning you of their existence as you drive. The whole point is not to generate revenue, but to ensure you reduce your speed.

© SUSAN LEGG

A red "L" may help you get more slack when driving.

ROADS AND MOTORWAYS

Ireland has an extensive network of roads and motorways. The road network is focused on Dublin, with most roads to the rest of the country connected here. Larger cities and towns have bypass roads, which literally pass by the city or town center so you can avoid the traffic in the center. Major roads are called motorways or national roads, and national roads are grouped as primary routes (numbered 1–33 and 50) or secondary routes (numbered 51–87, with a few exceptions).

Motorways are similar to highways in the United States and have the fastest speed. They are indicted by the prefix *M* followed by one or two numbers. All of the motorways are part of or form the national primary roads. The national primary roads are prefixed by *N,* followed by one or two numbers. The N1–N11 roads radiate counterclockwise from Dublin, and the N12–N33 are cross-country roads. The national secondary roads are also prefixed by *N* and are followed by higher numbers (51–87). These roads are often bumpier and worse quality than the regional roads, although there are generally good road signs. These roads may be narrow and winding, with poor visibility at times. However, the roads you really need to watch out for are the local roads, called *boreens* (narrow, rural lanes), which can be difficult to drive on.

RENTING A CAR

Due to limited public transportation to the rural parts of Ireland, renting a car is really your best option for a visit to Ireland. If you live here and live in a rural area, you will probably have to buy a car. The cheapest way to rent a car is to make sure to book well in advance. Call various companies, organize rental

BRINGING YOUR CAR INTO IRELAND

The Irish drive on the left side of the road, and the steering wheel is situated on the right side of the car. As such, it will be a little bit difficult to drive your American car in Ireland. But if you do plan to import your car into Ireland, there are three things you need to do before you will be allowed to drive: pay Vehicle Registration Tax (VRT), purchase car insurance, and pay motor tax. You will also be required to have a valid license to drive your car. This means you will need a full Irish license if you are a resident in Ireland.

When you first bring your car into Ireland, it will be subject to VRT and must be registered with the Revenue Commissioners. The rate of this tax depends on the size of your car's engine (it usually works out to about 25 percent of the expecting selling price). The good news is if you have owned your car abroad for more than six months and are moving permanently to Ireland, you are exempt from this tax. However, if you sell the car within 12 months of arriving in Ireland, you have to pay the full tax. People who are not resident in Ireland and foreign students studying in Ireland are also exempt from this tax.

If you are required to pay this tax, you will have to do so before you are allowed to drive in Ireland.

You will also have to wait to receive your car's registration certificate proving you have paid this before you can drive. Seven days after your car arrives in Ireland you have to book an appointment with the National Car Testing Service (NCTS). This test inspects your car to not only ensure it matches your registration documents, but to ensure it is safe for the road and the environment. You will need to provide proof of ownership, proof of address, date of arrival and departure from Ireland, proof of insurance, and proof of date of purchase. Incidentally, any car you own while living in Ireland will be required to pass the NCTS test and have proof of that stuck to the car's windshield while driving.

Once your car has been registered and the VRT paid, you will receive a receipt for the paid VRT showing your car's registration number, as well as a form RF100 to use when applying to pay motor tax. If you are importing a new car (less than three months old), you will also have to pay Value Added Tax (VAT) at 21 percent when you register the car. If you are importing an old car (more than four years old), you will need to have evidence of the car's previous registration, such as a foreign certificate of registration.

through your travel agent, or—for some of the best deals—look online. Rent by the week with unlimited mileage. The best place to pick up is at an airport, although the bigger rental companies have locations in the cities as well.

Make sure you have insurance of some kind (as I mentioned before, Ireland has a high incidence of traffic accidents). Collision Damage Waiver (CDW) insurance limits your financial responsibility in the case of an accident. Super CDW insurance allows you to "buy down" your deductible so you aren't financially responsible for anything in the event of an accident. Alternatively, you can opt

Bicycle taxis are available for getting around Dublin.

for your credit card to cover you. If you choose this option, be sure to call your credit card company and make sure it covers you in Ireland, as there are a very limited amount of rental agencies that do. Ask how it works and what the worst-case scenario would be. If you choose this option, you will have to decline all coverage from your car rental company, which means they have the right to place a hold on your card for the full deductible, and, in the case of damage, you will have to sort out the details with your credit card company. This usually involves you paying up front and your credit card company reimbursing you later.

Most car rental companies require your state-issued driver's license and don't need an international driving license, although you will have better luck with a wider variety of car rental companies if you do have an international driving license. Keep in mind that fuel prices are considerably higher in Ireland than in the United States, and you will have to return your car to the rental company with a full tank of gas.

DRIVER'S LICENSE

American citizens are allowed to drive in Ireland with a U.S. driver's license as long as they are a tourist, not a resident. Once you decide to become a resident, you have to apply for an Irish driver's license. If you will also be driving in other countries, Spain and Italy, for example, you will need to go into your local auto club, such as AAA, and get an International Driving Permit. This permit is a special driving license that allows you to drive abroad without further tests or applications.

Getting a driver's license in Ireland is one of the most convoluted, complicated, nonsensical processes I have ever come across. Before you can get your

PARKING RULES

Parking regulations in Ireland, particularly in Dublin city center, are strictly enforced. Parking meters operate in city center areas, and you should check the signs for rates you pay. Typically these rates run about €1.30-1.90 per hour. These meters are usually called "Pay and Display," with a single meter serving about 20 spaces. These modern machines are solar powered, and you will recognize them by a blue circle with a white letter *P*. As you insert your coins, the parking expiry time will be displayed. After you press the green button, the machine will print a two-part ticket – one to stick to your car's windshield and the other for you to retain.

Multistory car parks (parking lots) are available in many city centers (typically costing €1.50-2.50 per hour). These often have displays indicating how many spaces are available in each lot. Some of the car parks accept credit cards, including Stephen's Green and Royal Surgeons; however, some only accept cash. Outside of the city centers disc parking is in operation. Discs can be bought at local shops. You purchase one for each hour, scratch off the time you arrived on the disc, and put it on your dashboard.

Discerning where you can and can't park on streets can be confusing. One yellow line on the pavement means no parking Monday-Saturday during business hours. A double yellow line means no parking anytime. A broken yellow line means short stops are okay. If you park in a space you're not allowed to, one of your tires will be clamped, and you will have to call the number on the clamp boot and pay a stiff fine in order to leave. Okay, I know it makes no sense to clamp your car to make it stay there when the whole point is to make you leave, but, as you're probably learning, many things in Ireland don't make much sense. There will also be many times when cars double park alongside each other just to "pop into the shop." Yes, it holds up traffic, but people do it anyway.

© SARAH-JANE SWEENEY

Parking signs lead you in the right direction.

full license you must first apply for a provisional license (a learner's permit). To do this you simply apply to take a written theory test from your local motor tax office or online (www.dtts.ie/). Once you pass the test, you should include your test certificate with your application form (as well as proof of a passed vision test from a qualified optometrist) to receive your learner's permit. No actual driving experience is necessary (thus the high amount of road accidents in Ireland).

Once you have your learner's permit you will be required to have a qualifying adult with you at all times when driving. The qualifying adult must have had a full license for at least two years. Now, this may seem silly to add, but in Ireland it is relevant: The qualifying adult must be in a capable state; i.e., you can't pick your dad up from the pub when he is legless drunk. Next you should book driving lessons from a professional driving instructor in order to learn how to drive safely. This is not a rule but sort of a suggestion that, incidentally, most people do not follow. It is expensive and time-consuming, and most people don't bother with it (again, netting Ireland a high amount of road accidents).

One you feel comfortable with driving, you should apply for your full driver's license. This is where it gets really tricky. National fail rates are about 47 percent. That means that nearly one out of every two people who take the test fails. Not only that, you will have to wait months for the privilege of doing so. In the past, wait times were up to 62 weeks (my husband waited almost 10 months), but with the help of some private firms, average wait times are now about 18 weeks. The best advice I can offer is to apply for your test well in advance. You can find out how long your wait will be online (www.rsa.ie/Utility/Contact-Us/Driving-Test-Centres/). If you fail your driving test, as a high percentage of people do, the Road Safety Authority shuffles you out the door, allowing you to keep driving and just reapply to take the test again later.

The cost of a driving test is €85, although this fee goes up from time to time. You must be 17 years old to apply for a provisional license. Both provisional and full licenses are issued on colored paper that is laminated on one side: green for a provisional and red for a full license.

Before you drive your car, you should make sure the car has the tax disc placed on the windscreen, you have valid insurance, that the insurance disc is visible on the windscreen, and that your National Car Test (NCT) sticker is on your windscreen. Your L sticker should also be properly displayed on the front and back of the car. It's a lot of stuff to have stuck all over the windshield of a car, but it's the law, and you will pay a stiff penalty if you don't have any of them visible to the gards (police).

Public Transportation

Ireland has good public transportation in the city centers, particularly in Dublin, but the rural areas are a bit difficult to get around without a car. Bus Éireann (Irish Bus) is the national bus company, covering local, rural, and national routes, and Iarnród Éireann (Irish Rail) is Ireland's rail network, covering the major cities and towns across the island. Single, return, weekly, monthly, and annual passes are issued for public transportation options.

BUSES

All the major cities and even the smaller towns and villages are served by Bus Éireann's extensive bus network or by private buses and coaches. The name of the city the bus journey ends at is listed on the front of the bus, making it a bit easier to find which one you need to take. You do not need to book seats ahead of time for long-distance travel. All of the major cities and towns are served by local Bus Éireann buses, with the exception of Dublin, which is served by Bus Átha Cliath (Dublin Bus).

COMMUTER TRAINS

Ireland has a few suburban railway networks in operation: Dublin, Cork, Galway, and Limerick Suburban Rail. The Dublin service is composed of five lines: Northern Commuter (Dublin Pearse to Dundalk), South Eastern Commuter (Dublin Connolly to Gorey), South Western Commuter (Dublin Heuston to Portlaoise), Western Commuter (Dublin Pearse Docklands to Longford), and the Dublin Area Rapid Transit (DART). DART links Dublin city center with 30 stations along the coast outside of Dublin, from Howth in the north to Greystones in County Wicklow in the south. Services run 6:30 A.M.–midnight, although the services are less frequent on Sunday. Single tickets from Dublin city center to Howth cost €2.20. Cork, Limerick, and Galway also have suburban rail lines, linking the city centers with the surrounding suburbs. All lines are owned and operated by Iarnród Éireann, and prices vary according to how far, what time, and what day you are traveling.

LUAS

Dublin also has a light rail tram network. The Luas runs two tram lines: The green line runs from Sandyford north to St. Stephen's Green, and the red line runs from east Tallaght to Connolly Station via Heuston Station. Trams run Monday–Friday 5:30 A.M.–12:30 A.M. They depart every five minutes during peak times and every 15 minutes during nonpeak times. On Saturday the tram operates 5:30 A.M.–12:30 A.M., and on Sunday it runs 7 A.M.–11:30 P.M.

Fares are based on travel zones, costing €1.60–2.40 for a single ticket. You can get reduced prices for passes from a newsagent if you purchase ahead of time, or a daily pass will cost €5.30, a weekly pass will cost €19.10, and a monthly pass will cost €76 from the ticket machines.

DAILY LIFE

PRIME LIVING LOCATIONS

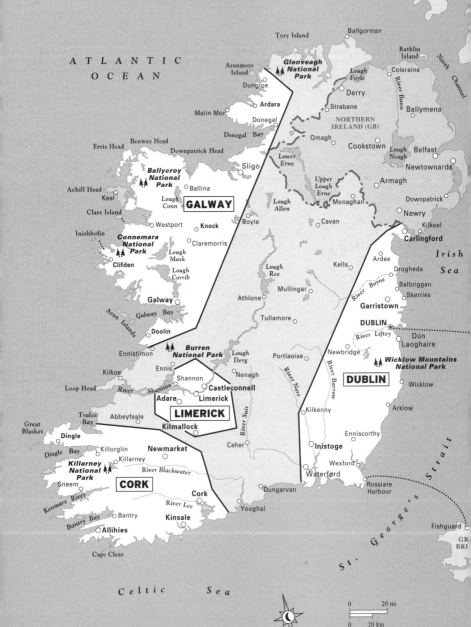

OVERVIEW

One of the startling things you'll notice about Ireland is the difference between urban and rural living. The population density of this diverse nation is hugely unbalanced, with a wide gap dividing rural and urban Ireland. Regional imbalances in population trends, employment, income, and social networks have long been a feature of Ireland. Dublin is, of course, the focus of the country's commercial, industrial, educational, administrative, and cultural center. Cork city is Ireland's main city for processing and marketing agricultural products, as well as large-scale industrial developments from its harbor. The smaller towns of Waterford, Dundalk, and Drogheda are small regional areas with industrial functions. Limerick city shares the success of Shannon Airport and Shannon Industrial Estate, and the towns of Galway and Sligo both have some regional success and offer an urban atmosphere.

The unprecedented economic boom in Ireland in the 1990s led to an increase in the population and economy of the main urban cities and a decrease in some of the rural villages. During these boom years, the high-tech and

internationally traded companies based themselves in Dublin or scattered throughout a few of the smaller cities (namely Cork and Galway), contributing to a decline in rural areas and a burgeoning of urban cities.

Of the 6.9 million hectares (17 million acres) of land mass in Ireland, about 4.2 million hectares (10.4 million acres) are used for agriculture (64 percent). So if you're looking for a little slice of countryside, Ireland is certainly full of it. In contrast, the main cities offer a cosmopolitan vibe, with access to shopping, cafés, theater, pubs, and cultural amenities. Of course, you have to balance that with overcrowding, smaller housing, and absolutely abysmal traffic.

Your choice for where to move in Ireland will naturally be a very personal one but will be based on these two options: rural or urban. While finding the area that suits you may not be easy, there are certainly many options available. Are you looking for the excitement of a bustling city like Dublin or the calm of the peaceful countryside like Knock? Do you want to be surrounded by rolling green hills like Glendalough or by wind-lashed beaches and the expansive Atlantic Ocean near Galway? Is being close to the cultural heritage, art exhibits, and theater of Limerick or Cork important to you, or the prehistoric forts, holy wells, and crumbling stone walls that surround Tara? The great thing about Ireland is that most everywhere in the country is within about three hours of each other, so even if you live in a peaceful village in County Galway, you're not that far from the bustle of Dublin city.

I should explain that the names of the main cities in Ireland are also the names of counties—Dublin city is in County Dublin, Galway city is in County Galway, and so on. The city is the main hub, while the county includes the suburbs, surrounding towns, and the contiguous countryside, which is peppered with farms, grazing cattle, and expanses of green pastureland.

Irish suburbs can range from upper to lower class, but they are typically comfortable areas with housing estates offering a common grassy area for children to play on. Irish housing estates are different from American neighborhoods in that they are typically attached to each other in long rows of terraced houses, similar to what Americans would call town houses, or long rows of semidetached houses, which are houses that are attached to another house on one side. Semidetached houses are typically larger and cost more than a terraced house. Fully detached houses are rare to find in the cities but are available in the suburbs and throughout rural Ireland, although this added element of space and privacy will cost you more.

No matter what you choose, Ireland offers a plethora of possibilities to suit any personality and any lifestyle. Here is an overview of the most popular expat options.

Dublin

Dublin city is the capital of Ireland and the hub of County Dublin. This metropolitan city appeals to the young and the old, to the urban and the suburban, to the history buffs and the modern revelers, and it has been inspiring poets and writers like Oscar Wilde and James Joyce for hundreds of years. The economic growth of the last decade has resulted in Dublin becoming modern and fashionable, and even the more recent economic downturn hasn't negated this. The economic growth also resulted in an explosion of multiculturalism—about 10 percent of Dublin's population are foreign nationals, and you will find Chinese herbalists situated next to traditional Irish pubs.

Dublin is the seat of Irish politics and finance, and the center of culture, art, and theater. Handsome Georgian squares and buildings overlook cobbled streets and green parks. In fact, Dublin has more green space per square kilometer than any other European capital city. So not only are you smack dab in the middle of a bustling city, you are also never far from the green areas of Dublin's city parks.

Dublin is also one of Europe's most youthful cities, with about 50 percent of its citizens being younger than 25. Many of the young and highly educated workforce in Dublin are employed in pharmaceuticals, technology, computers, and telecommunications. The city features a thrumming vibe and a sophisticated polish crowning a good-humored, dry-witted group of people.

If you are looking for a bit more space, you will find plenty of well-connected suburbs surrounding Dublin. Here you'll find less traffic, bigger houses, and more grass. Whether you choose the city or the suburbs of Dublin, be aware that this is not only the most popular place to be, but it is also the most expensive city to live.

Cork

Cork city is nestled within the borders of County Cork, a diverse, unspoiled county full of color and contrasts, rich farmlands and river valleys, sandstone hills and wind-lashed coastlines. In fact, Lonely Planet listed Cork in the top 10 Best in Travel 2010, describing Cork as being "at the top of its game: sophisticated, vibrant and diverse." I would describe Cork as the icing on the cake that is Ireland. No matter where you go, from city center to the smallest

Cork's beautiful marina

outlying village, you will find friendly people with a lyrical accent offset by a view of spectacular beaches, mountains, or rolling countryside.

In recent years Cork city has begun nonchalantly pushing Dublin out of the way as the premier city in Ireland. This Rebel County marches to a different beat than the rest of the country and has an individuality you won't find elsewhere. Whether you want modern art galleries, avant-garde theater, or stunning historic buildings, you will find them in Cork. Within the city you will catch a small-town intimate spirit blended with the energy of a modern city. There are three spectacular Gothic cathedrals and a pedestrianized shopping area with colorful shops, cafés, pubs, and boutiques. A thriving arts scene features events and exhibitions throughout the year, culminating in the famous Guinness Cork Jazz Festival.

Galway

Galway city is the beating heart of County Galway. The City of the Tribes, as it is known by the Irish, is lined with colorful shop fronts, traditional pubs, and cobbled lanes, lending a medieval quality to this cosmopolitan city. It is the soul of a creative and diverse cultural scene, featuring a free-spirited, bohemian atmosphere that is unlike any other place in Ireland.

Galway is the fastest growing city in Ireland and one of the most multi-cultural. You will see Chinese shops, Caribbean markets, and Polish pubs all

EXPAT INTERVIEW WITH SCOTT SIMONS

In 1975, Californian Scott Simons stopped off in Ireland to visit a friend after a trip around Europe. He fell in love. Not just with the stunning green countryside or the affable, charming people. He fell in love with an Irish girl.

The economy in Ireland at the time was poor, so they moved to America, where they stayed for 14 years. But Ireland had gotten into Scott's blood. Years of trips to visit his wife's family led them to discover Dungarvan, a rural coastal town midway between Cork and Waterford. "The land of opportunity," Scott said. "It was an exiting and adventurous time for us."

Dungarvan is nestled beneath the Knockmealdown Mountains, next to Dungarvan Harbor in the heart of County Waterford. Scott and his wife moved to a rural location about 10 minutes outside of Dungarvan, where they eventually designed and built their dream house. After the move, Scott had so much information about moving to Ireland that he began writing a website to help other expats. He named the website www.move-toireland.com, and it is still up and running today.

Scott moved to Dungarvan in 1992, and loves it even more now than when he first arrived. "I grew up in big cities – New York, Philadelphia, Minneapolis, Los Angeles – but at heart I'm a country mouse." Scott said. "My impressions have only grown stronger that this [Dungarvan] is one of the great places to be on Planet Earth. Blessed, that's me. I'm here till they cart me away in a box, and, I trust that box will be buried on Irish soil."

Rural Ireland is very different from urban Ireland. You may have acres of land before you see another house. Sheep and cows dot the pastureland. Tractors block the roads. It is quiet, peaceful, remote, and tranquil. Scott chuckles and says, "Everyone in a rural community knows your business. And you know everyone else's." While this is a worldwide thing, not necessarily Irish, in Ireland there is an openness, a friendliness to other cultures that new people find very enticing.

"The U.S. is a Messianic society," Scott reflects. "The weight of the world is on the U.S.'s shoulders, and it views itself, still, as the pilgrims. And that informs everything the country does; everything is of vital importance. In Ireland, they kick it down a few notches. No messy complexes. It's just a more relaxed attitude toward everything."

Scott's advice is to not take everything so seriously. Living in rural Ireland will certainly curb you of that. After a few days of the biting wit of the local farmer or a laugh with your neighbor about the cows on the farm, you're sure to start living life at a more relaxed pace.

"Just get involved," Scott recommends to newcomers. "In a big city you make your community through churches or your hobby, but here your neighbors are your community, and it's a wonderful experience." Rural Ireland doesn't have any expat clubs or societies other than the local pub. But there are certainly loads of local activities that people are sure to enjoy: drama or sports – bicycling, hiking, fishing, rowing, or even surfing. "Forget about the expat stuff," Scott says. "Just get involved with your neighbors. You're part of community. Make your contribution."

PRIME LIVING LOCATIONS

within the city center. The main university in the west, the National University of Ireland, Galway, is situated here, lending Galway a boisterous student presence throughout the school year. During the summer months, the city is bombarded by arts, music, film, and language festivals and fairs.

Radiating out from Galway city are arterial links to the suburbs, the adjacent towns and villages, and, beyond that to the west, the Gaeltacht, one of the main Irish-speaking areas in Ireland. Galway is known as the most "Irish" city in Ireland, with over 10 percent of the population speaking the Irish language fluently. If you're looking for a big-town feel with a laid-back ambience, Galway is the place to go. Despite the big-town look and feel, however, there is a definite small-town mentality in Galway; it is easy to know somebody who knows somebody else, so anonymity isn't that easy. You won't get lost in the press of the city, nor will you stand out as a blow-in—the Irish people's expression for somebody whose family hasn't lived in the area for generations—like you would in a smaller village.

Limerick

The city of Limerick is gracefully situated across several curves and islands of the River Shannon, which flows majestically under Limerick's three bridges and out through the rest of County Limerick. This lively city has enjoyed an economic and cultural renaissance after some bad press brought on by various media nicknames and the success of the book *Angela's Ashes,* offering numerous sports events, stunning historic sites, and a rich heritage to be explored.

The turbulent history of the area has left behind ancient artifacts, monuments, and stone edifices that lay testament to what the city and county have faced in the past, adding to its charm today. The city features a medieval core, but the addition of Georgian archaeology is visible in various historic buildings. Today Limerick is one of Ireland's leading tourist and business hubs. Shannon Airport is situated nearby, bringing in tourists from America and beyond, and the University of Limerick lends a young student population to the city.

Limerick is regarded as the sports capital of Ireland. Rugby, Gaelic football, soccer, and hurling are all very popular here, and many of Ireland's most commemorated All-Ireland League teams are located here. In fact, Limerick was designated as a European City of Sport for 2011 by the European Capitals of Sport Association (ACES).

Rural Ireland

Rural Ireland is very different from urban Ireland. The smaller villages are basically service centers providing shopping facilities for the rural community. Semidetached and detached houses, as well as some apartments, are typically centered around the village center, but most people in the community live on rural farms or houses on peaceful lots of land within close proximity to the village. The larger towns are also service centers, but in addition to having shopping areas in the town center, they also have industrial, administrative, and commercial functions.

While the larger cities offer a bustling vibe with culture, arts, and a social scene, the rural towns and villages that speckle the face of Ireland are more subdued and peaceful than their urban counterparts. Certain services are available in the cities that aren't in the villages. For example, garbage collection isn't available in many rural areas. You will have to take your garbage to the local authority dump. You may not have any neighbors nearby, but perhaps that's exactly what you're looking for.

Rural Ireland has changed hugely over the last decade. Previously, Ireland was an agriculturally dependant nation, producing beef, pork, lamb, and cheese on a multitude of farms. Now, however, agriculture no longer dominates rural economic activity, as the landscape of the country expands to include tourism, travel, and more transportation.

Rural areas are, of course, still dotted with farms, but these farms are interspersed with holiday homes, golf courses, and scenic tourist destinations. In fact, many rural towns are tourist destinations in themselves; for example, picturesque Adare in County Limerick, a historic village lined with thatched cottages and historic stone buildings, or the town of Blarney, which is home to the famous Blarney Castle and the Blarney stone.

While many of Ireland's rural towns and villages that are close enough to urban areas have expanded, pushing the development of transportation, education, community, and social services, and putting all existing infrastructure under strain, others have declined as their citizens have moved closer to the urban towns that promise jobs.

PRIME LIVING LOCATIONS

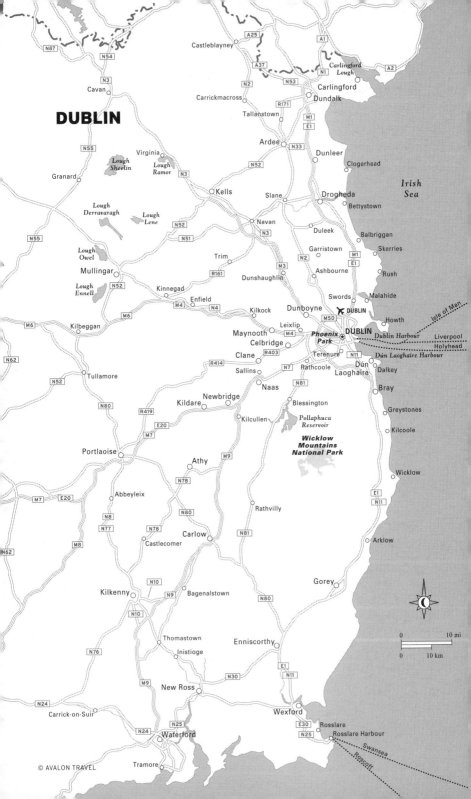

DUBLIN

Ireland's capital city, Dublin, *Baile Átha Cliath* (town of the hurdled ford) in Irish, is the heart of the nation. It is the seat of Irish commercialism, politics, finance, administration, and education; where most jobs are available; and where much of the country's culture and art is found. Daily life here moves at a brisker pace than the rest of the country, with a vibrant social scene for expatriates and tourists alike. The city buzzes with energy, combining urban chic, lush parkland, sweeping coastline, charming pubs, and elegant Georgian architecture to create an eclectic blend of beauty that is hard to resist.

The famous Irish writer James Joyce immortalized Dublin in his books *Dubliners, Ulysses,* and *A Portrait of the Artist as a Young Man.* He was quoted as saying that he chose Dublin as the setting for his books because it was a "center of paralysis," where nothing ever changed. Joyce would be shocked to see Dublin today, after the 1990s economic boom of the Celtic Tiger brought massive development and expansion to the city. The historical

© SARAHJANE SWEENEY

areas and buildings have been rejuvenated, new shopping centers built, and cultural and artistic sites restored. In 2009, Dublin was reported by UBS, a global financial company, to be the fourth-richest city in the world. Dublin now blends a modern, contemporary vibe with a sense of the history the city still retains.

Fueled by the economic boom, Dublin has grown to be the largest metropolis in Ireland, with approximately 25 percent of the country's population residing here. The arrival of new ethnic groups, including Polish, Chinese, Pakistanis, Nigerians, and Russians, has created a multicultural atmosphere, particularly in the north side of the city. In 2008, Ireland had the highest migration rate in the EU. Although this has certainly slowed down with the recent recession, the city is more international than ever before. Polish markets and Asian herbal shops now share space with ancient Irish pubs and 18th-century town houses, creating an eclectic, progressive atmosphere.

Young people from all nationalities fill the city, and the whole place seems to be perpetually transitioning from old to new. The sounds of ongoing construction can be heard on almost any street corner, and heavy traffic clogs the roads during rush hour. Although the DART transit system has eased some congestion, it can be difficult to get in and out of the city center.

If you decide that Ireland is where you want to live but don't really know where to start, Dublin is your best launching point. Not only is it modern and offers access to all amenities and conveniences you are used to in a metropolitan city, it is also within easy access to rest of Ireland. You will have a better chance of finding employment, and your salary will certainly be higher here than in the rest of the country.

The Lay of the Land

Dublin lies on Dublin Bay and the mouth of the River Liffey, overlooking the Irish Sea, with Great Britain situated beyond that. The River Liffey bisects the city center into the Northside and the Southside, and two canals, the Royal Canal in the north and the Grand Canal in the south, compose a semicircular arch around the city center. The city is fringed by a low mountain range to the south and is surrounded to the north and west by lush, flat farmland. Dublin's main central locations, including O'Connell Street, Grafton Street, Dame Street, Temple Bar, and Trinity College, are all within walking distance of each other, making Dublin compact and easily accessible on foot.

BOOK OF KELLS

The ancient Book of Kells is an illuminated manuscript written in Latin and featuring lavish decorations that combine traditional Christian symbolism with ornate swirling motifs, such as seen in Insular art. There are vivid figures of humans, mythical beasts, animals, Celtic knots, and interlacing patterns adorning the pages.

The book was created by Celtic monks around A.D. 800 and has been on display in the Old Library at Trinity College Dublin since the mid-19th century. The manuscript features the four Gospels on vellum (prepared calfskin) in a script called "insular majuscule."

The Book of Kells's place of origin is attributed to a monastery on Iona, an island off the west coast of Scotland. After a Viking raid in 806, the Columban monks took refuge in the monastery at Kells, County Meath. It is assumed by scholars that the Book of Kells was partially written in both locations.

In 1953 the book was bound into four volumes. Two volumes are on display to the public; one displaying the books' ornate decoration and the other showing two pages of the script. The displays are regularly changed to show different pages.

The Old Library building at Trinity College, where the Book of Kells is housed, is open Monday-Saturday 9:30 A.M.-5 P.M. and Sunday 9:30 A.M.-4:30 P.M. during the summer and noon-5 P.M. during the winter. Entrance is €9 for adults, and children under 12 are free.

The Book of Kells is located at Trinity College, Dublin.

COURTESY OF TOURISM IRELAND

PRIME LIVING LOCATIONS

HISTORY

Dublin was first established by Vikings in A.D. 998 and was originally called *Dubh Linn* (black pool). Under Viking rule, Dublin replaced the seat of the Irish High Kings at Tara (County Meath) and became the political and commercial capital of Ireland, with the main seat of the Parliament of Ireland held here since 1297. The city remained in Viking hands until the conquest of the Normans in 1169. In 1169 the King of Leinster, MacMurrough, enlisted the help of an English earl, Richard Strongbow, to help conquer Dublin and restore his throne. While the conquest was successful, MacMurrough died soon after and passed the throne to Strongbow. Strongbow later gave the throne to the King of England, marking the beginning of 700 years of Norman rule.

The 18th and 19th centuries in Dublin were marked by the growth of many famous buildings and districts, including Merrion Square, Parliament House, and the Royal Exchange, which later became City Hall. This time was marked by a further segregation between Protestants and Catholics in not only Dublin, but throughout Ireland. Things changed dramatically when the Easter Rising occurred in April 1916. The Irish rebels occupied the post office on O'Connell Street and announced a new Irish Republic. The British crushed the rebellion and executed many of the rebels, alienating the Irish and making way for the War of Independence, which began in January 1919.

The War of Independence turned Dublin into a violent and bloody place, with Irish Republic Army officers and British troops often fighting in the streets and innocent civilians getting caught in the crossfire. Unfortunately, the success of Ireland's independence from England didn't result in peace, and a civil war broke out between the pro- and antitreaty factions. Fighting continued in the streets of Dublin, from which the city did not begin to recover until the 1930s, when new shops, theaters, cafés, and public buildings were constructed. During the Celtic Tiger years of the early 2000s the city evolved to become the thoroughly modern, bustling, cosmopolitan center that it is today.

CLIMATE

Like the rest of the country, Dublin has a temperate climate, with mild winters, pleasant summers, and moderate temperatures. The temperature rarely falls below 0°C (32°F) in the winter, with the average temperature in January hovering around 4.5°C (40°F). In the summer, the temperature rarely goes above 18°C (64°F), with the average temperature in July being 15°C (59°F).

Situated in a relatively protected area between the expanse of Irish land to the west and the Irish Sea the east, Dublin experiences less rain than the rest of Ireland—about 69 centimeters (27 inches) per year. The sunniest months statistically are May and June, and the driest month is July. The wettest month is December, which is compounded by occasional snow and hail. The city encounters long summer days and very short winter days. Usually it gets dark by 4 P.M. in the winter, but this just gives you more time for socializing at the pub.

GREEN SPACES

Dublin has more green spaces per square kilometer than any other European capital city. There are 1,500 hectares (3,700 acres) of parks, 3 hectares (7.3 acres) of public green space per 1,000 people, and 5,000 trees are planted annually. The main parks are the Phoenix Park just west of the city center, near Castleknock; St. Stephen's Green at the top of Grafton Street; and Herbert Park in Ballsbridge, in Dublin's south side.

The Phoenix Park is the largest enclosed urban park in Europe, encompassing 712 hectares (1,760 acres). This park offers large, grassy areas and tree-lined avenues, and features a herd of wild fallow deer. Áras an Uachtaráin, the residence of the President of Ireland, is located in this park, as is the Dublin Zoo, the residence of the U.S. Ambassador, and Ashtown Castle. Every summer the park hosts various concerts and festivals.

Herbert Park is tiny in comparison, just 13 hectares (32 acres), but it provides a good example of Dublin's smaller city parks, offering a variety of amenities. The park includes sites for football, tennis, boules, and croquet, and a children's playground was added in 2007.

St. Stephen's Green is adjacent to a shopping center and is surrounded by offices, flats, and government buildings. The park, spanning 9 hectares (22 acres), is roughly rectangular in shape and features an artificial pond and waterfall that is home to ducks, a garden circle with wide expanses of green grass, and, most notably, a garden for the blind featuring scented plants that are labeled in Braille.

lunchtime at the park, Dublin

© SARAH-JANE SWEENEY

PRIME LIVING LOCATIONS

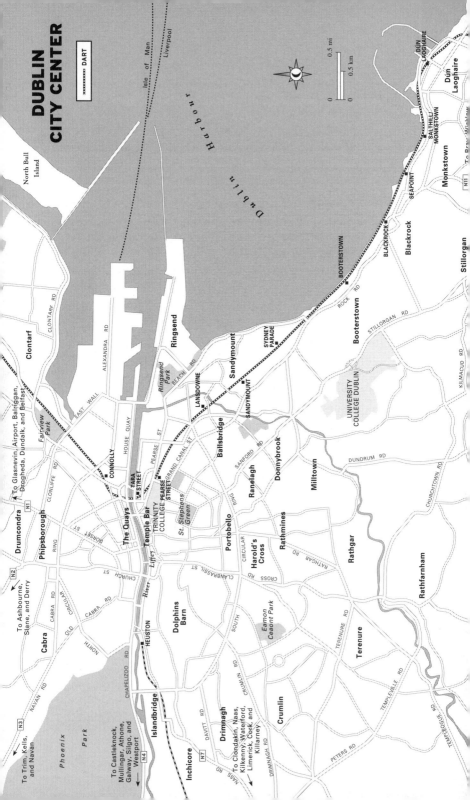

Where to Live

Just like any large city, Dublin offers an array of living options, from bustling city center flats to houses in the sprawl (well, relative sprawl) of the suburbs. Dublin is broken down into 24 districts; odd numbers are situated on the north side of the River Liffey and even numbers are on the south side. Housing can be expensive and difficult to find in the city center. Rapid development led to a sharp rise in accommodation prices, although the recession has helped level these prices out a bit.

You may end up choosing your accommodations entirely based on price. The average rent for a one-bedroom apartment in Dublin in 2010 was €765 per month. If you choose to share an apartment, the average rent is about €500 per month. Dublin is by far the most expensive place to purchase a house in the nation, costing on average €237,480 in late 2010. Of course, prices for both renting and purchasing vary depending on the location, if you want to share, etc. For example, buying a house in posh Ballsbridge will start around €750,000, while out on Clondalkin (west Dublin) you might get a house for €250,000. Keep in mind that this book was written as house prices were bottoming out in Dublin, so they may be subject to change.

The farther out of the city center you go, the cheaper it is. South Dublin, as a rule, is more expensive than north Dublin. Portobello, Rathmines, Ranelagh, and Harold's Cross in south Dublin are probably the nicest (and most expensive) areas in south Dublin, offering a variety of nice restaurants, green parks, and easy access into the city center via the Luas. The best areas in north Dublin are Drumcondra, Glasnevin, and Clontarf. You will also find more facilities for children and for families outside of the city center, such as parks, gyms, etc. For renting and flat sharing, a good resource is www.daft.ie.

CITY CENTER

Dublin's city center offers a mix of accommodations: apartments, town houses, semidetached houses, and terraced houses, as well as social housing. The city center is Dublin's commercial, education, and cultural hub. Original Georgian terraced houses sit next to high-rise concrete and glass blocks. Just south of the River Liffey lies Trinity College and the Bank of Ireland. Trinity College is virtually dead center in the middle of Dublin. It is surrounded by chic bookstores, shops, restaurants, offices, and lots of noisy traffic.

Ballsbridge and Embassy Row, near the Grand Canal, is an upscale suburb in the south side of the city center. If you want a house with a garden (and a large price tag), look here. This primarily residential area also features restaurants, hotels, and various embassies, including the U.S. embassy.

Between Trinity College and St. Stephen's Green are two little square parks—Fitzwilliam and Merrion Square—surrounded by magnificent Georgian town houses. This area is home to some of Dublin's most famous citizens, such as Oscar Wilde, William Butler Yeats, and Daniel O'Connell, although many of the houses are now government agencies or offices for lawyers and doctors.

Just south of these squares is Grafton Street and St. Stephen's Green. Grafton Street is the biggest shopping district in Dublin and offers some of the best hotels, restaurants, and shops. The apartments in this area feature impressive Georgian architecture, and prices can be quite steep.

Temple Bar is wedged between Trinity College and Dublin's Old City. During the day Temple Bar features art galleries, theaters, eclectic shops, and restaurants in a well-laid-out crisscross of cobblestone streets. At night, Temple Bar becomes the epicenter of partying, with bars, nightclubs, and pubs coming to life and young tourists (and Irish people) drinking copious amounts of alcohol. There are many hostels and student accommodations here, but this area isn't the best for permanently residing in if you're looking for a bit of peace and quiet.

West of Trinity College on Dame Street is Dublin's Old City. This neighborhood dates from Viking times and features cobblestone enclaves such as Dublin Castle, Christ Church, St. Patrick's Cathedral, and remnants of the city's original walls. There are chic boutiques and cafés lining the streets,

traditional Georgian houses in Dublin

and for the most part these are safe areas, although Christ Church can be a bit seedy at night. Adjacent to Old City is the Liberties district. This area is a bit more rundown than the Old City district but has recently begun to see a bit of urban renewal. The Liberties district's claim to fame is the Guinness Brewery.

On the north side of the River Liffey the Millennium Spire towers above O'Connell Street and the General Post Office, the headquarters of Dublin's stormy political efforts. O'Connell Street represents Dublin's theater district, with four theaters situated within a short walk of each other. The accommodations around here mostly comprise flats situated above shops and pubs or down alleyways. The main street is loud and noisy, but there are quieter side streets and small green parks available. Rent can be a bit higher here, but the close proximity to everything may balance that out for you.

The Quays, situated along the Liffey riverbanks on the north side, provide a trendy address for hotels, bars, and clubs. Modern accommodations are situated in the apartments and flats above these businesses. As with any accommodations near a bar or restaurant, this area can be noisy late into the night, although not nearly so much as Temple Bar.

Apartment or House Hunting

Many of the people in Dublin city center share a house or flat (apartment). This is the cheapest and most convenient way to live if you're on your own, but it obviously isn't the way to go if you have a family. There are a lot of choices for where to live, what amenities you will get, and who you will live with if you choose to share.

Rent in Ireland is payable monthly, although the price advertised is usually per week. Most landlords in Dublin require references, a deposit, and a lease of some sort. The average rent for a one-bedroom apartment in Dublin is €700–1,000 per month. If you plan to share, the average cost for a room is about €550 per month. This usually includes a washer and dryer unit, which basically means that it washes but doesn't dry (trust the radiators for that— I've rarely experienced a dryer that actually dries like an American dryer does). You will have to add electricity, gas, Internet, TV license, and any other bills to your rent.

The farther out of the city center you go, the cheaper it is. However, south Dublin is typically more expensive than north Dublin. Portobello, Rathmines, Ranelagh, and Harold's Cross in south Dublin are probably the nicest (and most expensive) areas in south Dublin, offering a variety of good restaurants, green parks, and easy access into the city center via the Luas. The best areas in north Dublin are Drumcondra, Glasnevin, and Clontarf. You will find more facilities for children and families outside of the city center, in both the north and south side, including parks, gyms, etc.

If you are intent on buying an apartment or house in Dublin, you should acquaint yourself with average property prices, as the property market in Ireland has been exceedingly tumultuous the last few years. In January 2011 the average property price in Dublin was €317,000. This price has steadily been dropping, so you may be able to get a good deal; however, there has been a leveling out in the market, so keep your eyes open.

Also, research the various laws necessary to buy a house in Ireland. Unlike in the United States, you have to hire your own lawyer (solicitor) to do all the legal paperwork. Also, there is no national property listing site in Ireland, so you have to register with individual agents who are only keen to sell the properties they have listed. It is a long and confusing process, but if you find the property at the right price, it might just be worth it.

Make sure to find a property that has a location that will suit you. Take a look at the *Housing Considerations* chapter in this book and walk yourself through the purchasing steps I have detailed. Make sure you are aware of any hidden fees that might surprise you before you purchase the property. It is also worth noting that, although there are no restrictions toward Americans buying a property in Ireland, you still have to make sure you have the correct visa and permits in place before being allowed to stay for longer than the permissible three months.

The North-South Divide

A north-south divide has traditionally existed in Dublin, with the River Liffey acting as the divider. The Northside is typically seen as the lower class–working class area of Dublin, while the Southside is seen as the middle-upper class area. This divide is accentuated by historic stereotypes. In the south the upper-middle class people are seen to swan around with posh, Dublin 4 (a play on the Southside, Dublin 4 district), faux-English accents, driving their expensive cars and wearing designer clothes. In the north, the working-class people are seen as being of a rougher sort, wearing track suits or hoodies and speaking with fast, whining accents. These stereotypes, just like all stereotypes, are not entirely accurate; for example, there are pockets of wealth and luxury on the Northside, such as the fancy estates in Howth and Clontarf, and the President of Ireland's (Mary McAleese) official residence in Phoenix Park.

The prosperous economic conditions of the Celtic Tiger has helped to level

LITERARY DUBLIN

Ireland has a tradition of being a nation of "saints and scholars," and in 2010 it was designated a UNESCO City of Literature. This tradition goes back thousands of years to the earliest Irish poetry in the 6th century and to the dark ages, when Irish monks began transcribing the bible. The most visible impact of Dublin's writers on literature began with Anglo-Irish literature in the 18th century. Jonathan Swift, a versatile satirist, was Ireland's first notable writer in the English language. He wrote *Gulliver's Travels* and *A Tale of Tube*.

In the 19th century Ireland saw a rise in poets and novelists, including John Banim, Gerald Griffin, Charles Kickham, and William Carleton. Their writing reflected the views of the middle class. James Clarence Mangen, a poet from Dublin's Fishamble Street, wrote *Dark Rosaleen* during this time, and shortly thereafter Bram Stroker coined the horror genre with his *Dracula*, followed by Sheridan Le Fanu, who wrote *Uncle Silas* and *Carmilla*.

Dublin writer and poet Oscar Wilde also became famous during this time. At the height of his fame he wrote the play *The Importance of Being Earnest*, which is still popular today, as well as four society comedies in the early 1890s, making him one of the most successful playwrights in late-Victorian London; London is where he spent much of his later life. Dubliner George Bernard Shaw wrote *Pygmalion, Major Barbara*, and *Caesar and Cleopatra*, and Samuel Beckett – also born in Dublin – wrote *Waiting for Godot* during this time.

As Irish nationalism began to increase near the end of the 19th century, the Gaelic Revival began, marking a new interest in the Irish language and Irish Gaelic culture. Patrick Pearse was a pioneer of the Gaelic Revival, followed by Pádraic Ó Conaire, Seosamh Mac Grianna, and William Butler Yeats. Yeats used Irish mythology in his writing and later became famous for writing *The Wanderings of Oisin and Other Poems*.

No Irish literary figure is more famous in the 20th century than Dubliner James Joyce, who wrote poetry, fiction, and drama. Joyce is known as the father of stream of consciousness, which is the style he uses in his famous work *Ulysses*. He also wrote *Finnegans Wake* and *Dubliners*.

The heritage of Ireland's famous literary authors is vibrant in Dublin today. The city has opened the Dublin Writer's Museum, which occupies an 18th-century town house in Dublin and presents manuscripts, paintings, letters, and rare editions of many famous authors. The James Joyce Cultural Center, located near Parnell Square in Dublin, exhibits an archive, various exhibits, and a reference library for literature enthusiasts.

PRIME LIVING LOCATIONS

the playing field, and the global financial crisis and Ireland's current recession have helped reduce the massive differences between property prices in north and south Dublin, resulting in a slight mellowing of the north-south distinction. However, you still won't be able to buy a reasonably priced house in Blackrock or Ballsbridge in south Dublin, and it is probably worth noting the location of your prospective accommodations when deciding on where to live in Dublin.

SUBURBAN DUBLIN

Just like any large city, Dublin has a network of smaller suburban towns that feed into the city center. Opting for the suburbs will give you more bang for your buck (or your euro), offering houses with gardens, nearby parks, family facilities such as playgrounds, swimming pools, and gyms, all with less traffic and costing less money. Of course, the trade-off is it takes longer to get to the city center, and you may not be a suburb sort of person.

About three kilometers (two miles) south of the city center lay the urban areas of Harold's Cross, Rathmines, and Rathgar. These middle-upper class suburbs feature tree-lined streets and detached and semidetached houses. Apartments are usually available, but more common are shared accommodations. The most popular areas are Blackrock and Dalkey to the south of Dublin along the coast, and Clontarf, Howth, and Malahide to the north.

On the Southside of Dublin is Donnybrook, one of Dublin's most exclusive suburbs. The suburb of Donnybrook in the Dublin 4 district is a highly sought after area to live. The area is about 3.5 kilometers (two miles) from the city center near the ferries, the Royal Dublin Society (RDS), and to University College Dublin, and is the home to RTÉ, the national broadcasting center. It is characterized by the various embassies that dominate the area. Expensive properties ring the tree-lined streets, including pretty brick-faced terraced houses, charming cottages, and expensive houses. This stylish Dublin suburb is the home to Donnybrook Stadium, numerous tennis clubs, a football club, a cricket club, and various retail shops, grocery stores, and a spa.

Drumcondra is a lovely residential area in the Northside of Dublin, four kilometers (two miles) from the city center. The River Tolka and the Royal Canal flow through Drumcondra, marking pretty patches of green areas and riverfront property. Drumcondra is most well-known for being the home of Croke Park, where Ireland's national Gaelic football and hurling games are played. During games the area overflows with sports fans, lending an almost riotous atmosphere and jam-packed pubs. The rest of the time, however, the suburb is peaceful and quiet.

Dundrum, a Southside suburb of Dublin, was originally a town in its own right. With Dublin's extensive urban sprawl, Dundrum is now a suburban village and district of Dublin. This suburb is about six kilometers (four miles) from the city center and is entirely self-contained. A main street offers retail shops, a post office, banks, and churches. There is a purpose-built shopping center containing a cinema, numerous retail shops, and restaurants. The Luas tram links Dundrum with Dublin city center via Taney Cross.

The suburb of Palmerstown is located seven kilometers (four miles) to the southwest of the city center, bordered by the River Liffey to the north, Lucan to the west, Ballyfermot to the south, and Chapelizod to the east. Palmerstown is a busy, well-populated suburb, thanks to its convenient location near the M50 motorway, which runs from north to south, and the N4, which runs from east to west. The Dublin Bus stops along both sides of the N4 with regular services into the city center. The amenities of Palmerstown are clustered along the old Lucan Road and called Palmerstown Central—Palmerstown Upper and Palmerstown Lower are mostly residential and are almost villages unto themselves.

Castleknock, situated on the Dublin–Navan road at the edge of the Phoenix Park, seven kilometers (four miles) from Dublin city center, is a convenient little suburb offering easy access to the city center and Dublin Airport. Mostly residential, this suburb is one of the nicest areas in the Northside of Dublin. Castleknock is convenient for reaching many parts of Dublin via the ring road. This suburb is most well-known for being where actor Colin Farrell is from.

On the east coast of Ireland, about 11 kilometers (7 miles) from Dublin city center, is Dún Laoghaire. This coastal village is surrounded by rolling hills and offers easy access to Dublin city center on the DART suburban railway. Fishing, golf, and sailing are all readily available, and there are two shopping centers offering a variety of retail businesses.

Situated north of Dublin, 15 kilometers (nine miles) from Dublin city center, is the commuter town of Swords. Swords is economically diverse, offering everything from upscale, private apartments to family-oriented houses to local authority (social) housing. There is a shopping center, a skate park with adjoining basketball courts and a football field, as well as several golf courses and a number of good schools.

The suburb of Dalkey is a pleasant coastal suburb situated 13 kilometers (eight miles) north of Dublin city. Dalkey was designated a heritage town in 1994 as it offers an understated charm due to its medieval streets, ancient castle, and famous landmarks. The area features a train station on the main street, from which you can walk to seven castles (three of which remain), a 10th-century church and graveyard, the Deilg Inis Living History Theatre, the town hall, and a heritage center. Retail shops are available along the main street, and the coastal road offers a pleasant drive along the water. Killiney Hill Park features a stunning view over Dublin city. The DART suburban train runs every 10–15 minutes to and from Dublin city center, taking about 25 minutes each way.

RURAL VILLAGES

In the peaceful countryside that surrounds Dublin are beautiful little villages that are ideal for serene living away from the bustle of the city. Most of these villages are within commuting distance to Dublin or at least near another larger town offering a bank, a post office, and a supermarket. Surrounding the village centers are expanses of quiet, green landscape for those who want more isolation.

Garristown

Garristown is an attractive little rural village in County Dublin, located on a hill that slopes down from west to east, with panoramic views of the Mourne Mountains in the north and Wicklow Mountains in the south. Situated 25 kilometers (15.5 miles) northwest of Dublin, the village only has 400 people, with one main street running from north to south that features a tree-lined mall on the western side. The village offers a renovated library, a primary and secondary school, a police barracks, and a number of churches.

The remnants of a windmill dating from 1736 dominate the landscape around Garristown and the scenic hill fort around the windmill is called Rath Esa after a princess in Celtic mythology who lived on the hill.

COURTESY OF TOURISM IRELAND

Wicklow is home to St. Kevin's monastic site.

Skerries

Skerries is a little fishing village situated 31 kilometers (19 miles) north of Dublin city center, in County Dublin. This peaceful village is a commuter village for many people who take the train into Dublin each day for work. In recent years Skerries has become a resort town and now offers golf, sailing, and motorcycling. Semidetached and detached houses are available in the town center, and traditional Irish cottages lay on the outskirts of the village.

Balbriggan

The seaside town of Balbriggan, County Dublin, is situated about 34 kilometers (21 miles) north of Dublin city center. Expect to see a beautifully restored castle, a lighthouse, an operational harbor, beaches, and lakes. There are also golf courses, parks, and shopping. Good transportation options are available into the city, including Dublin Bus and Irish Rail services. The River Bracken flows through the town, and numerous safe, sandy beaches are located on the coast, which dominates one side of the village.

Balbriggan is located next to the M1 motorway, which links Dublin to Belfast. The village experienced a population boom in the early 2000s when Dublin began extending out. Hundreds of new homes were built, and commuters established themselves in this peaceful village.

Carlingford

Carlingford is a tiny medieval village on the shores of Carlingford Lough on the Cooley Peninsula in County Louth. It is nestled under the stunning Slieve Foy Mountains and is situated 108 kilometers (67 miles) from Dublin city center, about one hour by car, although it is actually closer to Belfast at 80 kilometers (50 miles).

Carlingford is a magical village with well-preserved medieval streets and lanes that meander past colorful shops, cafés, and pubs, and lead to a scenic harbor. Walking and hiking trails, horse riding, sailing, windsurfing, and waterskiing are all popular here amid the beautiful natural landscape. A regular bus service (the 161) links Carlingford with Dundalk and Newry, although it does not run on Sundays or bank holidays.

Inistioge

Picture-perfect Inistioge in County Kilkenny is a little village situated about two hours by car from Dublin, 134 kilometers (83 miles) away. It is, however, closer to the large town of Waterford, which is just 34 kilometers (21 miles) away. Inistioge has an 18th-century stone bridge with ten arches spanning the River Nore.

The village is nestled in the Nore River Valley and faces the river, offering two spacious greens and numerous pubs. Hiking trails and scenic roads crisscross the river valley around the village. This remote village is surrounded by verdant green countryside, woods, and rural houses, but it is difficult to reach using public transportation.

Getting Around

Dublin is compact and easily navigable on foot, and it is connected by an extensive network of buses, trains, and trams. If exploring farther than the city center, the DART will connect you to the coastal towns and villages, and there are numerous trains and buses that connect Dublin to the rest of Ireland. Dublin city center has absolutely appalling traffic, so your best option is to walk or take a bicycle if you can. Time your travel so you can elude rush hour and the most congested traffic times.

BUSES

The main public transportation in Dublin is the bus, called *Bus Átha Cliath* (Dublin Bus). The Dublin city bus is a double-decker bus painted in blue and yellow, and the tourist bus is painted green. City buses run 6 A.M.–11:30 P.M., with less frequent service on Sunday. Buses heading to the city center have *An Lár* (city center) on the front. Ticket prices begin at €1.15 for the first three stages, which will get you to most city center locations, and go up from there depending on how many stages you are traveling through. The most expensive ticket is €4.60 for traveling to the outer suburbs of Dublin.

Night buses are available for 22 routes after 11:30 P.M. Monday–Friday. Nitelink buses leave from the triangle formed by Westmoreland Street, College Street, and D'Olier Street in the city center. Ticket prices begin at €5. (Note: All ticket prices are correct as of April 2011 but are subject to change.)

When you get on the bus, tell the driver where you want to go. The driver will tell you the fare. Try to have the correct change in coins, as drivers do not accept notes, and you will not get change. Instead, the driver will issue you a receipt for your journey, which you can take to the head office to get your change. This is an ingenious move by Dublin Bus, as I have never known anybody to actually go get their change. Make sure to keep your receipt, as you are liable to get a €50 penalty if you don't have proof of your ticket when asked by an official.

Bus Éireann links Dublin with the suburbs and the rest of Ireland from Bus Áras, the central bus station on Amiens Street. You can find more information about arrivals and departures on www.buseireann.ie.

LUAS

Dublin's Luas is a light rail tram running two lines around Dublin. The green line runs from Sandyford north to St. Stephen's Green, and the red line runs from east Tallaght to Connolly Station via Heuston Station. Trams operate

The Luas is a light rail tram in Dublin.

Monday–Friday 5:30 A.M.–12:30 A.M., leaving every 4–5 minutes during peak times and every 10–15 minutes during nonpeak times. On Saturday the tram runs 6:30 A.M.–12:30 A.M., and on Sunday it runs 7 A.M.–11.30 P.M. Electronic displays are located next to the tram lines telling you when the next tram is due to arrive.

If you plan to use the Luas a lot, you should purchase a smart card. Smart cards are similar to London's Oyster card. The fares are slightly cheaper than standard fares and allow you to pay as you go, rather than buying longer-term passes. You can purchase the smart card online or at a Luas ticket agent for €10, which includes a €3 nonrefundable fee for the card, €3 of credit, and €4 for a refundable "reserve fund," which allows travel even when there is insufficient credit for the journey.

Ticket fares for the Luas differ depending on your travel zone and what type of pass you buy. Fares start at €1.60 and go up to €2.40 for single travel tickets. A daily pass costs €5.30, a weekly pass costs €19.10, and a monthly pass costs €76 from the ticket machines. Here's a tip, though: You can get a reduced price on passes if you purchase ahead of time from a newsagent.

DART

The Dublin Area Rapid Transit (DART) is a commuter train that runs along the coastal towns of Dublin, linking 30 stations around Dublin Bay, from Howth in the north to Greystones in County Wicklow in the south. Services are available 6:30 A.M.–midnight, although the services are less frequent on Sunday. Single tickets from Dublin city center to Howth, the last stop, cost €2.20.

BICYCLE

Dublin has a pay-as-you-go bike scheme available throughout the city center, which is very handy during rush hour. There are 450 bicycles stationed at 40 locations for your use. Simply purchase a €10 smart card, use your credit card to pay a €150 refundable deposit, and away you go. Just return the bicycle to another station to stop the charges. The fee can be paid online or at any of the stations. The first 30 minutes are free, and you pay €0.50 for each half hour after that.

TAXIS

Taxis are readily available throughout Dublin city center. You can hail them in the streets or find them at taxi ranks. There is a taxi rank on O'Connell Street, St. Stephen's Green, Grafton Street, and College Green. Taxis are not cheap and will cost you even more during rush hour traffic, but they are useful for getting in and out of the city from the suburbs. Fares are based on how far you go and how long it takes. Global Cabs (01/473-1333) dispatches cabs if you call in advance, as does Dublin-Dial-A-Cab (01/80-80-800). When you can afford it, traveling by taxi can be a fun and educational experience. The taxi drivers are normally very cheerful and chatty, and are more than willing to disperse stories or little bits of history as they drive through town. I have never been ripped off by an Irish taxi driver, but as with any large city, ensure the meter is turned on prior to departing.

TRAVEL PASSES

Bus and Luas passes are available to purchase from Dublin Bus offices or ticket agents (you will see their signs in shop windows). If you will be using the bus a lot, purchase a Dublin Bus Prepaid smart card (similar in principle to the Luas smart card), which saves you time and money, and allows you unlimited use of the bus for either one month or one year. Alternatively, you can buy 1-, 3-, 5-, and 30-day Rambler Tickets for nonconsecutive days of travel, a good option if you are just visiting.

Rail passes are available from DART or suburban train stations. The Adult Short Hop (bus and rail) is valid for unlimited travel for one day on Dublin Bus, DART, Luas, and suburban trains. The Bus-Luas Pass offers unlimited travel on both the Dublin Bus and the Luas. The Family Bus and Rail Short Hop is valid for one day of unlimited travel on all bus and rail services for a family with two adults and two children under 16.

TRAIN

If you will be going farther afield than Dublin, intercity trains are available from Dublin's two train stations: Heuston Station and Connolly Station.

© SARAH JANE SWEENEY

Dublin bikes are for hire on the streets.

Heuston connects Dublin to the west (Mayo and Galway) and the south (Limerick, Cork, and Waterford). Connolly Station connects Dublin to the north (Belfast in Northern Ireland) and the northwest (Sligo). These two stations are not currently connected by train, but the number 90 Railink bus links them via Bus Áras (the main bus station) and costs €0.90. You can find information on arrivals and departures at www.irishrail.ie.

DUBLIN AIRPORT

Dublin Airport is the busiest airport in Ireland, offering frequent flights regionally, nationally, and internationally. The airport is located in Collinstown, about 10 kilometers (six miles) north of Dublin city. It is currently served by local and private buses and taxis, but plans for a railway called Metro North have been proposed to link the city center to the airport from St. Stephen's Green. The airport has two terminals offering extensive short- and medium-haul flights. About 40 departures leave daily from Dublin to London's airports, and there are more than 30 departures to other UK airports. Aer Lingus, Ireland's national airline, serves many major U.S. hubs, and Eithad Airways, the national airline of United Arab Emirates, flies twice a day to Abu Dhabi.

CORK

Celtic Sea

10 mi
10 km

© AVALON TRAVEL

CORK

Cork, *Corcaigh* (marshy place) in Irish, is one of those cities—like Paris or New York—that buzzes with the brazen confidence of a city that is absolutely certain of its place in the world. Cork is sophisticated, diverse, and vibrant, and its citizens know it. The city has long dismissed Dublin as only second-rate compared to the arts, music, and restaurant scene in Cork. In fact, I once heard it said that this patriotic lot define themselves as non-Dubliners first and as Corkonians second. This Rebel County has a history of standing out from the rest of the country: They have Murphy's instead of Guinness, the *Examiner* rather than the *Independent* newspaper, and an entirely different accent.

Corkonians refer to Cork as the "real capital of Ireland" and have begun to reference Cork with the tongue-in-cheek moniker of the People's Republic of Cork. This term has taken on a cult-like association following the Corkonian pro-independent movement. You will often see people adorning themselves with T-shirts, hats, and other items proclaiming this proudly. During the spring 2011 visit of Queen Elizabeth II to Ireland, a friend of mine in Cork

COURTESY OF TOURISM IRELAND

saw the queen's helicopter flying over. "It's a great honor for her to be in the People's Republic," he said, proud that she would visit the most important county in Ireland.

There is a rivalry over the "real" capital of Ireland that has been raging between Cork and Dublin for years, emulating that of London and Manchester or Barcelona and Madrid. Dubliners think Corkonians are too cocky, and Corkonians think Dubliners are just jealous. The famous soccer player Roy Keane is from Cork, as is Hollywood star Cillian Murphy, compounding that rivalry. Most citizens of Cork see themselves as distinctly different (dare I say better?) than the rest of the country, and this is reflected in the strut and swagger of the city, making it a truly interesting place to be.

While County Cork is full of color and contrasts, from the sandstone hills in the west to the bays and coves of the Atlantic, the city itself is cosmopolitan, modern, and cultured, and the sanguine people are a genuinely welcoming bunch. Urban renewal began in 2005 with Cork's stint as European Capital of Culture, and new buildings, bars, and arts centers sprang up throughout the city center, giving the city a face-lift and injecting vitality and animation into it.

The Lay of the Land

Cork city is the Republic of Ireland's second-largest city. The city was originally built around several little islands formed by channels of the River Lee. Many of these channels were spanned in the 18th century to form the main streets that you see in Cork today. Now there are two channels branching out from the western end of the city and converging at the eastern end of the city. These channels create an island on which the city center is located, the River Lee flowing around the estuary to Lough Mahon, on to Cork Harbor, and eventually out to the Celtic Sea.

Cork city is a major Irish seaport, with quays and docks dotted along the banks of the River Lee on the eastern side of the city center. The city center features narrow, 17th-century cobbled alleyways; grand, 19th-century Victorian buildings, such as the Central Markets; and modern masterpieces like the Cork Opera House.

Surrounding the city in County Cork are rich farmlands and river valleys in the east, sandstone hills in the west, and beyond that the stunning Atlantic coast, cradling beautiful bays and remote coves with soft golden sand and rocky bluffs. The county is relatively unspoiled, its towns and villages unsophisticated but lively and friendly, welcoming to visitors from Ireland and abroad.

HISTORY

Historically Cork is said to have been founded by Saint Finbarre, who established a monastery that left behind evidence of the earliest human settlement in Cork. Subsequently, the monastery was raided by Vikings, who settled the area that is now known as the city of Cork. By the 12th century, the Vikings had intermarried with the native Irish and become known as the Ostmen, establishing Cork as an important trading center. However, in A.D. 1177 the city was again sacked, this time by the Normans. The Normans constructed

TITANIC

On April 11, 1912, the doomed liner *Titanic* stopped at her last port of call in Queenstown, now called Cobh, in Cork, on her maiden voyage. The *Titanic* was built in the Harland and Wolff shipyard in Belfast, Northern Ireland, and was designed to be the most luxurious, opulent ship of the time. The first-class section was graced with a swimming pool, gymnasium, squash court, Turkish bath, and electric baths. The ship was equipped with three electric elevators, electric lights, and two radios.

Titanic departed from Southampton in England to New York on her maiden voyage on April 10, 1912. She reached Cobh the next day but was too big to be anchored in the harbor. As a result she was anchored in Roches Point, the outer anchorage on the southeastern tip of Cork Harbor. The doomed ship added a total of 123 passengers at Cobh: three first-class passengers, seven second-class travelers, and the rest in third class (steerage). At 1:30 P.M. the *Titanic* departed from Cobh to the strains of "A Nation Once Again" and "Erin's Lament," played on the bagpipes by passenger Eugene Daly. There were 1,308 passengers and 898 crew members, according to the Cobh Heritage Center, making a total of 2,206 people on board as the *Titanic* embarked on her ill-fated voyage.

On Sunday, April 14, around 10:30 P.M., after just three days at sea, the ship scraped an unforgiving iceberg on the right side, buckling the hull and popping out rivets below the waterline. The iceberg proved to be disastrous for the magnificent ship, and within 10 minutes the five forward compartments were 14 feet underwater.

While there was space for the majestic ship to carry 48 lifeboats, only 16 were actually on board, and within an hour, most of these lifeboats had been filled and lowered into the water. The ship sank at 2:20 A.M. on Monday, April 15, 1912. Most of the passengers died from exposure while floating in the ice-cold waters while wearing their life jackets. Approximately 705 *Titanic* passengers survived, most of whom were women and children from first and second class.

a wall on the south island of the River Lee, eventually extending the wall so the entire city was enclosed.

In 1491 a man named Perkin Warbeck arrived in Cork, claiming to be the rightful king. He tried to overthrow Henry VII and was eventually executed. In 1798, an undercurrent of dissension and dissatisfaction erupted into the 1798 Rebellion. During Ireland's War of Independence, Cork played a major role in the conflict, with ambushes, reprisals, shootings, and murders marking this period. These events earned Cork the moniker Rebel Cork, and even today the area is fondly called the Rebel County.

Cork saw a huge influx of French Protestants arrive in the late 17th and early 18th centuries, establishing what is now called the Huguenot Quarter and French Church Street. This was also a period of mass building, and the city built Christ Church; St. Anne's Church, with the Shandon Bells; the Customs House; the Corn Market; and the Butter Market.

When the potato famine devastated most of the country in the 19th century, Cork's population exploded as people from the countryside moved to the city to avoid poverty or to emigrate—Cork was the main port for emigrants leaving Ireland to the United States and other countries. During the early 20th century, the city of Cork suffered horribly from the War of Independence and the subsequent civil war. In 1920 the British Black and Tans shot and killed the Lord Mayor of Cork, Thomas MacCurtain. His successor, Terence McSwiney, was subsequently arrested and died on hunger strike later in the year. On December 11, 1920, the Black and Tans started a fire that gutted the city center, engulfing over 300 buildings. Cork was also a stronghold for the anti-treaty forces during the Irish Civil War. Cork was retaken by pro-treaty forces in August 1922, but guerilla warfare raged throughout the county until April 1923, when the anti-treaty side finally called a cease-fire.

CLIMATE

Cork's climate, like the rest of the country, is mild and changeable, with temperate winters, moderate summers, and an abundance of rain throughout the year. Temperatures below 0°C (32°F) or above 30°C (86°F) are rare. In January, the average temperature is 5.3°C (41.5°F), and in July the average temperature is 14.6°C (58.3°F). There are on average 151 rainy days throughout the year. Despite this, Cork is one of Ireland's sunniest cities, having nearly four hours of sunshine each day. Cork is also one of the foggiest cities in Ireland, having an average of 100 days of fog per year, mostly during the morning or winter.

ARTS

Cork has a thriving arts scene, with music, dance, theater, film, and poetry all playing a prominent role in its modern cultural infrastructure. Every year Cork hosts festivals, events, and celebrations that draw thousands of visitors to this vibrant city. The Cork School of Music; the Crawford College of Art and Design; The Institute for Choreography and Dance, a national contemporary dance company; the Triskel Arts Centre; the Cork Academy of Dramatic Art (CADA); and the active theater components of many courses at University College Cork (UCC) contribute to the arts scene of Cork. Corcadorca Theater Company, where Cillian Murphy attended before becoming famous, is in Cork, as is the RTÉ Vanbrugh String Quartet. There is also a thriving literary community focused on the Munster Literature Centre and the Triskel Arts Centre.

In June, Cork celebrates the Cork Midsummer Festival, a 16-day summer festival celebrating contemporary arts and culture. The festival combines local, national, and international events, including street entertainers, international artists, and local talent; popular music; a circus; and visual and conceptual art. During the last weekend in October the city hosts the annual Guinness Cork Jazz Festival, which takes over the entire city. More than 1,000 musicians play at 80 music venues ranging from local pubs to the magnificent Cork Opera House. This is one of Ireland's largest festivals, with music ranging from traditional Irish to Dixieland.

Cork Pride takes place in Cork in June, celebrating gay pride in Ireland. The Cork Decades Festival, fondly called the biggest fancy dress party in Ireland, occurs for one week in August. During this week the pubs of Cork city center re-create the illusion of times past with the pubs decorated to reflect their decade and staff dressed to match. In September the Beamish Cork Folk Festival celebrates traditional Irish music, artists, and dancing, showcasing the very best fiddle, pipe, flute, and accordion music at

the Crawford Art Gallery in Cork

© SARAHJANE SWEENEY

PRIME LIVING LOCATIONS

FAMOUS PLACES IN CORK

Cork is home to many famous architectural and historic sites that represent the culture and diversity of this sophisticated city.

ENGLISH MARKET

The English Market, one of the oldest of its kind, having opened as a market in 1788, is a covered market with entrances on St. Patrick's Street, Grand Parade, and Princes Street in Cork city center. The various stalls sell wares from the exotic to the humble, offering traditional Cork foods, such as meats, cheeses, fish, and chocolate, alongside international foods such as Greek olives and Indian spices.

THE SHANDON BELLS

The Church of St. Mary is home to one of Cork's most famous attractions, the Shandon Bells, known throughout the world because of *The Bells of Shandon*, a poem celebrating the bells of the church written by Francis Sylvester Mahony, a Cork man writing under the alias Father Prout. The church itself consists of two types of stone sourced from the relics of other landmarks: red sandstone extracted from the original Shandon Castle and white limestone from the North Mall Franciscan Abbey. The red and white represent the colors of Cork. A clock featured on the tower is known locally as the Four Faced Liar. Due to the different thickness of the wood used in the clock facing, each face tells a slightly different time.

ST. FINBARRE'S CATHEDRAL

St. Finbarre's Cathedral is a French-Gothic cathedral of the Church of Ireland in central Cork. The current cathedral is the most recent in a string of cathedrals that have graced the location since the time St. Finbarre is said to have founded the settlement of Cork. The triple-spired cathedral features marble mosaics from the Pyrenees, elaborate carvings, and over 1,260 stunning sculptures built into the fabric of the building itself.

THE BLARNEY STONE

One of Ireland's most mythical attractions, the Blarney stone is made of bluestone and is set into the battlements of Blarney Castle, Blarney, about eight kilometers (five miles) from Cork city. Hundreds of thousands of visitors flock to kiss the Blarney stone – also called the Stone of Eloquence – every year, hoping to receive the "gift of gab" that the stone is reputed to give. The picturesque village of Blarney is designed in the Tudor style, and the stunning garden grounds of Blarney Castle offer a welcome escape from the crowds.

Blarney Castle Tower

the open-air Céilí Mór. The Cork Film Festival celebrates a wide range of film, including big budget movies, world cinema, independent films, short films, and documentaries.

Where to Live

Cork city center is dominated by bewildering one-way streets; pedestrianized shopping areas crisscrossing Grand Parade, St. Patrick's Street, and Oliver Plunkett Street; and bow-shaped bridges linking the canals and islands that adorn the city. Rent in the city center costs about €500–700 for a one-bedroom, fully furnished apartment and about €700–1,000 a month for a two-bedroom, fully furnished apartment. Rental properties in Cork usually come furnished, although you may find unfurnished houses in the suburbs.

A two- or three-bedroom terraced house in the inner city area of Cork will cost anywhere from €800 to €1,500 a month. The average asking price for a property in Cork city in 2011 was €240,000, and €219,000 in County Cork, representing a reduction in price of about €145,000 from peak 2007 prices. A three-bedroom house in Cork city suburbs sells for around €155,000–250,000. This book was written when house prices were continuing to fall in Cork, so they may be subject to change, although the rate of property value decline has slowed down in Cork as of May 2011.

St. Patrick's Street is one of Cork's pedestrianized streets.

PRIME LIVING LOCATIONS

CITY CENTER

The pedestrianized shopping district of Cork is located around St. Patrick's Street and Oliver Plunkett Street, both of which are situated in the island formed by the north and south channels of the River Lee. This area is dominated by pubs, restaurants, cafés, and shops, and features numerous small flats located above the many shops and pubs. Perpendicular to Oliver Plunkett Street is the Grand Parade area, and behind this is Cork's famous English Market, one of the oldest markets of its kind, having opened as a market in 1788.

Grand Parade is a wide, tree-lined avenue that was built over a channel of the River Lee. The Grand Parade area and the area just behind it to the west are important archaeological sites in Cork. The southeastern side of the historic wall of Cork runs along the western side of the Grand Parade, and a section of the wall is visible inside the gates of Bishop Lucey Park. This area is filled with offices, financial institutions, and Cork's Central Library, and there are a number of small flats available above shops and banks.

Just west of here is Washington Village, home of Saint Finbarre's Church, where Cork was first settled. On the north bank of the River Lee is the historic Shandon area, a quiet neighborhood that is towered over by the Church of St. Anne, home to the famous Shandon Bells. The narrow streets and alleyways of this neighborhood are dotted with attached houses and apartments that suit young professionals.

Off the city center's main island is Cork's City Center North area. This area adopts a faintly bohemian air, with numerous hotels, pubs, and shops lining MacCurtain Street and lovely apartments and flats available for rent. Along the Western Road on the South Bank is University College Cork, a Tudor-Gothic building with a beautiful riverside quadrangle. The area is active and vibrant due to its student population and offers an array of student housing, apartments, and attached and semidetached homes.

SUBURBAN CORK

Like any big city, Cork offers an array of suburbs surrounding the city center. The suburbs cater to young professionals and families. You will have access to a larger house with a yard, nearby parks, large supermarkets, and retail shopping centers, but keep in mind you will have to deal with a horrendous commute every day.

The Cork suburb of Blackpool, 2.5 kilometers (one mile) from the city center, has a large concentration of social housing areas, apartment blocks, and working-class estates. As such, it is certainly more affordable, and you may get more bang for your buck here than in many of the more affluent

ACCENT AND DIALECTS

You wouldn't think with an island so small you would get accents and dialects so diverse. But the first time you hear a Cork person speak, it may take you several seconds to register that the person is actually speaking English. As Irish comedian Tommy Tiernan so eloquently puts it, "The Cork accent...It sounds a bit like Tinkers trying to speak French."

The Cork accent displays patterns of tones and intonation that rise and fall, with the overall sound leaning toward an unusual musical quality. The pitch is higher than the standard Irish accent, so it sounds like the person speaking is eternally surprised. It has been described as anything from lyrical to whiny. Indeed, the uniquely singsong cadence is beloved by some and mocked by others.

While the Cork accent is recognizable as an Irish accent, it is not the leprechaun-sounding accent you might hear in Hollywood's version of an Irish accent. Corkonians speak fast, running their words and their sentences together in one long jumble with no pauses or punctuations: "How are you" becomes "how-arhoo." Most notably, consonants are crisp, while vowels are soft. The accent boasts a strong Irish *r*, which is like the standard *r*, only with the back of the tongue raised slightly so it sounds more like a pirate's "ar-rrghh." The *th* sound doesn't even exist in Cork. Instead of *thirty-three* it is *tirty-tree,* and instead of *the* it is *dee.*

English spoken in Cork has a variety of words that are distinctive to the city and surrounding areas. While many standard Irish-English words originated from the Irish language, many words from Cork were encountered at home and abroad and interjected into everyday use over the years.

The popular term *langer* describes somebody who is a bit of an eejit (idiot), or you can say *langers* to describe how drunk you are. Corkonians says "I will ya" as a sarcastic way of saying "no" and use the phrase "up back of leap" to indicate "in the middle of nowhere." The word *boy* (pronounced by-eee with a Cork accent) is used to address most everybody, and Corkonians tend to add the word *like* to the end of most sentences – "Will we stop at the pub, like?" (unlike West Coast American teenagers who add *like* to the beginning of their sentences).

This distinctive accent, combined with the diacritic words that make Cork English so unique, are familiar throughout the island. A Dubliner will know a Corkonian simply by the way he speaks. These lyrical patterns of tone and intonation are peppered with Cork's colloquial style, making the Cork accent and dialect unique and distinct, even in Ireland.

neighborhoods. Nicknamed the Belfast of the South, Blackpool has a high concentration of industries such as brewing, distilling, and tanning, and features numerous retail shops.

The suburb of Mahon is situated on the eastern side of Cork, three kilometers (two miles) from the city center. It used to be a peninsula of verdant green fields and housing estates, but it has been developed in the past few years and is now a central suburb of Cork. The South Ring Road runs through the area, entering near the Jack Lynch Tunnel, which runs under the River Lee, and gives easy access to Cork city. Mahon is mostly residential, with housing estates packed together into a dense network of suburban streets. There are three schools and a library available in the area, and Cork's biggest shopping center, the Mahon Point Shopping Centre, offers commercial services to the residents.

Three kilometers (two miles) to the west of Cork city center is the suburb of Wilton. Wilton is dominated by Cork University Hospital (CUH) and is home to the Wilton Shopping Centre. Surrounding the hospital and the shopping center are mostly modest residential streets. The main bus routes between Wilton and Cork city are numbers 8 and 14.

Douglas is a suburb of Metropolitan Cork, situated just four kilometers (2.5 miles) south of the city center. The town began as a farming community but developed as a suburban area during the late 18th and 19th centuries. A number of estates were built here, including Grange House, Donnybrook House, Castletreasure House, and Maryborough House, which is now used as a hotel. The town features numerous schools, shopping centers, and cinemas, and a wide variety of housing that caters to families is available. Most of the housing developments are private, but there are some areas of social housing. Douglas's main claim to fame is that it is the birthplace of actor Cillian Murphy.

Situated about eight kilometers (five miles) west of Cork city is the commuter town of Ballincollig. The town boasts a castle, a number of historic churches, and a variety of good schools. A bypass road wraps around the town from Cork to Killarney, reducing traffic through the town center.

The picturesque satellite town of Midleton is a bustling market town in Metropolitan Cork. The town is situated in East Cork, about 22 kilometers (13.6 miles) outside of Cork city center. It offers an array of rich resources, including fine food and lively pubs. Legend has it that Midleton is where whiskey was invented, and you won't want to miss visiting the Old Midleton Distillery, a restored 18th-century distillery open to visitors. The town has a private college, numerous churches and historical buildings, a prominent library, and various retail shops. It offers a wide selection of semidetached and detached houses with fenced yards, as well as apartments and flats. Cork's suburban rail line connects Midleton to Cork city center.

RURAL VILLAGES

The countryside surrounding Cork city and county offers a plethora of rural villages situated in peaceful locations. These villages have shopping facilities and the most basic of necessities, but you may have to go into Cork city or one of the bigger towns to find services such as garbage pickup or fast Internet access.

Cobh

Just 22 kilometers (14 miles) from Cork city center is the pleasant seaport town of Cobh (pronounced "cove"). The town is situated on Great Island, one of the three islands in Cork Harbor, all of which are joined by roads and bridges. The town is located on the southern slopes of a hill overlooking Cork Harbor and the surrounding beaches. The streets climb and wind around the slopes up to the top, which is crowned by the 47 bells of St. Coleman's Cathedral.

For those who desire to live outside the bustle of Cork city center but still want to be part of a vibrant community, Cobh offers numerous amenities, including a retail park; a swimming pool; a marina and harbor; various shops, restaurants, and cafés; and a wide variety of schools and churches. A regular commuter train links Cobh with Cork city, stopping at Fota, Carrigaloe, and Rushbrooke stations.

Kinsale

Kinsale, County Cork, is a charming village set at the mouth of the River Brandon. The village has a maze of narrow streets that drop steeply from the hills into the seafront's harbor. Situated 27 kilometers (17 miles) south of Cork city, this historic village has been around since the 17th century and features numerous historic sites, including historic forts, castles, churches, and museums. Its Georgian houses sit majestically over the winding streets, which become crowded with tourists during the summer months.

Kinsale is known for its many gourmet restaurants and leisure activities, such as yachting, sea angling, and golf. There are numerous art galleries and antiques shops, and a yachting marina is located near the town center. Bus Éireann buses link Kinsale to Cork via Cork Airport. The countryside surrounding Kinsale offers numerous holiday homes and B&Bs, as well as farms and rural houses.

Newmarket

The market town aptly named Newmarket is situated in the northwest of County Cork, near the Blackwater River on a glen in the shadow of the Mulmuaghreirk Mountains. Newmarket is located 63 kilometers (39 miles) from Cork city in the Barony of Dulhallow.

The town can best be described as sleepy, although it could also be described as peaceful and quiet. Not a lot happens here, but the area is pretty, and it is an easy commute to Cork. There are no hotels here, which means not as many tourists, but the main high street offers most amenities, including restaurants, pubs, and a bank. The town is surrounded by the serene, beautiful Island Wood, which offers secluded walking trails, as well as scenic golf courses, lakes, mountains, and rivers.

Allihies

For a truly rural village cradled in an area steeped in myths and legends, try Allihies, West Cork, in County Cork. Allihies is 143 kilometers (89 miles) from Cork city center, taking about two and a half hours by car. The village is set within the majestic Beara Peninsula in the shadow of the Caha Mountains, surrounded by scenic lakes and rugged coastline, as well as mountains and valleys rich in archaeological sites. Sheltered sandy beaches rim the village, which overlooks the Atlantic Ocean.

Allihies is composed of three pubs, a small grocery store, and a post office. Originally a mining settlement and producer of copper, Allihies has now become famous for its jaw-dropping scenery, sandy beaches, and outdoor summer activities, including swimming, horse riding, fishing, and scuba diving. The village is so rural you will need a car to get around.

Dingle *(An Daingean)*

Dingle, *An Daingean* (fortress) in Irish, is a charming medieval town situated in County Kerry. The town is 150 kilometers (93 miles) from Cork city center and takes about two and a half hours to drive. It is the most westerly town in Europe and is often referred to as the last parish before America. This little village is located in the Gaeltacht region and has retained much of what makes it traditionally Irish: thatched cottages, traditional pubs playing Irish music, and a close-knit community. The town has hilly streets lined with brightly colored terraced houses, interspersed periodically with a traditional pub. In fact, the entire social life of the town revolves primarily around the pub: In the winter there are quizzes and card games, and in the summer the pool tables are stashed away to make room for the tourists who flood the town.

The major industries in this little village have historically been fishing and farming, but tourism has become increasingly important. Dingle Mart, a livestock market, serves the surrounding countryside. The nearest train station is in Tralee, 52 kilometers (32 miles) away; however, regular buses depart from Dingle for Killarney, Dublin, Cork, Limerick, and the rest of Ireland.

Getting Around

Cork city center is compact and best navigated on foot, and I definitely recommend walking rather than driving. Even if you do have a car, you will want to park it elsewhere. The network of one-way streets, pedestrianized districts, lack of parking, and abominable traffic make it difficult to negotiate by car. Prepaid park-and-scratch stickers or pay-and-display parking is required if you can find parking at all. Like Dublin, Cork offers a range of transportation options for getting around the city, the suburbs, and the surrounding county.

BUSES

Green and red Bus Éireann buses operate throughout Cork's main suburbs, colleges, shopping centers, and historic buildings in the city center, and are numbered 1–19. The Central Bus Terminal is located in Parnell Place, in the center of the city. There are 18 different bus routes in the city center and 17 to the suburbs, most running Monday–Sunday 7:15 A.M.–midnight.

An airport bus departs every 30 minutes from Arrivals to the main hotel and tourist areas of Cork. The number 5 bus takes you from Kent Railway Station into the city center. Two buses provide circular services through the north and south areas of the city. Services to the suburbs, including Glanmire, Carrigaline, and Ballincollig, as well as long-distance buses, are available from the bus terminal at Parnell Place. Six buses depart daily to Dublin, and hourly

© SARAH JANE SWEENEY

Bus Éireann operates throughout Cork.

services depart from the bus station to Killarney-Tralee, Waterford, Athlone, and Shannon Airport–Limerick–Galway. There is also a Euroline bus that departs daily from Cork's bus station to Victoria Coach Station in London via South Wales and Bristol.

Bus Éireann buses cost €1.60 for a single adult ticket and €1 for a single child's ticket. An adult day-saver pass is available on all Bus Éireann buses for €4.40. You should purchase your ticket from the driver using exact change. Weekly city service tickets cost €17.50 for adults, €15.50 for students, and €7.70 for children. Monthly city service tickets cost €62 for adults, €55 for students, and €33 for children. Weekly and monthly tickets should be bought at the Bus Éireann office. A three-day Cork Rambler ticket is available from the Travel Center in Cork's Parnell Place Bus Station. The ticket allows three consecutive days of unlimited travel between June and September, costing €25.

Cork city operates the Cork City Tour Bus, offering hop-on and hop-off service as it circles the city's main historical landmarks and sites. Bus Éireann operates buses for tourists from Parnell Place to Blarney Castle, the town and harbor of Kinsale, Cobh in Cork Harbor, the Jameson Heritage Center, and Youghal. Organized coach tours operate to Kerry and West Cork.

Numerous private bus companies operate services to and from Cork city. Citylink departs from Cork for Limerick and Galway, and Aircoach operates to Dublin city center and Dublin Airport.

TRAIN

Cork's main train station is located at Kent Station, in the city center. The trains are operated by Iarnród Éireann (Irish Rail, www.irishrail.ie). Cork's train and bus station are not located in the same area—you will have to walk about 5–10 minutes to get from one to the other. Trains depart from Kent Station for destinations throughout Ireland from here, usually via Dublin or Limerick Junction. Trains leave hourly for Dublin (11 trains a day), offering a number of connecting services and stopping at the many towns along the way. Intercity trains depart to Killarney, Tralee, and Galway via Limerick Junction and the western corridor.

The Cork Suburban Rail network serves the commuter towns in Metropolitan Cork and County Cork. There are currently three lines in operation, with plans to open additional stations in the future. The suburban trains depart from Kent Station and link Little Island, Mallow, Midleton, Fota, and Cobh in Metropolitan Cork. The suburban network offers special day and weekly fares throughout the year.

CAR

While driving in Cork might be all right for the seasoned Irish driver, I definitely wouldn't recommend it for a tourist or as a regular way of getting around. There are a series of one-way streets that are narrow enough for a horse and carriage, but not for two cars going in opposite directions. After confusion sets in, you will be forced to pay a pretty steep fee to park at a parking garage. That being said, there are some parking areas available in the city center; just be sure to check the closing times before you leave your car. Cork also operates a parking disk and a park-by-phone system on the streets. Purchase the disk from any shop, enter the date and time on your disc, and display it on your dashboard.

International and local car rental companies are readily available from Cork Airport and throughout the city center. Cork city and county are bisected by a number of National Primary roads. The Cork South Link road links the Kinsale road with the city center, and the Jack Lynch Tunnel extends the N25 South Ring Road under the River Lee. The N27 extends south from the city, the N20 extends north, the N22 extends west, and the N8 extends east. The M8 motorway links Cork with Dublin in about two and a half hours.

CORK AIRPORT

Cork city and county are well served by Cork Airport, one of Ireland's main regional airports. The airport is located on the south side of Cork city in Ballygarvan and features 20 airlines flying to over 65 destinations, with over 60 flights operating each day. Airlines include Aer Lingus, Ryanair, Wizz Air, Iberworld, and Jet 2. Cork Airport is the third-busiest airport in Ireland, after Dublin and Shannon, and has opened a second terminal to handle the increase in passengers. Cork Airport has a relatively short runway, which currently prevents transatlantic flights, but flights frequently depart to the UK and Europe.

GALWAY

ATLANTIC OCEAN

Irish Sea

N56

Ardara
N56

Killybegs

Donegal

N15

Ballyshannon

Bundoran

N15

N16

N76

SLIGO
Sligo

N59

Irishcrone

Ballycastle

R314

R315

Bangor

N59

Ballina

N26

N17

N4

Lough
Allen

Ballycroy
National
Park

Lough
Conn

Pontoon

N58

N26 Swinford

R293

Achill
Island

Castlebar

Newport

N59

N5

IRELAND WEST
AIRPORT KNOCK

N5

N61

Clare
Island

Westport

Loiusburgh

N60

R323

N17

Knock

Ballintubber

Claremorris

Ballyhaunis

Castlerea

R335

N84

Ballymoe

N60

N63

Ballinrobe

N83

Roscommon

Lough
Mask

R364

Connemara
National
Park

Lough
Corrib

Headford

Tuam

N63

Athl

Clifden

Connemara

N59

N84

N17

Monivea

M6

Carna

Moycullen

GALWAY

Athenry

R336

Barna

Galway

Oranmore

M6

N65

Inis Mór

N67

N18

N65

Aran Islands

Inishmaan

Lisdoonvarna

Gort

N52

Inisheer

Doolin

Lough
Derg

Ennistimon

N18

0   10 mi

0   10 km

© AVALON TRAVEL

GALWAY

The city of Galway, *Cathair na Gaillimhe* (stony city) in Irish, is known by many names: the City of the Tribes, the capital of Connacht, the tourist gateway to the west, the jewel of the west, the bilingual capital of Ireland. Irish poet William Butler Yeats went so far as to call it the Venice of the West. But whatever you call it, Galway is irresistible. On Ireland's stunning west coast, this bohemian, laid-back city features a cosmopolitan, artistic atmosphere and is the cultural heart of the country. It is the soul of what really sums up all that is "Irish." There is no other city in Ireland where the wild, natural beauty and the vibrant heritage and traditions can so clearly be seen and felt.

Like Dublin, Galway was fueled by the economic boom in the early 2000s and is now the fastest growing city in Ireland—and one of the fastest growing in Europe. Galway is Ireland's third-largest city, featuring an energetic urban vibe and a thriving commercial community. A labyrinth of cobbled, winding medieval lanes radiates from Shop Street, the city's pedestrianized shopping

district, which is lined by colorful shop fronts, cafés, and pubs. The city is packed with students during the college year and with festivalgoers attending Galway's many arts, music, film, and language festivals during the summer. Galway is renowned for its easygoing, laid-back atmosphere offset by a lively nightlife and picturesque scenery.

Lay of the Land

County Galway is divided into two: the flat eastern area, with small lakes and rivers, and the western area of Connemara, known for its rocky bogs, mountains, and fjords. Galway city is majestically situated in the middle of the two sections, on the River Corrib between Lough Corrib and Galway Bay. Galway is the only official city in the Province of Connacht, in the west of Ireland, and is surrounded by the Irish midlands to the east and the wild Atlantic Ocean to the west. County Galway exhibits a stunning natural landscape with rugged mountains, boglands, and vistas from the coastline of the nearby Aran Islands. Its mild, damp climate perpetuates the growth of palm trees and fig trees, which would normally not be found at such high latitudes.

HISTORY

The history of Galway is uncertain and often disputed, and nobody even knows for sure how the city got its name. It is theorized that the name comes from the term *Gall*, which is what the Irish people called foreigners. The English

Fishing in one of the many lakes in Connemara.

GALWAY HOOKERS

From their thick impastos of richly textured and coloured paints you can all but taste the very salt of the spray, wipe its pearls from sun kissed brow, hear the thump of the wave's crest on the bow, brace for the shudder of going about under the whack of a soaked and heavy canvas sail, the muscle powered heft of rope and rudder, cleat and anchor."

– Ian Hill on the work of Irish artist and sculptor James G. Miles on the Galway hookers

The Galway hooker was an 18th-century boat originally constructed about 200 years ago for the unique needs of fishermen in the Atlantic off the west coast of Ireland. The boats were created to sail in shallow waters so they could navigate the areas around south Connemara. The Galway hooker can best be identified by its sail formation, which consists of a single mast with one main sail and two foresails.

The Galway hooker refers to four classes of boats, all of which are named in Irish: the *Bád Mór* (big boat) ranges in length from 10.5 to 13.5 meters (35–44 feet), the smaller *Leathbhád* (half boat) is about 10 meters (28 feet) long, the *Gleoiteog* is about 7–9 meters long (24–28 feet) and has the same sails and rigging as the larger boats, and the *Púcán*, which is similar in size to the *Gleoiteog* but has a lug mainsail and a foresail.

Both the *Bád Mór* and the *Leathbhád* were used to carry turf to be burned as fuel from Connemara, across Galway Bay, and on to County Mayo, the Aran Islands, and the Burren. The boats often returned laden with limestone in order to neutralize the acidic soil of Connemara and Mayo. There is also an unofficial class called the Boston hooker, which was created by Irish settlers in Boston. When they needed a fishing craft, they built the hooker they remembered from home, fitting it with a cockpit floor over the ballast for fishing.

There has recently been a revival in the interest of the Galway hooker, with a plethora of artwork, songs, and sculptures dedicated to the beautiful sailboat. Every year the festival of Cruinniú na mBád is held, in which Galway hookers race across Galway Bay from Connemara to Kinvara.

© JOHN MOLLOY

a Galway Hooker - a traditional sailing boat in Galway Bay

settlers who arrived in the Galway area were called *Clann-na Gall,* which means foreign clan, and evolved into *Gaillibh,* which means foreigner's town. The other theory is that the city got its name from *Gaillimh,* which means Galway River. The river Gallimh got its name from the daughter of a Fir Bolg chieftain who drowned here.

What is historically known is that Dún Bhun na Gaillimhe (Fort at the Mouth of the Gaillimh) was built in 1124. Galway was later captured by Richard de Burgh and became a prosperous town adept at trade with Spain, France, and the Caribbean. As the population grew, walls were eventually built around the town. During medieval times, Galway came under the rule of the 14 Tribes of Galway—two Irish tribes and 12 Anglo-Norman tribes— thus the name City of the Tribes. Galway traded in wine, spices, salt, and fish, quickly becoming a primary port after London and Bristol.

In 1477 Christopher Columbus visited Galway, praying at St. Nicholas Collegiate Church before setting sail to discover the New World. Today there is an inscription near the Spanish Arch in Galway that reads: "On these shores around 1477, the Genoese sailor Cristoforo Colombo found sure signs of land beyond the Atlantic."

The 17th century saw Galway support Catholic troops against the English crown, resulting in a battered economy for centuries to come. The decline in Galway's economy was exacerbated in the 19th century, when the Great Famine decimated the west of Ireland and much of the population died or emigrated. The city was left relatively unscathed during the War of Independence, as Galway was the western headquarters for the British Army, and their forces were so strong that the Irish Republican Army could do little to damage them.

CLIMATE

Perched on the Atlantic Ocean, Galway's climate is a bit more temperamental than the rest of Ireland. Like the rest of the country, the temperature is mild, but the rainfall is drastically higher in Galway, receiving 45 inches of rainfall a year (compared to 27 inches in Dublin). The weather here is changeable and unpredictable; you may wake up to bright sunshine, but by the time you get out of bed, dark, angry clouds may be lashing fat drops of cold rain. Prevailing winds sweep the city from the North Atlantic, and severe windstorms often pummel the city in late autumn and early spring. Rain is most common in the winter but is expected during the summer also, although May and September often end up being nice months.

Thanks to its northerly location, Galway receives long summer days. On the flip side, it also receives short winter days. In the summer the sun rises around 4 A.M. and lasts until about 11 P.M. In the winter, daylight starts around 9 A.M. and is gone by 4 P.M.

LANGUAGE

Galway is considered by many to be the most "Irish" of Ireland's cities. It is the only city you might hear Irish spoken on the streets or in the shops. Nearly 10 percent of Galway's population are fluent Irish speakers, although they mostly converse in English. This level of Irish speakers may be due to its close proximity to the Galway Gaeltacht, one of Ireland's Irish-speaking areas. People here speak a dialect of Connacht Irish. The strongest dialect is found in Connemara and the Aran Islands, which is very different from general Connacht Irish.

There are several Irish-language organizations based in Galway that contribute to the bilingual atmosphere, including the National University of Ireland, Galway, which offers Irish-language courses, and Gaillimh le Gaeilge, which develops and promotes the Irish language in the Galway area. The success of Gaillimh le Gaeilge has been so great that now there are hardly any streets that don't have businesses featuring signs in the Irish language, or at least in English and Irish.

Since Galway has so successfully accepted its Irish heritage, culture, and language, a variety of organizations have been established to celebrate this. The National Irish Language Theater, *Taibhdhearc na Gaillimhe,* was set

© JOHN MOLLOY

an ancient, Celtic grave marker

GALWAY FESTIVALS

Galway is renowned throughout Europe, and indeed the world, as Ireland's cultural heart. Every year Galway hosts festivals, events, and celebrations drawing thousands of visitors to this vibrant city. Every July Galway hosts the Galway Arts Festival, celebrating artistic excellence and featuring hundreds of artists, performers, writers, and musicians creating theater, art, music, comedy, and literature for over 100,000 visitors. The festival culminates in the Macnas Parade, a festival parade that features acting, dancing, and music.

Preceding the Galway Arts Festival is the Galway Film Fleadh (festival in Irish). This six-day international festival attracts actors, directors, artists, and cinematographers of all backgrounds and generations to share a mutual love of cinema. At the end of July, the Galway Races, a horse-racing festival, begins. The festival runs for seven days, starting on the last Monday in July every year. The Galway Races are the subject of poems, songs, and talk shows, and are famous worldwide.

In September Galway celebrates the Galway International Oyster Festival, which is a food festival begun by Galway's Great Southern Hotel. The main events include the Guinness Irish Oyster Opening Championship, the Guinness World Oyster Opening Championship, and two Oyster Opening Championships, as well as a beauty pageant and a Mardi Gras party.

The Volvo Round the World Ocean Race occurs in Galway in July, and at the end of July and the beginning of August, Galway celebrates the Galway Hooker Festival, saluting the iconic Galway sailing boats.

In June Galway features the Salthill Air Show; the Little Havana Festival, which celebrates Latin culture; the Salthill Guinness Harp Festival; and the Galway Sessions, featuring various Irish music at pubs throughout Galway. In May Galway celebrates the Galway Early Music Festival and Connemara Bog Week, which is centered on the very best of traditional Irish music. Every

up in the city center, producing Irish plays and hosting events in the Irish language for all ages. Conradh na Gaeilge, a nongovernmental organization that promotes the Irish language in Ireland and abroad, is available in Galway to teach Irish-language classes and promote events in the Irish language. Áras na nGael, on Dominic Street; Tigh Choilí; and Tigh Taaffes pubs offer traditional Irish music amid a very Irish atmosphere. Galway offers four primary schools and one secondary school taught through the medium of Irish. The national Irish-language television station TG4 and radio RTÉ Raidió na Gaeltachta are based in Connemara, just outside of Galway. The National University of Ireland, Galway, holds the archive of spoken material for the Celtic languages, further enriching the culture and heritage of Ireland in Galway.

Galway offers a variety of living options, from modern city-center flats to houses with yards in the suburbs. The River Corrib flows through the center

March, Galway, along with the rest of the country, celebrates the most Irish of holidays – St. Patrick's Day. This is preceded by Seachtain na Gaeilge (Irish Week), a two-week festival that promotes the use of Irish language and culture.

This is just a snapshot of the festivals that Galway hosts every year.

This vibrant, cosmopolitan city is renowned for hosting festivals. In the summer, a week rarely goes by without a celebration of art or community. If you are lucky enough to visit during one of these festivals, you can take in a celebration of art, culture, food, sport, comedy, or music.

COURTESY OF TOURISM IRELAND

The Galway Races are held every year in July.

of the city to Galway Bay, with lovely houses perched on either side. Many of the city center accommodations are situated over shops and pubs, especially on the main street, so beware before you sign a lease that you might also be signing up for late-night noise when the pubs and clubs let out and early-morning banging when the delivery trucks arrive.

Where to Live

Galway offers a variety of unique neighborhoods and streets. You will pay about €650–700 for a one-bedroom apartment in the city center, or around €800–1,000 for a three-bedroom house in the suburbs. If you are looking to rent a room in an apartment or house, you will spend around €350–400 per month. Rental properties in Galway are typically furnished, although you may find unfurnished houses in the suburbs. A one-bedroom property in Galway city costs an average of €148,000, while a three-bedroom property costs an average of €199,000. Of course, prices for buying or renting property depend largely on the location you want to be in. The city center is the most expensive area, and anywhere near the water is bound to be more expensive than out in the suburbs. This book was written when house prices were bottoming out in Galway, so they may be subject to change.

CITY CENTER

Galway city center offers a good mix of student housing, apartments, flats, town houses, and terraced houses. Around Shop Street, Galway's main pedestrianized area, there are numerous apartments and flats situated in the old brick buildings above the brightly colored shops, cafés, and pubs. The narrow alleyways that extend from Shop Street crisscross Galway's streets and feature more apartments and flats. On the weekends, the Galway market opens just off Shop Street, behind St. Nicholas's Church. You can purchase locally made crafts or fresh vegetables, herbs, cheeses, or chocolates, as well as an array of ethnic food, from Madras curry to Japanese sushi. The Docklands neighborhood is located around Galway's docks and is home to trendy shops and boutiques, and new modern apartments.

Galway's Latin Quarter encompasses some of the city's most historic landmarks. The area starts at St. Nicholas's Church, extending onto O'Brien's

Shop Street is often packed with pedestrians.

COURTESY OF TOURISM IRELAND

Bridge, along the River Corrib, down to the Spanish Arch, and then up along Middle Street to Buttermilk Lane. The entire area is identified by some of Galway's best-loved pubs and restaurants, as well as locally owned businesses. There are a multitude of modern apartments and flats, but no houses.

The Claddagh neighborhood is situated just across the river from the Spanish Arch near the Dominican Church of St. Mary on the Hill. It was once a fishing village outside of the city walls, separated from the city by the River Corrib. This historic area is where the claddagh ring originated. The homes in the Claddagh are now very valuable, with some of the highest property prices in Galway, due to their close proximity to the city center and sweeping views across Galway Bay.

The Spanish Arch neighborhood is located to the left of the River Corrib, where the river meets the sea. The arch is what is left over from a 16th-century bastion, which was added to the city's walls to protect merchant ships from looting. This area is surrounded by pubs, restaurants, and boutique shops. The neighborhood benefits from modern apartments and a stunning view out toward Galway Bay.

Situated on the banks of the River Corrib, near the National University of Ireland, Galway, is Nun's Island. The area is formed by a small canal that branches off the Corrib as it flows through Galway city to the sea. It is named Nun's Island due to the enclosed community of Poor Clare sisters whose monastery is located here. The area is also home to a modern theater that hosts the Galway Youth Theater, and the stunningly beautiful Galway Cathedral. There are many lovely terraced and semidetached houses in this area, and it is within walking distance of numerous shops, the market, and the amenities of Shop Street.

Eyre Square is the focal point of the city center, surrounded by shops, hotels, pubs, and restaurants. Just up the hill from Eyre Square is the Prospect Hill neighborhood. Prospect Hill offers flats and apartments, as well as terraced houses, all within an easy walk to Eyre Square and Shop Street. Around the corner from Eyre Square is the Woodquay neighborhood, featuring a pub, a hostel, and a number of cafés and boutique shops. Passing Woodquay, you head out to Terryland, which is characterized by a retail park, a supermarket, and fast food restaurants. This area represents the end of the city center, and after Terryland you head into the suburbs.

SUBURBAN GALWAY

Galway has an intricate network of suburbs surrounding the city center. If you don't mind the commute, living in the suburbs will buy you a larger house with a yard, nearby parks, large supermarkets, and access to gyms. Between the National University of Ireland, Galway, and University College Hospital is the Newcastle neighborhood. Newcastle is 1.5 kilometers (one mile) from the Eyre Square, and it is debatable whether it is actually the city center or suburbs, as it is only a 10–15 minute walk from Eyre Square. The area is almost entirely residential, with a few corner shops on various streets. There are semidetached houses, terraced houses, and apartments available, so if you're looking for a house with a yard or a large, modern apartment, but you still want to be near the center of Galway, Newcastle is the place to go. The houses range from basic to modern, so you are bound to find a room, apartment, or house well within your budget.

Just on the other side of Newcastle, one kilometer (0.5 mile) from the city center, located next to University College Hospital, is the Shantalla neighborhood. While Galway city is generally a very safe area, Shantalla is one of the more run-down parts of central Galway. The houses are old and the yards unkempt; however, this does mean the rental and purchase prices are a bit lower here. The area offers semidetached houses, terraced houses, and apartments, all available within walking distance of the city center.

Probably the nicest and most affluent suburb of Galway is Salthill. In the past, Salthill was a small seaside resort situated three kilometers (1.5 miles) outside of Galway city. In modern days, it has grown so much it has now been incorporated as a suburb of Galway city. The area offers a wealth of amenities, including the giant Leisureland complex, which features an indoor heated swimming pool, a children's pool with a pirate ship, a waterslide, an outdoor amusement park, and a health and fitness center with a gym. A long promenade extends down the seashore, offering pubs, restaurants, and boutique shops. Salthill Park and Quincentennial Park add to the greenery of the area, and you can play tennis or golf at any of the nearby clubs. For outdoors enthusiasts, swimming, sailing, snorkeling, and fishing are available. As expected, rent and property prices are much higher here, but you do get what you pay for. It is one of the safest, prettiest suburbs of Galway.

Just behind Salthill is Taylors Hill, just two kilometers (one mile) from the city center. It offers beautiful detached and semidetached homes close to Salthill and the amenities of Galway city, but at a smaller price tag than Salthill itself. The area offers local amenities such as churches, shops, and good public schools.

Knocknacarra, on the west side of Galway city center, is adjacent to Salthill. The area is five kilometers (three miles) from the city center. Mostly residential, it also offers good public schools, corner shops, and a few pubs. Buses regularly run from Galway city center to Knocknacarra in about 10 minutes.

As I mentioned before, there are not really any dangerous or dodgy parts of Galway. It is a mostly laid-back, bohemian city with an affable charm to it. That being said, there are some neighborhoods in the Westside that are noisy, rowdy, and a bit run-down, including parts of Rahoon, Ballinfoyle, and Castlepark.

About eight kilometers (five miles) from Galway city along the R336 coast road is Barna, a quiet seaside village with a rocky pier and a large wooded area, Barna Woods. Barna is also home to Silver Strand, one of Galway's most popular, beautiful beaches overlooking the Burren Hills in County Clare and, on a fine day, the Aran Islands. Barna was previously a satellite of Galway city, but due to its expansion, it has now become a suburb. Officially Barna is considered part of the Gaeltacht, the Irish-speaking part of Ireland, but due to its proximity to Galway city, it is primarily an English-speaking village. The village of Barna offers all necessary amenities for a family, including good schools, churches, shops, and entertainment. The prices for rent and for purchasing property are more reasonable than in the city center, and you will have a choice ranging from modern apartments to grand, detached houses. The drive from Barna into Galway city center only takes about 15 minutes, but figure that you will have to contend with traffic, which may double or triple your driving time.

The suburban town of Oranmore lies nine kilometers (5.5 miles) from Galway city center. This quaint little town is situated in the shadow of Clanricarde Burke castle, next to the Galway Road as you drive to Galway from Dublin. Next to the castle lies a large megalithic dolmen from 2000 B.C. Just like any suburban town, Oranmore offers a variety of accommodations, from basic apartments to large family homes with yards. Rinville Park offers access to a picnic and barbecue area, as well as a playground for the children. Walking routes crisscross the nearby woodland and farmland, and views of the stunning Galway Bay can be seen. Oranmore is an easy drive or bus journey into Galway city, but remember the traffic on the Galway Road can lengthen your commute.

Situated approximately 10 kilometers (six miles) from Galway city is the satellite town of Claregalway. Once a rural village on the outskirts of Galway city, this suburban town has become a thriving town with a rapidly expanding population. The town is a throughway for those commuting into Galway, as it sits at the junction of the N17 and N18 national primary routes and leads straight into Galway's city center. The focal point of the town is the Claregalway Shopping Center, a supermarket, and a hotel, and the area is surrounded by numerous residential areas with nice detached and semidetached homes.

The suburban village of Moycullen is 13 kilometers (eight miles) outside of Galway city. Like many other suburban villages around Galway, Moycullen is becoming a suburb and is an easy commute into the city. The village offers large, modern houses with fenced yards for families, a small shopping area, and a number of pubs and restaurants. The area is rich in historical remains, including churches, wells, and cairns, and there are numerous amenities for outdoors enthusiasts, including 11 coarse-fishing lakes, horse riding, and walking trails.

RURAL VILLAGES

The city and county of Galway are surrounded by sleepy little villages and picturesque rural landscapes ideal for those not comfortable living in the city. Even the most rural villages offer amenities such as a grocery store, commercial shops, a gas station, and a post office, although some of the most rural areas might not offer banking services, garbage services, or very good Internet and television reception.

THE CLADDAGH RING

The Claddagh Ring originated in the fishing village of Claddagh, situated just outside of Galway's city walls and separated by the River Corrib. The ring is attributed to many myths and legends, but most frequently to a man named Richard Joyce, of Claddagh. Joyce was engaged to be married after a trip to the West Indies, but he was captured by Algerian pirates during his journey there. He was sold as a slave to a Moorish goldsmith, who trained him in his craft. Joyce pined for his sweetheart in Ireland and crafted the Claddagh ring for her. In 1689, William III of England demanded all British subjects enslaved in Algiers be released. Joyce's master offered him his daughter's hand in marriage and half his wealth if he would stay, but Joyce declined and returned to Ireland to marry his sweetheart, presenting her with the Claddagh ring he had designed.

The Claddagh ring is now given as a token of love, friendship, eternity, or engagement, but historically it was usually given as a wedding ring, drawing on the story of Richard Joyce and his marriage to his sweetheart. The Claddagh ring shows two hands holding a heart, which wears a crown. The elements of the ring are explained as: the heart represents love, the hands represent friendship, and the crown represent loyalty. This is explained in the motif "let love and friendship reign".

The ring is traditionally worn in three different ways. On your left wedding ring finger means you are engaged. On the right ring finger with the heart pointing down to your fingers means you are free of any attachments. On the same finger with the heart turned around means you are involved with somebody.

Clifden

Clifden is situated in the beautiful Connemara region, beneath the rugged Twelve Ben mountain range, near the Roundstone Bog and the golden beaches ringing the nearby Atlantic Ocean. Clifden is located 78 kilometers (49 miles) northwest of Galway city and is widely regarded as the capital of Connemara. The town is situated on the Owenglen River where it flows into Clifden Bay.

Clifden offers a serene beauty and a tranquil splendor for anybody looking for a bit of isolation within an easy commute of Galway city. By car Clifden can be reached by the N59 from Galway or Westport, and regular coaches connect Clifden with Galway city, Dublin, and the rest of Ireland. This small market town and fishing center is dominated by the dual spires of its Catholic and Protestant churches. It offers numerous retail shops and is known for its production of traditional tweed and its array of holiday homes for tourists. The area around Clifden features numerous walking trails and scenic drives, and the sea-facing Clifden Castle can be reached by the farm track near the Sky Road. Each year the community organizes the Connemara Pony Show and the Clifden Community Arts Week.

Knock

Situated on Ireland's western seaboard, in County Mayo, 71 kilometers (44 miles) from Galway, is the little village of Knock. If you're looking for a bit of peace and quiet, a slice of tranquil repose surrounded by rolling green farmlands, and an endless sky, Knock is the place to go. This village is a perfect example of rural Ireland and is what misty-eyed visitors might view as "traditionally" Irish. Conventional Catholic values still hold strong in this close-knit community, everybody attends church on Sunday, and family is still considered paramount.

One street bisects the center of the village, there is one roundabout (rather than a stop sign), thatched-roofed cottages surround the village, and tractors regularly roll down the streets. Knock is predominantly an agricultural-based community, with sheep, cow, and pig farming the main forms of employment.

It is literally a blink-and-you'll-miss-it village, featuring three pubs, a tiny school, a post office, and some tourist shops celebrating Knock's heralding glory—the Knock Shrine. The Knock Shrine is now an internationally recognized pilgrimage site for Catholics who believe an apparition of the Virgin Mary occurred here. Due to this, the village gets busier during the summer months, becoming more lively and atmospheric than in the winter.

Doolin

The remote seaside village of Doolin is actually in County Clare, next to County Galway, 73 kilometers (45 miles) from Galway city center. Perched amid the green Irish countryside in the Burren, a region characterized by its karst landscapes, Doolin is a traditional Irish village that is widely regarded as the capital of traditional Irish music. The village has escaped commercialization and retains a certain charm in its houses, streets, pubs, and ambience.

Doolin has about 200 or so residents living within the village and the surrounding rural areas, and offers a wide range of housing that suits families or young professionals. The village consists of a Catholic church, numerous retail shops, some B&Bs, restaurants, and a post office. Down the road from the main village center, centered around Fisherstreet, is O'Connors Pub and Paddy's Doolin Hostel. About one kilometer (0.5 mile) from the village center is the village harbor, from which the ferry crosses to the Aran Islands.

The Aran Islands

The Aran Islands are composed of three islands located off the coast of Galway. Inis Mór is the largest island and the most populated, Inishmaan is less inhabited and does not have any cars, and Inisheer is the smallest, wildest, and most remote of the three islands.

The Aran Islands are one of the only places in Ireland you will regularly hear the Irish language. Although English is understood, the residents are geographically and historically cut off from the rest of Ireland, maintaining a different set of ideals, principles, and social structure than the rest of the country.

All three islands are very rural, with one main village center on each. Getting around the islands is usually done by bicycle, horseback, or by just walking. On the cliff tops of the islands are ancient forts such as Dún Aengus on Inis Mór and Dún Chonchúir on Inishmaan, featuring some of the oldest archaeological remains in Ireland.

Living on any of the Aran Islands is entirely different from what you would find anywhere else in Ireland. The schools have a pupil-teacher ratio of 2 to 1, a 100 percent transfer of students to university, total immersion in the Irish language, and a life steeped in tradition and culture.

While there isn't any public transportation on the islands, there are two ferries that depart from Doolin to the Aran Islands, Island Ferries departs from Rossaveal, and O'Brien Shipping ferries tourists between Galway Bay and the islands. Aer Arann offers regular flights from Connemara Airport.

Ardara

The rural village of Ardara in County Donegal is located on the southwestern coast of Ireland in a wide valley where the Owentocher River enters Loughros More Bay. This quiet village is 232 kilometers (144 miles) from Galway but is only 28 kilometers (17 miles) from Donegal town. Ardara is absolutely tiny, with one main street winding up and down rocky hills lined with colorful boutiques and charming arts and retail shops. The village center can literally be explored in minutes. If you're looking for isolation in the heart of a heritage town, Ardara is the place to go.

This quiet village offers long stretches of unspoiled beaches, spectacular scenery, and friendly hospitality from its people. The area is famous for many crafts, including knitting, hosiery, embroidery, and the manufacturing of the distinct Donegal tweed for jackets and suits. In the region surrounding Ardara there are brown-trout lakes, the nearby caves of Maghera, and the magnificent Glengesh Pass.

Getting Around

Galway city center is best navigated on foot or by bicycle. Much of the city center is pedestrianized, making driving down the narrow, traffic-laden, one-way streets a living nightmare. Add to this the parking difficulties, and you will soon realize you are better off just walking. Buses are readily available to take you within the city center or farther afield to any of Galway's suburbs, but there are no trams or metro trains available. Taxis are convenient and can be found on the street or at taxi ranks. Taxi ranks are available at Eyre Square and Bridge Street, but do keep in mind they can be a bit expensive.

The website www.galwaytransport.info offers up-to-date travel information for Galway's city and regional buses. There is a summary map of various bus routes in the city, as well as detailed maps of individual routes, maps of available taxi ranks, and detailed directions for reaching popular locations using public transportation.

BUSES

Galway buses are efficient and inexpensive, and cover the entire city center as well as the suburbs around Galway. Buses also link Galway city to the rest of the country. There are two city center buses: Bus Éireann (www.buseireann. ie), Ireland's national bus company, provides service to most of the city and suburbs, and City Direct provides service to the north side of Knocknacarra.

Bus Éireann bus numbers 1–9, except 6, operate from the bus stop in Eyre Square to city center and inner suburb locations.

Buses operate in the city center Monday–Saturday 7 A.M.–10:30 P.M., and Sundays and holidays have limited routes operating 10:30 A.M.–10:30 P.M. Bus Éireann buses cost €1.60 for an adult and €1 for a child single ticket. An adult day-saver pass is available on all Bus Éireann buses for €3.50. You should purchase your ticket from the driver using exact change. Weekly city service tickets cost €17 for adults, €15.50 for students, and €7 for children. Monthly city service tickets cost €55 for adults, €47.50 for students, and €26 for children. Weekly and monthly tickets should be bought at the Bus Éireann office in Ceannt Station (the Galway Travel Center). City Direct tickets cost €1.80 for adults, €1.30 for children age 13–16, and €0.90 for children up to age 12 (children under 3 are free). Weekly and monthly tickets are available at their website, www.citydirectgalway.ie/fair.htm. Fares should be paid directly into the box next to the driver, and no change is given.

Regional buses link Galway with the suburbs and various towns and villages surrounding the city. Bus Éireann operates daily commuter buses throughout the region, and a route planner is available on their website. Going east, Citylink (www.citylink.ie) operates daily services between Galway and Connemara, via Moycullen, Rosscahill, Oughterard, Maam Cross, Recess, Canal Bridge, Clifden, Cleggan, and Letterfrack. The Sleepzone Hostel Bus operates a daily bus around the Connemara Loop, stopping at various tourist destinations as it loops back to Galway.

Going north, Burkes operates buses from Galway to Tuam, Dunmore, Milltown, and Headford. The Feda O'Donnell bus departs daily from Galway to Sligo and Donegal from Eyre Square. Healy's operates buses from Galway to Castlebar and Westport.

Going east, the Brendan Boyle bus operates every day from Galway Cathedral to Ballygar, Newbridge, Mountbellew, Moylough, Abbeyknockmoy, Turloughmore, and Lackagh. The commuter bus, Mountbellow Bus Company, operates daily between Galway and Mountbellew. Going south, Citylink operate daily services from Galway to Limerick and Cork, and JJ Kavanagh departs to Shannon Airport and Limerick. The website www.irishtransport. info offers a targeted bus search for all private and public buses operating throughout the nation.

TRAINS

Galway is well connected with Ireland's main cities by train. Iarnród Éireann operates from Galway's train station, Ceannt Station. The station is located just off Eyre Square in the center of Galway. Six trains depart Monday–Saturday (four on Sunday) from Galway to Dublin's Heuston Station, stopping at intermediate stations along the way. The train to Dublin departs every two hours and takes about two and a half hours. The website www.irishrail.ie gives precise departure and arrival times. Special fares can be found at this website, but expect to pay more during weekday peak times.

Galway also has the Galway Suburban Rail line, operating on the railway east of Galway. This line offers 14 services between Athenry and Galway on the weekdays, with 11 services from Galway and 10 services from Athenry operating on Sunday. Early morning and late services run between Athlone and Galway, serving the towns of Ballinasloe, Woodlawn, and Attymon. Morning and evening InterCity services operate from Limerick to County Galway's towns of Gort, Ardrahan, and Craughwell. In the evenings services continue to Athlone and on the Heuston Station in Dublin.

CAR

While driving in Galway city is not recommended, having a car to drive around the towns and villages in the area is. There are three national primary roads that serve the city and the surrounding area: The N17 heads north toward Tuam, Donegal, Letterkenny, and Derry; the N6 heads east toward Athlone and Dublin; and the N18 links Galway to Shannon, Limerick, and Cork in the south. The main motorway is the M6, which radiates to the east toward Athlone and Dublin. Galway is linked to the western area of Lough Corrib by the N59, and the R337 links the northern shore of Galway Bay and Connemara.

GALWAY AIRPORT

Galway is served by national and international flights to and from Galway Airport. The airport is located in Carnmore, 7.5 kilometers (4.5 miles) north of Galway city center. The runway can only handle turboprop aircraft and small executive jets, so the airport is limited in flights. The regional airline Aer Arann operates short flights to Dublin, Edinburgh, Waterford, London Luton, London Southend, and Manchester, and seasonal flights to Lorient, France.

PRIME LIVING LOCATIONS

LIMERICK

Limerick, *Luimneach* (bare marsh) in Irish, is the third-largest city in Ireland and the capital of the midwest region. Conquered by the Vikings in the 9th century, Limerick features a distinctly medieval air that resounds in its ancient, cobbled streets. Later, Georgian architecture was added, including St. John's Square, Pery Square, and stone-faced Georgian offices and town houses, successfully blending the city's dark, medieval architecture with the neat lines of Georgian architecture.

A decidedly modern atmosphere has descended on the city as it has blossomed in the 21st century, successfully blending both new and ancient aspects. Limerick city offers cultural attractions, sports amenities, and a lively atmosphere. This progressive city is now a contender for the primary economic region of Ireland, outside of Dublin and Cork. This is driven by the University of Limerick, Dell, Vistakon, Wyeth, the close proximity of Shannon Airport, and Shannon Development, an economic development agency.

COURTESY OF TOURISM IRELAND

Limerick is famous throughout the world for its passion for sports and is considered the sporting capital of Ireland. Gaelic football, rugby, golf, hurling, and soccer are just some of the sports that occur here throughout the year. Thomond Park Stadium, home to Munster Rugby, is located in Limerick, as is the University of Limerick Sports Arena, which hosted the 2010 Special Olympics Ireland Games; the Gaelic Grounds, which are the headquarters of Limerick GAA; the Limerick Racecourse; and the new Greyhound Stadium. This passion for sport combined with such an excellent sporting infrastructure helped crown Limerick the European City of Sport, 2011 by the European Capitals of Sport Association (ACES).

The Celtic Tiger years of Ireland saw a noticeable increase in the immigrant community in Limerick, and as such, the city features a distinctly multicultural atmosphere. It is also an established university city, with educational establishments including the University of Limerick, Limerick Institute of Technology, Mary Immaculate College, and the Limerick School of Art and Design. The high proportion of students in Limerick gives it a subtly bohemian, cosmopolitan vibe.

Unfortunately, Limerick also has a dark, gritty side to it. You will almost certainly hear Limerick referred to as Stab City, an unfortunate moniker that Limerick has earned thanks to ongoing gang feuds and violent incidents. However, these incidences are typically confined to a number of housing estates in the suburbs of Limerick, not to the city center. Limerick is a city in perpetual motion, morphing into a progressive powerhouse. The city has known hard times and has some dark areas, but it is a city in harmony with itself, one that is working toward a better station in life.

The Irish government has begun to address these problems with projects to regenerate these disadvantaged neighborhoods. In addition, the city center is experiencing a renaissance, and the 21st century has seen the refurbishment and restoration of old buildings and the construction of new ones. The skyline has transformed with additions such as The Clarion, Ireland's tallest hotel; the River Point; and the development of the Opera Center. In the 1990s King's Island was refurbished, as was Steamboat Quay and Abbey Bridge, and the Georgian House was opened in Perys Square. Limerick City Council has also unveiled a €50 million regeneration plan that will pedestrianize and remodel Limerick city center, transforming it into a vibrant city center.

Lay of the Land

Limerick city is known as the riverside city, lying at the top of County Limerick on the picturesque River Shannon, just before the river uncoils into an estuary and then carries on to the Atlantic Ocean. The city overlooks the majestic King John's Castle, an early-13th-century Norman castle. It is bisected by the mighty River Shannon, Ireland's largest river, which flows beneath Limerick's three bridges. County Limerick extends out from the city to the south, east, and west, with County Clare situated to the north. Low-lying farmland surrounds the city, framed by rolling hills and squat mountains in the southern and eastern boundaries of the county. The city and county are both filled with historic and archaeological sites and monuments, including the Lough Gur Neolithic Settlement, King John's Castle, St. Mary's Cathedral, and Bunratty Castle.

HISTORY

Limerick city began as a Viking colony established in the 9th century on an island between the River Shannon and the Abbey River. The city has witnessed battles between Vikings and Irish, Irish and Scots, and Irish and English, and has been captured and retaken numerous times throughout its turbulent history. In the late 12th century, the English took over and began developing Limerick, and in 1197 a charter was granted by the English declaring Limerick a city.

King John of England, who visited in 1210, ordered the construction of a castle (King John's Castle) and a bridge (Thomond Bridge). Under the peace imposed by the English, Limerick became a prosperous trading town. English settlers arrived and established a settlement on King's Island called Englishtown. The native Irish settled across the Abbey River in what was called Irishtown. In the 13th century a stone wall was built around Englishtown and was later extended to include Irishtown, making Limerick a walled city.

In 1316 Edward Bruce of Scotland captured Limerick, but the occupation was short-lived, and the English ousted the Scots by 1318. The 15th and 16th centuries saw Limerick as a city isolated from the rule of the English. While England remained in control, tensions arose between those loyal to the Catholic Church and those loyal to the Church of Ireland.

By the time the 17th century occurred, tensions were bubbling over, and the city was besieged four times, culminating in the famous Treaty of Limerick on October 3, 1691. The first siege occurred in 1642 when the Irish Confederates took King John's Castle from the English garrison. But in 1651, Oliver Cromwell recaptured Limerick after the city was decimated by the plague.

The next siege took place in 1690. The Catholic king of England, James II, had been deposed and came to Ireland, where Irish and French troops supported him. James II and his troops were defeated at the Battle of the Boyne, and James fled the country. The remaining soldiers took refuge behind Limerick's walls, but the city was besieged by William of Orange. William of Orange's troops later withdrew to Waterford but returned again in 1691. Following the massacre of the 850 defenders, Limerick fell, and the famous Treaty of Limerick was signed using a large stone set in the bridge as a table.

During the Great Famine in the 19th century, the population of Limerick city rose slightly as people fled to the city's workhouses, which offered accommodations and employment to those unable to support themselves.

Limerick played a role in the independence of Ireland in the early 20th century, when Sinn Féin gained popular support after the executions following the Easter Rising in 1916. Conflicts erupted in the streets between the general population and the English troops, and subsequent murders and assassinations occurred as the Irish fought for their independence from England.

After the treaty was signed between England and Ireland, establishing the Republic of Ireland, Limerick was split into pro- and anti-treaty factions. In July 1921, the two factions opened fire on each other, and William Street became a battle zone. The pro-treaty forces flattened the Ordnance Barracks and captured the Castle Barracks. The city lay in ruins until rebuilding began in 1925, after the Irish Civil War had finished.

CLIMATE

Due to its location on the south of Ireland's west coast, Limerick has a climate that is damp and moderate, similar to the rest of Ireland. The weather is very changeable and unpredictable, but you can usually expect rain on any given day, even in the summer. May has the most sunshine, although there is a spike in rainfall during this month. July is typically the warmest month, with an average daily temperature of 15.7°C (60.3°F). The coldest, wettest month is January, with an average daily temperature of 5.4°C (41.7°F). There is an average of 22 days of rain during the month of January, and an average of 16 days in both June and July.

ARTS, CULTURE, AND HERITAGE

Limerick is the arts and culture capital of the midwest region, offering a vibrant city that is home to the Irish World Academy of Music and Dance, the Irish Chamber Orchestra, the Island Theatre Company, the historic Belltable Arts Centre, the University Concert Hall, and the Millennium Theatre at

LIMERICK OR LIMERICKS?

While the exact origin of limerick poetry isn't known, they are often associated with Limerick the city and county due to their matching names. In the history of Irish literature, however, the town of Croom, in the heart of County Limerick, was the meeting place of the Maigue Poets, the Gaelic poets of the 18th century who wrote short satiric verses that were eventually called limericks. Written in their native Irish, the Maigue Poets produced works of poetry that were famous throughout Limerick, eventually spreading to Counties Cork, Clare, and Tipperary.

A limerick is a type of comedic poem consisting of five anapestic lines: the first, second, and fifth have three metrical feet and rhyme with each other, and the third and fourth have two metrical feet and rhyme with each other. Traditionally, limericks are said to be bawdy and obscene, but they can be traced back to the 14th century in England when they were used in nursery rhymes for children. For example, here is a well-known limerick from 1774:

Hickory Dickory Dock

A mouse ran up the clock

The clock struck one

And down he run

Hickory Dickory Dock.

Limericks are popular rather than literary and were made famous by Edward Lear in the mid-18th century after the publication of his book *Book of Nonsense* in 1845, and his follow-up in 1872. His books were entirely filled with silly limericks written as nonsensical themes and utilizing wordplay.

Limericks are easy to write if you get the rhyme and rhythm patterns correct. They use an AABBA rhyme pattern, and the rhythm pattern goes like so: three DUMS, three DUMS, two DUMS, two DUMS, three DUMS. For example:

There once was a man from Limerick

(da DUM da da DUM da da DUM)

Who had a horrible tick

(da DUM da da DUM da da DUM)

He twitched off the dock

(da DUM da da DUM)

And sank like a rock

(da DUM da da DUM)

And that was the end of Derrick

(da DUM da da DUM da da DUM)

Ideas for limericks can come from anywhere, often introducing a person and a place, for example, your city, state, country, or name.

Limerick Institute of Technology. The city also hosts numerous festivals and fairs each year, including the annual Limerick International Music Festival in May, which features various concerts from music around the world; the Limerick Bike Parade in June, which takes place from King John's Castle to People's Park; and the Lough Gur Summer Solstice Festival in June.

Limerick's turbulent history and rich heritage are evident in its castles, ancient walls, and notable museums. King John's Castle was built in the 13th century on King's Island, in the center of medieval Limerick. The castle was besieged four times in the 17th century but has been carefully restored for visitors to see its massive gatehouse, corner towers, and battlements.

St. Mary's Cathedral is Limerick's oldest church, more than 800 years old, and is situated near King John's Castle on King's Island. The church began as a palace, and a few pieces from the original building are still erect. Most of the present-day structure is from the 15th century and includes ornate wood carvings and an impressive altar. There are five chandeliers hanging from the ceiling, a belfry with eight bells, and a large organ. Today the church still operates as a place of worship.

Just 23 kilometers (14 miles) outside of Limerick city in County Limerick is the Lough Gur archaeological site. Lough Gur is a horseshoe-shaped lake situated beneath limestone hills outside the town of Bruff. Surrounding the lake are numerous megalithic remains, including the largest grange stone circle in Ireland, a dolmen (a portal tomb), the remains of small farmsteads built on three crannogs (the Irish word for artificial island), numerous Stone Age houses, ring forts, and one hill fort. The Lough Gur archaeological site represents a significant pre-Celtic site, with remains dating back to 3000 B.C.

A LOVE AFFAIR WITH RUGBY

Whether you love rugby or don't even understand it, if you move to Limerick you will be swept up in the remarkable passion the city holds for this sport. Limerick is a renowned sporting city, famous for its zeal for rugby in particular. Munster is where the heartbeat of the Irish game resides, and the streets of Limerick become awash in red when celebrating their Munster team. The people feel a breathless sort of enthusiasm, a stomach-churning anxiety at the start of each game. The essence of the game of rugby is known throughout Ireland and beyond as synonymous with the Limerick people.

Rugby has been played in Ireland since the first club was established at Trinity College in Dublin in 1854. There are now both amateur and professional teams, and each of the provinces of Ireland have their own team—Munster, Leinster, Ulster, and Connaught. These teams primarily concentrate on the Heineken European Cup, which is played in the iconic Thormond Park Stadium, although competitions within Ireland are important as well.

The All-Ireland League, the national league for the 48 senior rugby clubs in Ireland, dominates the city of Limerick, with three clubs winning the competition

13 times. Secondary schools in Limerick compete in the Munster Senior and Junior Cups, with Crescent College taking the Senior Cup nine times.

For all its perceived violence, rugby is often considered an elitist game, but in Limerick this sport crosses all religions and classes, binding the people behind a passion so fiery it is world-renowned. The devotion to the Munster rugby team in Limerick is the stuff of legend, and many say the opposing team most fears "the sixteenth man" (the crowd).

Where to Live

Limerick city center is mostly filled with flats and apartments rather than houses, most of which are situated above pubs and shops or in apartment blocks. The city center itself is quite safe, but some of the suburbs are gritty and even quite dangerous, and these should be avoided at all costs, most notably the Moyross, St. Mary's Park, Ballinacurra Weston, and Southill housing estates in the north and south suburbs of Limerick.

In the city center it will cost you about €600–750 for a new, modern, one-bedroom apartment. Apartments and flats in older buildings are a bit less expensive, running about €550–650 per month for a two-bedroom. Rental properties throughout Limerick are usually furnished, although you may find unfurnished houses in the suburbs. Renting a room is generally pretty inexpensive, costing about €200–300 per month, fully furnished.

The outskirts of the city center are ringed with streets filled with terraced houses. Don't be surprised if city center houses don't feature a backyard, or even a front one. You will have to look farther out in the suburbs for this. Renting a terraced house costs about €700 a month for a three-bedroom.

Limerick city center offers a variety of choices for purchasing property, ranging from apartments to town houses to detached houses. Prices here are more affordable than the rest of the country, and prices typically depend on size and location. The average apartment price in the city center ranges €150,000–250,000, while house prices can be anywhere in the range of €170,000–400,000, depending on where you buy and what you are looking for. This book was written when house prices were bottoming out in Limerick, so they may be subject to change.

CITY CENTER

Limerick city center is filled with apartment blocks, flats situated above shops and pubs, town houses, and terraced houses, and there is a variety of student

LIMERICK REGENERATION

In September 2006, two young children were severely injured when a petrol bomb was thrown into the car they were playing in at Moyross Housing Estate, an underprivileged, crime-ridden neighborhood located in the northern suburbs of Limerick city. These sorts of actions were a near daily occurrence in the disadvantaged areas of Limerick. Fortunately, this particular incident propelled the government to hire former Dublin city manager John Fitzgerald, who is originally from Limerick, to produce a report on solutions for the housing-, poverty-, and crime-related problems that had emerged in the disadvantaged areas of Limerick.

Compounding the problems of criminal and antisocial behavior is the fact that 42 percent of Limerick housing is social housing (compared to just 9 percent in Galway). Unemployment in these areas is five times that of the national average, and there is a large amount of one-parent families and a low level of educational attainment.

Following the publication of the Fitzgerald Report in 2007, the Irish government launched a multimillion-euro project to regenerate the poorest neighborhoods of Limerick. Issues such as criminality were addressed, adding policing to the areas, with plans to regenerate the economy and infrastructure to create employment, and develop coordinated responses to social and educational problems in order to break the cycle of disadvantage.

Two Regeneration Agencies have been created to deal with the regeneration of the north and south sides of Limerick. The agencies submitted proposals to the government for the regeneration of these areas, and on June 18, 2010, the government approved the first of 26 separate projects. The first project will inject €337 million into the communities, adding new housing, community facilities, and road infrastructure for Moyross, St. Mary's Park, Ballinacurra Weston, and Southill housing estates.

Overall, the government will spend about €1 billion on the Limerick Regeneration Plan. The funds will address the problems with violent crime and build the currently weak infrastructure, adding new transport links and commercial businesses for employment opportunities, making Limerick a safer city.

housing available near the university. O'Connell Street is the main street running through the city center. Work is currently underway to update the street, so construction is ongoing in many parts of this area. At the end of O'Connell Street is Patrick's Street. This street is dominated by shops on the bottom floor, with a range of flats rising to four stories above. Cutting just west of Patrick's Street is Arthur's Quay, a quiet little area presided over by the Arthur's Quay Shopping Center, with a variety of coffee shops, restaurants, pubs, and shops. Arthur's Quay Park overlooks the River Shannon, Curragour Falls, and Clare Hills, and a new dam was built to allow boats access between the Abbey River and Shannon Estuary. Limerick's riverside walk passes through the leafy greenery of this park along the River Shannon.

Numerous flats and apartment blocks are available to rent or purchase in this area.

Thomas Street and Bedford Row, in the city center, offer excellent apartments and flats above pedestrianized streets. The Thomas Street Center is a development of retail units and offices, and is surrounded by numerous boutiques, restaurants, and pubs.

Just around the corner is the popular Limerick Milk Market. This all-week, all-weather market has been around for over 150 years and was redeveloped in 2010, offering major markets on Friday, Saturday, and Sunday; occasional markets throughout the week; a new food pavilion; and a variety of

There are numerous golf courses out past the suburbs.

events. People gather here every day, particularly on the weekends, to buy fresh produce, as well as attend antiques and craft fairs, lunchtime concerts, food tastings, barbecues, and fashion shows.

Across the River Shannon on King's Island is the medieval quarter, over which towers the impressive King John's Castle. Also in this area is St. Mary's Cathedral, the Treaty Stone, Hunt's Museum, and the Limerick Museum. The medieval district is a beautiful old area filled with cobbled roads and narrow alleyways. The houses are a mixture of terraced and semidetached, and an old housing estate called St. Mary's Park is here.

The People's Park, located by Pery Square, is the principal park in Limerick and is a pretty little area presided over by imposing Georgian architecture. The park itself features a museum and an art gallery, expanses of green lawns, a playground for children, a library, and two gazebos. The Georgian houses around the park are set on long, wide, elegant streets. This development extended the city south of the Abbey River and the medieval city, and is named New Town Pery, after the speaker of the Irish House of Commons, Edmund Sexton Pery, who was the impetus behind the development. The Customs House, the Town Hall, and the Granary buildings are all situated here.

SUBURBAN LIMERICK

Just 1.5 kilometers (one mile) north of the city center by the Westfield Park is the North Circular Road. This area, as well as the suburban areas around Glenview, Farranshone, and Belfield, offers some of the nicest, most upmarket houses in Limerick. The wide streets are lined with palm trees and flowering bushes, and most of the houses are either detached or semidetached with yards and parking spaces.

Two kilometers (one mile), or a 10-minute walk from the city center on the main Ballinacurra Road, is the suburb of Ballinacurra. The area is peaceful and mostly residential, featuring a variety of bungalows, semidetached houses, and detached houses, as well as streets lined with colorful, terraced houses.

The suburb of Dooradoyle lies three kilometers (two miles) to the south of Limerick city center. The area features the Crescent Shopping Center, with a 12-screen cinema, various restaurants and retail shops, the offices of Limerick County Council, and a public library. The Dooradoyle Leisure Club features a swimming pool, sauna, steam room, and gym facilities. The Midwestern Regional Hospital is located on the outskirts of Dooradoyle on the St. Nessans Road. Numerous suburban homes and apartments are located throughout the area. Many of the houses are semidetached or detached and have fenced yards.

On the Dublin Road, just east of the city center and home to the University of Limerick, is a little suburban town called Castletroy. Castletroy is 6.5 kilometers (four miles) from central Limerick and offers a variety of student accommodations, cheap flats, and apartments. Because of the proximity to the university there is a young, urban vibe. The area is the largest suburb in Munster and one of the fastest growing in Ireland. It is a predominantly middle-class suburb with a number of charming semidetached and detached houses with large, green yards. Historically, the entire area was separate from Limerick and consisted of a little village called Annacotty. However, with the creation of the University of Limerick and the ensuing growth of Limerick city, Annacotty was swallowed and is now part of Castletroy. The Newtown local shopping center, the main shopping center, is located off the Dublin Road and features 24 retail shops, various restaurants, and an eight-screen cinema.

Castletroy was originally composed of the housing developments of Kilbane, Castletroy Heights, Monaleen Heights, and Monaleen Park, all of which were surrounded by rich farmland. These houses are now some of the most sought after properties in the area. The popular Castletroy Golf Course sits at the edge of Castletroy, dividing it from Monaleen.

RURAL VILLAGES

A stunningly beautiful network of roads links Limerick's rural villages and towns. The peaceful country roads and lanes meander through forests and mountains, castles and historic sites, and verdant, green countryside. The rural villages that intersperse these stunning sites range from tiny dots with little more than a pub and a post office to thriving market villages with commercial shops, grocery stores, and banks.

Castleconnell

Castleconnell is a scenic little village perched on the banks of the River Shannon. It's located 11 kilometers (seven miles) from Limerick city on the borders of Counties Clare and Tipperary. Due to its close proximity to Limerick city, the village has begun to increase in size in recent years, with new shops, business premises, and a lot of new housing developments in the village center. The village is punctuated by pretty bungalows painted in pastel colors, ivy-covered stone buildings, and manicured bushes and trees. Surrounding the village are quiet, rolling hills dotted with rural houses and bungalows in peaceful locations, and quiet lakes popular for fishing.

Castleconnell is home to the Irish Harp Center, run by famous harpist Janet Harbison and her husband. A former convent has been converted to a beautiful hotel, the Castleoaks House Hotel, which is popular for weddings. The village has a historic stone church, and the ruins of the Castle of Connell are situated on

© SUSAN LEGG

It is not uncommon to see tractors on rural roads.

a rocky outcrop overlooking a bend of the river. The village has a train station on the Limerick–Ballybrophy railway line, but it runs a skeletal service and is usually pretty quiet.

Adare

The village of Adare is located 18 kilometers (11 miles) outside of Limerick city on the River Maigue. Nestled amid the lush Irish countryside, Adare is widely regarded as Ireland's most picturesque village. The tree-lined main street is populated with thatched cottages and historic stone buildings, and the village holds medieval monasteries, a Norman castle, and numerous architectural ruins. Situated in the town center is the stunning Adare Manor, a historic

The villages surrounding Limerick are scenic and picturesque.

manor house featuring winding woodland paths, riverside walks, stone-walled gardens, and a golf course.

Adare is an easy commute from Limerick city, taking about 20 minutes to drive by car. Alternatively, Bus Éireann buses leave every half hour from the village center for Colbert Station in Limerick city. The journey takes about 30 minutes, depending on traffic.

Kilmallock

The medieval town of Kilmallock is a walled town, with almost 70 percent of the wall still standing today. This rural town is rich in archaeological sites, including excavations at Tankardstown and church, castle, and abbey ruins. Kilmallock was known as the crossroads of Munster and was an important Norman town between the 13th and 17th centuries. Today this historic tradition still exists with a museum, heritage center, and history trail available in the town.

Kilmallock is situated 35 kilometers (22 miles) from Limerick city. It is bisected by one main street and lined by pastel-colored terraced houses on one end and retail shops, restaurants, and pubs at the other end. Every once in a while you will see imposing stone structures or arches where the gates and walls of the medieval city still stand.

Getting Around

Limerick city center is best navigated on foot. The cobbled, medieval streets suffer terrible traffic, and the narrow roads compound the problem. Numerous streets are fully or partially pedestrianized, including the main street, O'Connell Street, between William Street and Roches Street. This complicates matters further if you are trying to drive, as does the ongoing construction that is working to further pedestrianize streets, widen footpaths, and improve the infrastructure of the city center. If you do decide to drive, parking can be difficult to find. On-street parking utilizes parking disks, which you should purchase ahead of time from a shop, or a pay-by-phone system.

Buses depart from the Bus Éireann bus station at Colbert Station, located at Parnell Street in Limerick's bustling city center. Limerick's buses connect you to the towns and villages in County Limerick, to Shannon Airport, and throughout the rest of the country, but there are no trams or trains available. There are 11 taxi ranks located throughout the city center, but keep in mind they can be a bit expensive.

BUSES

Local bus transport is available from Bus Éireann, Ireland's national bus operator. There are 12 buses that operate throughout the city center, and numerous buses depart from the Bus Éireann bus station next to Limerick's Colbert Railway Station. Fares cost €1.60 for a single adult ticket, €1 for a single child ticket, and €0.75 for a student single ticket. You can purchase a day saver for unlimited travel within the city for €3.50. An adult weekly ticket costs €17, and an adult monthly ticket costs €44. A student weekly ticket costs €15.50, and a student monthly ticket costs €47. Eurobus Limerick operates services from the city center to the university and Annacotty areas. Fares cost €1.20 for adults and €0.80 for schoolchildren in uniform.

Hourly services are available from Limerick's bus station to Dublin, Cork, and Galway, and there are daily services that depart for London via the ferry from Rosslare Europort. JJ Kavanagh & Sons (www.jjkavanagh.ie/) operates a bus service connecting Limerick to Shannon Airport and Dublin Airport.

TRAINS

Iarnród Éireann, Ireland's rail service, operates from Limerick's Colbert Station and links Limerick to numerous cities throughout the country. Ten direct trains leave daily for Dublin, and seven depart daily for Cork. Commuter services depart daily for Ennis, Ballybrophy via Nenagh, Waterford, and stations in County Tipperary. The Western Corridor line offers service from Limerick to Athenry, Limerick to Galway, and Collooney to Sligo. Many trains go through or transfer at Limerick Junction, a station situated about 35 kilometers (22 miles) outside of Limerick city center.

CAR

Limerick is strategically situated on the national primary road network. The city is linked to Ennis and Galway by the N18, with Cork by the N20, with Killarney by the N21 and N23, and with Dublin by the N7. Work is currently under way to build a dual-carriageway two-way motorway ring road that will loop around the city center and reduce travel times. The Limerick South Ring Road (N18) loops around the south of Limerick to the west, winding through the Limerick Tunnel and on to Shannon Airport. Numerous secondary roads link Limerick to the rest of the country.

SHANNON AIRPORT

Shannon Airport is located 25 kilometers (16 miles) outside of Limerick city on the N18 road, taking approximately 30 minutes by car. This airport is the second busiest airport in the country, featuring numerous transatlantic and international routes, including Boston, Chicago, New York, London, Amsterdam, Paris, and Moscow. Daily flights depart from Shannon Airport to Dublin Airport, taking just 45 minutes.

RESOURCES

Embassies and Consulates

UNITED STATES

Before moving to Ireland, you may be required to visit the embassy or one of the Irish consulates in the United States. There is only one embassy for Ireland, located in Washington DC; however, there are a number of consuls and honorary consuls available to help you with your paperwork and prepare you for your move to Ireland.

CONSULATE GENERAL OF IRELAND IN ATLANTA

Suite 260, Monarch Plaza
3414 Peachtree Road NE
Atlanta, GA 30326
tel. 404/554-4980
fax 678/235-2201
www.consulateofirelandatlanta.com
Jurisdiction: Georgia, North Carolina, South Carolina, Florida, Tennessee, Mississippi, Alabama

CONSULATE GENERAL OF IRELAND IN BOSTON

535 Boylston Street
Boston, MA 02116
tel. 617/267-9330
fax 617/267-6375
www.consulategeneralofirelandboston.org
Jurisdiction: Maine, Massachusetts, New Hampshire, Rhode Island, Vermont, Chicago

CONSULATE GENERAL OF IRELAND IN CHICAGO

400 N. Michigan Avenue
Chicago, IL 60611
tel. 312/337-1868
fax 312/337-1954
www.irishconsulate.org
Jurisdiction: Alabama, Arkansas, North Dakota, South Dakota, Illinois, Indiana, Iowa, Kansas, Kentucky, Louisiana, Michigan, Minnesota, Mississippi, Missouri, Nebraska, Oklahoma, Ohio, Tennessee, Texas, Wisconsin

CONSULATE GENERAL OF IRELAND IN NEW YORK

345 Park Avenue, 17th Floor
New York, NY 10154-0037
tel. 212/319-2555
fax 202/980-9475
www.consulateofirelandnewyork.org
Jurisdiction: Connecticut, Delaware, Florida, Georgia, New Jersey, New York, North Carolina, Pennsylvania, South Carolina, West Virginia

CONSULATE GENERAL OF IRELAND IN SAN FRANCISCO

100 Pine Street, 33rd Floor
San Francisco, CA 94111
tel. 415/392-4214
fax 415/392-0885
www.consulateofirelandsanfrancisco.org
Jurisdiction: Alaska, Arizona, California, Colorado, Guam, Hawaii, Idaho, Montana, Nevada, New Mexico, Oregon, Utah, Washington, Wyoming

EMBASSY OF IRELAND

2234 Massachusetts Avenue NW
Washington DC 20008-2849
tel. 202/462-3939
fax 202/232-5993
www.embassyofireland.org

HONORARY CONSUL GENERAL OF DENVER

Mr. James M. Lyons
1200 17th Street
The Tabor Center #3000
Denver, CO 80202
tel. 303/623-9000
fax 303/623-9222
jlyons@rothgerber.com

HONORARY CONSUL GENERAL OF LOS ANGELES

Mr. Finbar Hill
1631 Beverly Boulevard
Los Angeles, CA 90012
tel. 714/658-9832
fax 714/374-8972
icla@ireland.com

HONORARY CONSUL GENERAL OF MISSOURI
Mr. Joseph B. McGlynn
1015 Locust Street, Suite 710
St. Louis, MO 63101
tel. 314/727-1000
fax 314/727-2960
jbm@mcglynnlaw.com

HONORARY CONSUL GENERAL OF TEXAS
Mr. John B. Kane
2630 Sutton Court
Houston, TX 77027
tel. 713/961-5263
fax 970/925-7900

HONORARY CONSUL OF FLORIDA
Ms. Cynthia Byrne-Hall
255 8th Street South
Naples, FL 34102-6123
tel. 239/649-1001
fax 239/649-1972
chall@silveriohall.com

HONORARY CONSUL OF NEW ORLEANS
Judge James F. McKay III
1317 Jay Street
New Orleans, LA 70122
tel. 504/412-6050
fax 504/412-6053
JFM@la4th.org

HONORARY CONSUL OF PITTSBURGH
Mr. James J. Lamb
Ireland Institute of Pittsburgh
Regional Enterprise Tower
425 6th Avenue
Pittsburgh, PA 15219-5819
tel. 412/394-3900
fax 970/925-7900
info@iiofpitt.org

HONORARY CONSUL OF SEATTLE
Mr. John F. Keane
5819 St. Andrew's Drive
Mukilteo, WA 98275-4858
tel. 425/290-7839
fax 206/337-4147
jkeane@irishconsulseattle.com

IRELAND
Since Ireland is such a small country, there is only one embassy that handles all issues for U.S. citizens.

EMBASSY OF THE UNITED STATES IN IRELAND
42 Elgin Road
Ballsbridge, Dublin 4
01/668-8777
Emergency after-hours tel. 1/630-6200
fax 01/668-8056
http://dublin.usembassy.gov/

Planning Your Fact-Finding Trip

TRAVEL IN IRELAND
The official website of the Irish Tourism Board is www.discoverireland.com. The website offers an incredibly comprehensive list of information for accommodations, attractions, activities, and events. In addition, information and websites for the main tourist cities and towns is available on the website. (Each of the autonomous regions, cities, and most towns have their own tourism websites to help you plan your trip.) The following websites are privately or publicly owned and include valuable information for your fact-finding trip.

www.irishtourism.com
www.authenticireland.com
www.myguideireland.com
www.exploringireland.com

RESOURCES

GUIDED TOURS
Budget Tours
PADDYWAGON TOURS
5 Beresford Place Lower Gardiner Street
Dublin 1
Ireland
01/823-0822
fax 01/823-0765
info@paddywagontours.com
www.paddywagontours.com
Paddywagon Tours offers great value for the money for your tour of Ireland. The Irish drivers pepper the tours with funny, lighthearted stories about Ireland. Tours range from 1- to 10-day trips around the country, and Paddywagon Tours also offers special tours celebrating holidays, such as St. Patrick's Day, Easter, or Christmas.

SHAMROCKER TOURS
Kinlay House Dublin 2/12 Lord Edward Street
Dublin 2
Ireland
01/672-7651
info@shamrockeradventures.com
www.shamrockeradventures.com
Shamrocker Tours offers budget tours that cater to backpackers, students, and young professionals. The tours feature 100 percent Irish guides who are good at telling the stories and history that encompass Ireland. There are six different tours available, ranging 3–7 days and departing for various regions throughout the country.

Culture and Heritage Tours
CULTURE & HERITAGE TOURS
Clarion Village
Clarion Road
Ballytivnan
Sligo
Co. Sligo
Ireland
071/913-8949
info@irishcultures.eu
www.cultureheritagetours.ie
Culture & Heritage Tours offers diverse and exciting luxury tours that are given throughout the 32 counties of Ireland. The company specializes in organizing tours for small groups and for travelers wishing to experience an authentic tour of Ireland. Tours include those centered on fairies, ghosts and graveyards, medieval Ireland, and Georgian Ireland.

HERITAGE ISLAND
Marina House
11-13 Clarence Street
Dun Laoghaire
Co. Dublin
Ireland
01/205-4998
fax 01/284-4845
info@heritageisland.com
www.heritageisland.com
Heritage Island takes you on a tour of the best visitor attractions and heritage towns on the island of Ireland. Tours include historic houses, castles, monuments, caves, and parks, and are available for every region within Ireland.

Gastronomy Tours
THE HIDDEN IRELAND ADVENTURE
P.O. Box 40034
Mobile, AL 36640
tel. 251/478-7519
fax 251/478-7519
info@hiddenirelandtours.com
www.hiddenirelandadventures.com
The Hidden Ireland Adventure's food tour offers cooking instructions in the West Cork region of Ireland. The tours include visiting the landscape of West Cork and County Kerry, as well as the farms surrounding Ballymaloe.

LYNOTT TOURS, INC.
205 Mineola Boulevard, Suite 1B
Mineola, NY 11501
tel. 1 800/221-2474
www.lynotttours.com/i-foodie.htm
Lynott Tours is a luxury travel company based in New York that offers food and wine tours throughout Ireland. This company offers the flexibility of picking your own hotels, car rentals, and sightseeing options, while organizing tastes of locally sourced food and traditional recipes in Ireland. Lynott Tours also offers a variety of other tours for travelers to choose from.

Golf Tours

GOLF TOURS IRELAND
55 Bladon Drive
Malone Road
Belfast
BT9 5JN
Northern Ireland
1800/345-1109
sales@golf-tours-ireland.com
www.golf-tours-ireland.com

Golf Tours Ireland offers golf tours that range from the basic to the luxury, including castle lodgings or luxury boat trips. You can choose from a variety of preorganized trips, or the company can customize tours according to what you want.

IRISH GOLF TOURS
34 Sweetbriar Lawn
Tramore
Co. Waterford
Ireland
051/381-728
fax 051/381-961
info@irishgolftours.com
www.irishgolftours.com/

Irish Golf Tours specializes in providing custom-designed golf holidays to those wishing to explore Ireland's natural beauty and experience the world-renowned parkland golf courses. Golf tours are tailor-made to suit your needs, so you experience your dream golf vacation in Ireland. An online tour planner helps you select your specifications.

Making the Move

LIVING IN IRELAND
www.citizensinformation.ie
www.movetoireland.com
www.transitionsabroad.com
www.livinginireland.ie
www.livingabroadin.com/Ireland/ireland_making.html
www.irishabroad.com/Irish-World/Expats/Moving-to-Ireland
www.garda.ie/controller.aspx?page=31

HOUSING CONSIDERATIONS
www.myhome.ie
www.daft.ie
www.irishpropertymarket.com
www.housingireland.com
www.propertyireland.net

DEPARTMENT OF JOBS, ENTERPRISE AND INNOVATION
23 Kildare Street
Dublin 2
01/631-2121
info@djei.ie
www.djei.ie

IRISH DEPARTMENT OF FOREIGN AFFAIRS
80 St Stephen's Green
Dublin 2
01/478-0822
www.dfa.ie

Language and Education

IRISH INSTRUCTION IN IRELAND

COMCHOISTE NÁISIÚNTA NA GCOLÁISTÍ SAMHRAIDH (CONCOS)
Indreabhán, Co. Galway
091/505-760
eolas@concos.ie
www. concos.ie

CONRADH NA GAEILGE
6 Sráid Fhearchair
Baile Átha Cliath 2 (Dublin)
Ireland
01/475-7401
eolas@cnag.ie
https://cnag.ie/index.php?page=home
Irish-language courses are available at different branches throughout the country.

GAEL-LINN, FORAS NA GAEILGE
26-27 Merrion Square
Baile Átha Cliath 2 (Dublin)
01/676-7283
fax 01/676-7030
info@gael-linn.iol.ie

IONAD FOGHLAMA CHLÉIRE
Carraig an Éisc
Oileán Chléire
An Sciobairín
Co. Chorcaí (Co. Cork)
Ireland
028/3919
eolas@cleire.com
www. cleire.com

OIDEAS GAEL
Gleann Cholm Cille
Contae Dhún na nGall (Co. Donegal)
Ireland
074/973-0248
eolas@oideas-gael.com
www. oideas-gael.com

OIDHREACHT CHORCA DHUIBHNE
Baile an Fhirtéaraigh
Trá Lí
Co. Chiarraí (Co. Kerry)
066/56100
cfcdtteo@iol.ie

NATIONAL UNIVERSITY OF IRELAND, GALWAY
Áras Mháirtín Uí Chadhain
An Cheathrú Rua
Co. na Gaillimhe (Co. Galway)
091/595-101
fax 091/595-041
treasanimhaoil@tinet.ie

NUI GALWAY INTERNATIONAL SUMMER SCHOOL, IRISH LANGUAGE
Irish Language Centre, Áras Mháirtín Uí Chadhain
National University of Ireland, Galway
091/495-442
summerschool@nuigalway.ie
www.nuigalway.ie/international-summer-school/irish_language.html

TAISCE ÁRAINN
Árainn Mhór Island
Contae Dhún na nGall (Co. Donegal)
075/21593
foghlaim@arainnmhor.com

UNIVERSITIES
There are numerous universities throughout Ireland, catering to students from Ireland as well as abroad. Four of these universities are classed as constituent universities of the National University of Ireland, located in Dublin, Cork, Galway, and Maynooth. In addition, there are a number of smaller city universities, as well as Trinity College.

DUBLIN CITY UNIVERSITY
Dublin 9
Ireland
01/700-5000
www.dcu.ie

TRINITY COLLEGE, DUBLIN
College Green
Dublin 2
Ireland
01/896-1000
www.tcd.ie

UNIVERSITY OF LIMERICK
Limerick
Ireland
061/202-700
www.ul.ie

National Universities of Ireland
NATIONAL UNIVERSITY OF IRELAND, GALWAY
University Road
Galway
Ireland
091/524-411
www.nuigalway.ie

NATIONAL UNIVERSITY OF IRELAND, MAYNOOTH
Maynooth
Co. Kildare
Ireland
01/708-6000
www.nuim.ie

UNIVERSITY COLLEGE CORK
College Road
Cork
Ireland
021/490-3000
www.ucc.ie

UNIVERSITY COLLEGE DUBLIN
Belfield
Dublin 4
Ireland
01/716-7777
www.ucd.ie

EDUCATION INFORMATION RESOURCES
NATIONAL EDUCATIONAL WELFARE BOARD (NEWB)
Head Office
16-22 Green Street
Dublin 7
01/873-8700
info@newb.ie
www.newb.ie

Employment

ADECCO
1 Mill View House, Mill Road
Blanchardstown
Co. Dublin
01/820-8824

CAREERS REGISTER
49 St. Stephens Green
Dublin 2
01/500-5900
info@careers-register.com
www.careers-register.com

CITY AND COUNTY ENTERPRISE BOARDS
www.enterpriseboards.ie/index.aspx#

EDEN RECRUITMENT
2 Crampton Quay
Dublin 2
01/474-4500
jobs@edenrecruitment.ie
www.edenrecruitment.ie

LABOUR RELATIONS COMMISSION
Haddington Road
Dublin 4
01/613-6700
info@lrc.ie
www.lrc.ie/docs/Welcome/4.htm

MINISTER FOR JUSTICE AND LAW REFORM
94 St. Stephen's Green
Dublin 2
info@justice.ie
www.justice.ie

STEP ONE STAFFING SOLUTIONS
Killakee House
Belgard Square
Tallaght
Dublin 24
01/404-5511
info@stepone.ie
www.stepone.ie

Health

PRIVATE HEALTH INSURANCE

Ireland currently has three private health insurance companies. Buying private health insurance provides quicker access for health care in Ireland. Fortunately, private health insurance policies cost less than in America.

DEPARTMENT OF HEALTH
Hawkins House
Hawkins Street
Dublin 2
01/635-4000
www.dohc.ie

HEALTH INSURANCE AUTHORITY
Canal House
Canal Road
Dublin 6
01/406-0080
www.hia.ie

HIBERNIAN AVIVA
www.aviva.ie
Information about rules and coverage for private health insurance in Ireland is available from:

QUINN-HEALTHCARE
www.quinn-healthcare.ie

VOLUNTARY HEALTH INSURANCE BOARD (VHI)
www.vhi.ie

SAFETY

All emergency numbers in Ireland are called by dialing 999. Alternatively, the European standard 112 can be dialed. These numbers are free but should only be used in the case of a genuine emergency.

AMBULANCE, FIRE DEPARTMENT, AND/OR POLICE
999 or 112

AN GARDA SÍOCHÁNA HEADQUARTERS
01/666-0000

FIRE AND RESCUE
Dial 112 or 999 and ask to be put through to the fire service.

GARDA CONFIDENTIAL NUMBER
1800/666-111

MARINE AND COASTAL EMERGENCIES
Dial 112 or 999 and ask the operator to put you through to the Garda Costa (Coast Guard).

POLICE DEPARTMENT NONEMERGENCY
Check www.garda.ie/ for the phone number of the local departments.

Finance and Legal Matters

BANKS
ALLIED IRISH BANKS (AIB)
Bankcentre
Ballsbridge
Dublin 4
01/660-0311
www.aib.ie

BANK OF IRELAND
Bank of Ireland
New Century House
Mayor Street Lower
Dublin 1
1850/753-357

SOLICITORS
AIDAN T. STAPLETON & CO. SOLICITORS
Parliament Buildings
38 Parliament Street
Dublin 2
01/679-7939
info@astapleton.com
www.stapletonsolicitors.ie
A law firm specializing in immigrations, offering comprehensive services about green cards, work permits, business permission, and visas.

BRYNE WALLACE
2 Grand Canal Square
Dublin 2
Ireland 1/691-5000
fax 1/691-5010
info@byrnewallace.com
www.byrnewallace.com
Byrne Wallace is one of the largest and most dynamic law firms in Ireland. The practice is increasingly international, serving North Americans through a New York office. They are a full-service law firm offering services for banking and financial, capital markets, employment, consumer, and family business law.

FITZGERALD SOLICITORS
6 Lapps Quay
Cork
021/427-9800
fax 021/427-9810
law@fitzsols.com
www. fitzsol.com
A full-service law firm offering all services that an expat might need when moving to Ireland, including taxes, purchasing property, or starting a business.

LACY WALSH SOLICITORS
77 Strand Road
Sandymount
Dublin 4
01/206-0230
info@lacywalsh.ie
www.lacywalsh.ie
A business-specializing law firm dealing with legal matters such as buying property, setting up a business, or corporate restructuring.

Communications

TELEPHONE AND INTERNET
BT IRELAND
1800/924-925
www.btireland.ie

DIGIWEB
1890/940-400
www.digiweb.ie

EIRCOM
1800/503-303
www.eircom.net

MAGNET
1800/819-999
www.magnet.ie

METEOR
Bill pay: 1905 from your phone (free) or +353 1/430-7085 from abroad (charges apply) Prepay: 1747 (charges apply) from your phone, 1890/808-585 from a landline (charges apply), or +353 1/430-7066 from abroad (charges apply).
www.meteor.ie

02 IRELAND
Bill pay: 1909 from your phone (free) or +353 61/203-501 from abroad (charges apply).
Prepay: 1747 from your phone (charges apply), 1850/601-747 from a landline (charges apply), or +353 61/203-501 from abroad (charges apply).
www.o2.ie

SMART TELECOM
1850/945-549
www.smarttelecom.ie

TELECOM ÉIREANN
1 Heuston South Quarter
1800/400-000

RESOURCES

THREE
083/333-3333
www.three.ie

UPC
1890/940-624
www.upc.ie

VODAFONE IRELAND
Bill pay: 1907 from your phone (free) or +353
1/203-8232 (charges apply).
Prepay: 1747 from your phone (charges apply),
1850/204-020 from a landline, or +353 1/203-
8232 from abroad (charges apply).
www.vodafone.ie

EXPRESS MAIL SERVICES
AN POST
1850/575-859 or 01/705-7600
www.anpost.ie

DHL IRELAND
1890/725-725
www.dhl.ie

DX GROUP
0844/371-0000
www.thedx.co.uk

FEDEX IRELAND
1800/535-800
http://fedex.com/ie

NIGHTLINE DELIVERS
1890/321-890
www.nightline-delivers.com

NEWSPAPERS AND MAGAZINES
IRISH INDEPENDENT
Independent House
27 - 32 Talbot Street
Dublin 1
01/705-5333

IRISH TIMES
The Irish Times Building
PO BOX 74
24-28 Tara Street
Dublin 2 Ireland
01/675-8000

Travel and Transportation

BY AIR
AER ARANN
0818/210-210
www.aerarann.com
Aer Arann is Ireland's regional airline,
operating services from Ireland and the
Isle of Man to destinations throughout
Ireland, the UK, and France.

AER LINGUS
0818/365-044
www.aerlingus.com
Aer Lingus is Ireland's national airline,
operating a fleet of Airbus aircraft departing for Europe, North America, and
northern Africa.

CORK AIRPORT
County Cork
021/431-3131

DUBLIN AIRPORT
County Dublin
01/814-1111

IBERWORLD
0034/971-070-565 (in Spanish)
www.orbest.com
Offers flights to Spain.

IRELAND WEST AIRPORT KNOCK
County Mayo
094/936-8100

IRISH AVIATION AUTHORITY
01/671-8655
info@iaa.ie
www.iaa.ie
The IAA is a commercial company providing for air traffic management and
the safety regulation of the civil aviation industry in Ireland. All of Ireland's

airports are regulated by individual airport authorities.

JET 2
0044/203-031-8103
www.orbest.com
Offers cheap flights throughout Europe.

RYANAIR
0818/303-030
www.ryanair.com
Ryanair is Ireland's low-cost airline. Based in Dublin, Ryanair operates numerous aircraft to destinations throughout Europe and Morocco.

SHANNON AIRPORT
County Clare
061/712-000

WIZZ AIR
1800/818-839
wizzair.com
Offers cheap flights from Ireland to destinations in Eastern Europe.

BY BUS
AIRCOACH
01/844-7118
www.aircoach.ie

BUS ÁTHA CLIATH (DUBLIN BUS)
01/873-4222
www.dublinbus.ie

BUS ÉIREANN
info@buseireann.ie
www.buseireann.ie
Ireland's national bus and coach service.

LUAS
01/4161-4910
www.luas.ie

BY TRAIN
IARNRÓD ÉIREANN
1850/366-222
www.irishrail.ie
Iarnród Éireann is Ireland's national rail network. It is the only rail network in the country.

BY CAR
AA IRELAND
01/617-9999
www.aaireland.ie
Similar to the AAA in the United States, AA Ireland offers motoring advice on all aspects of driving, as well as sells car and home insurance.

Prime Living Locations

DUBLIN
www.visitdublin.com
www.travelinireland.com
www.travelireland.org
www.dublintourist.com
www.dublinsfaircity.com

Expat Clubs
AMERICAN WOMEN'S CLUB OF DUBLIN
www.awcd.net

EXPAT MEETUP
www.meetup.com/dublin-expats

EXPAT WOMEN
www.expatwomen.com/expat-women-countries/expat-women-living-in-ireland.php

INTERNATIONAL WOMEN'S CLUB OF DUBLIN
www.iwcdublin.ie

Real Estate Agents
LISNEY
24 St. Stephen's Green
Dublin 2
01/638-2700
dublin@lisney.com
www.lisney.com

O'CONNOR SHANNON
176 Lower Rathmines Road
Rathmines
Dublin 6
01/496-8111
www.oconnorshannon.ie

RESOURCES

REMAX IRELAND
3 Parnell Street
Waterford
Ireland
051/860-333
info@remax.ie
www.remax-ireland.com

TOM MAHER & CO LTD.
Main Street
Tallaght Village
Dublin 24
01/451-5622

Relocation Agencies
ALLEN REMOVALS & STORAGE
30A Hibernian Industrial Estate
Dublin 24
01/451-3585 or 01/878-0833
info@allenremovals.ie
www.allenremovals.ie

MAC DONALD PRICE
28 Marley Court
Rathfarnham
Dublin 16
01/295-1478
Relocation@MacDonald-Price.ie
www.clubi.ie/MacDonald-Price

THE RELOCATION BUREAU
93 Upper Georges Street
Dun Laoghaire
Co. Dublin
01/284-5078
info@relocationireland.com
www.relocationireland.com

CORK
www.cometocork.com
www.cork-guide.ie
www.iol.ie/~discover/orksee.htm
www.corktourist.com

Real Estate Agents
CAHALANE SKUSE AUCTIONEERS & VALUERS
26 Marlboro Street
Cork
021/427-9179
csav@indigo.ie
www.cahalaneskuse.com

ERA DOWNEY MC CARTHY
39 Grand Parade
Cork
021/490-5000
info@abetterchoice.ie
www.eraireland.com

HENRY O'LEARY, AUCTIONEERS, VALUERS & ESTATE AGENTS
1 Lamb Street
Clonakilty
Co. Cork
023/88-35959
property@hol.ie
www.hol.ie

Relocation Agencies
CELTIC RELOCATIONS
Maclear House 7 Ardbrack
Kinsale, Co. Cork
021/470-0762
www.celtic-relocations.com

IRISH REMOVALS CORK
Public Storage Centre
Bandon Road Roundabout
Bishopstown
Cork
021/454-3976 or 087/958-0779
www.irishremovals.ie
Relocation services also available in Dublin.

GALWAY
www.galwaytourism.ie
www.galway.net
www.galway-ireland.ie
www.galwayonline.com
www.galwaytourist.com

Real Estate Agents
CORRIB REAL ESTATE
An Fuarán Development
Moycullen
Galway
091 555685
info@corribrealestate.com
www.corribrealestate.com

O'DONNELLAN & JOYCE AUCTIONEERS
Mary Street
Galway
091/564-212
info@odonnjoyce.com
www.odonnjoyce.com

SPENCER AUCTIONEERS
Main Street
Oughterard
Co. Galway
091/552-999
info@spencerauctioneers.com
www.spencerauctioneers.com

Relocation Agencies
BEAZLEY REMOVALS
091/568-200
info@beazleymoving.ie
www.beazleymoving.ie/
Also available for relocation in Cork, Galway, Limerick, and Dublin.

RB RELOCATION
Doon
Kingston
Galway
091/524-793
info@rbrelocations.com
www.rbrelocations.com

LIMERICK
www.limerick.ie
www.limericktourist.com
www.limerickslife.com
www.limerick.com

Real Estate Agents
HICKEY O'DONOGHUE AUCTIONEERS LTD.
49 O'Connell Street
Limerick
061/310-022
info@hod.ie
www.hod.ie

JOHN SHAW AUCTIONEERS
No.1 Lower Mallow Street
Limerick
061/311-133
info@johnshawauctioneers.com
www.johnshawauctioneers.com

O'CONNOR MURPHY GUBBINS AUCTIONEERS
5 Shannon Street
Limerick
061/314-151
info@omg.ie
www.omg.ie

Relocation Agencies
CARELINE INTERNATIONAL MOVING & STORAGE
Whitehall
Parteen
Limerick
061/326-070 or 061/459-002
www.careline.ie
Relocation services also available in Cork, Dublin, Galway, and Limerick.

IRELAND RELOCATIONS JEANETTE MCDONNELL
Lurriga Patrickswell
Co. Limerick
061/355-929

RESOURCES

Public Holidays

Holiday	2011	2012
New Year's Day	Jan. 1	Jan. 1
St Patrick's Day	Mar. 17	Mar. 17
Easter Monday	Apr. 25	Apr. 9
May Holiday	May 2	May 7
June Holiday	June 6	June 4
Summer Holiday	Aug. 1	Aug. 6
October Holiday	Oct. 31	Oct. 29
Christmas Day	Dec. 25	Dec. 25
St. Stephen's Day	Dec. 26	Dec. 26

Clothing Conversion Chart

Ireland uses both UK and European sizes for clothing and shoe sizes. You will see the size on the label inside of the garment.

WOMEN'S CLOTHING

U.S.	UK/Ireland	Europe
4	6	34
6	8	36
8	10	38
10	12	40
12	14	42
14	16	44
16	18	46
18	20	48

MEN'S CLOTHING (SHIRTS)

U.S.	UK/Ireland	Europe
Small	34	87
Medium	36	91
	38	97
Large	40	102
X-Large	42	107
	44	112
	46	117

WOMEN'S SHOE SIZES

U.S.	UK/Ireland	Europe
3.5	2	35
4.5	3	36
5.5	4	37
6.5	5	38
7.5	6	39
8.5	7	40
9.5	8	41
10.5	9	42

MEN'S SHOE SIZES

U.S.	UK/Ireland	Europe
5.5	5	38
6.5	6	39
7.5	7	40.5
8.5	8	41
9.5	9	42
10.5	10	43
11.5	11	44
12.5	12	45

RESOURCES

Glossary

While the Irish speak English, they do have a variety of slang and references that might be completely lost on a newcomer. The following is a list of slang and common references that the Irish say in both Irish and English.

aubergine eggplant

arseways making a mess of things

bank holiday an official three-day weekend when banks are closed and everybody is off work

baile (BAL-ee) village or town

bap a round roll, similar to a hamburger bun

biro ballpoint pen

biscuits cookies

black pudding sausage made from curdled and boiled pig blood

blather to talk excessively

bog slang for toilet or a marshy area

bollocks slang for "balls" or a colorful way of exclaiming an expletive

bonnet hood of a car

boot trunk of a car

bother (BOH-her) road

brilliant a common way of saying "great"

bucketing or lashing raining hard

caravan a trailer or mobile home

céad míle fáilte (cayd-MEE-lay-FAWL-cha) one hundred thousand welcome

ceilidh or ceili (KAY-lee) a traditional music and dancing session

chemist pharmacist

chippy a fish-and-chips shop

chips fries

cider alcoholic apple cider

cill (kill) church

courgette zucchini

crisps potato chips

craic (crack) fun

culchie (CUL-chee) a shortening of the word *agricultural* and referring to those living in the countryside

daft crazy

deadly very good or a great time

dodder waste time

dole Irish welfare or unemployment

dosser lazy person

dual carriageway four-lane highway

dún (done) fort

eejit idiot

Éire (Air) the Irish name for the Republic of Ireland

en suite a private bathroom

eolas (OH-lahs) information

fag cigarette

fáilte (FAWL-chah) welcome

fair play well done

feck used instead of the other f-word; used commonly as an adjective and isn't meant to offend

fir (fihr) men; used on toilet doors

flannel a facecloth

freephone a toll-free telephone number

GAA Gaelic Athletic Association

Gaeltacht (GWALE-tahckt) the Irish-language speaking region (plural *Gaeltachtaí*)

gardaí (gar-DEE) the Irish police

gas funny

give out to scold

gone in the head mad, crazy

grand agreeing to something, as in "okay," or things will be fine

having the craic having a good time

he or she is such a me feiner he or she is so selfish

jammers packed

jammy lucky

knackered very tired

knickers a woman's underwear

langered or langers drunk

lift elevator

loo toilet

lorry truck

lose the head to lose control in anger

lough (lock) a lake or narrow sea inlet

manky dirty, unappealing

mince hamburger

mná (m'NAH) women, used on bathroom doors

mór (more) big

nappy diaper

RESOURCES

on the piss getting drunk
off license liquor store
petrol gas (fuel)
quay (key) a stretch of street along a river
queue (cue) a line
plaster a Band-Aid
rashers bacon
return ticket a round-trip fare
runners athletic shoes, sneakers
sellotape Scotch tape
shattered or wrecked tired
single ticket a one-way fare
slagging making fun of
slán goodbye
sláinte cheers
slí (shlee) path
soft old day a wet day
snog kiss
taking the piss making fun of
talking shite not making much sense

Taoiseach (TEE-shuck) Ireland's prime minister
Tánaiste (TAHN-ish-teh) Ireland's deputy prime minister
Taxi rank A taxicab stand on the street where you wait for taxis
teach (tock) house
Teachta Dala (TOCK-tuh DOLL-uh) a member of the Irish Parliament, (TD)
to let to rent
townland a small geographical division of land
tennis shoes
what's the craic? a common greeting
yer man that man there (whose name is unknown)
yer one that woman there (whose name is unknown)
yoke a broad term referring to just about anything; "that yoke there"
yonks a long time

Irish Phrasebook

The Irish language isn't heard much outside of the Gaeltacht, and unless you can spend a year or so living here, learning the language may be quite difficult. However, there are some common terms and phrases that are easy to pick up. The most important thing to learn is the pronunciation of this beautiful language. Once this is understood, Irish grammar is very well ordered (unlike English), having been perfected by Irish poets in the 12th century, and the language is a pleasure to speak. Keep in mind that Irish is a living language, and as such, you will always run into variations of Irish pronunciation and words. As Cole Porter said, "You say tomAto, I say tomAHto." Below I have included pronunciation and phrases for Connemara Irish, as this is a popular learner's dialect.

IRISH VOWELS

The Irish vowels include *a, e, i, o,* and *u.* There is no *y.* The vowels are divided into broad and slender vowels and long and short vowels. *A, o,* and *u* are broad vowels, and *e* and *i* are slender vowels. You can remember them easily by how they look: *a, o,* and *u* are broad, while *e* and *i* are slender. These vowels help distinguish how the closest consonants are pronounced. Short vowels are pronounced the same way they are in English, but long vowels use an accent mark called a *fada.*

Long vowels are pronounced as follows:

á "aw," as in sáile (SAW-lah, meaning sea water)

é "ay," as in séamus (SHAY-mus, meaning James)

í "ee," as in sí (shee, meaning she)

ó "oh," as in sólás (so-LAS, meaning solace)

ú "ooh," as in tú (too, meaning you)

IRISH CONSONANTS

Like with the vowels, there are broad and slender consonants in Irish, depending on the closest vowel. You will only rarely see a broad vowel on one side of a consonant and a slender vowel on the other side of the same consonant. An example of a broad and slender consonant is a broad *d,* which sounds like *d,* and a slender *d,* which sounds like a *j.*

Modern Irish consonants are: *b, c, d, f, g, l, m, n, p, r, s,* and *t.* The Irish language doesn't use *j, k, q, v, w, x, y,* or *z.* The letter *h* is very important for combining with certain consonants to change the pronunciation or to add to the beginning of a word for grammatical reasons. When an *h* is added to a word it is said to be aspirated, and this changes the pronunciation. For example:

bh when pronounced broad is "w," when pronounced slender is "v" or "vy"

ch when pronounced broad is "kh," when pronounced slender is "kh" or "khy"

dh when pronounced broad is "gh," when pronounced slender is "yih"

fh is always silent

gh when pronounced broad is "gh," when pronounced slender is "yih"

mh when pronounced broad is "w," when pronounced slender is "v" or "vy"

ph when pronounced broad is "f," when pronounced slender is "f" or "fy"

sh when pronounced broad is "h," when pronounced slender is "h" or "hy"

th when pronounced broad is "h," when pronounced slender is "h" or "hy"

There are also a few unfamiliar consonant groups that have pronunciations you would never be able to figure out on your own, including:

bhf "w," as in cá bhfuil tú (cah will too, "where are you?")

bh "v," as in mo bhean (moh van, "my woman")

mh "v," as in naomh (nave, "saint")

dh "y," as in dhá dhoras (yah yorahs, "two doors")

gh "y," as in mo gheansaí (moh YAN-see, "my sweater")

COMMON WORDS AND EXPRESSIONS

Hello *Dia dhuit* (DYEE-a gwitch; literally, "God be with you")

Thank you *Go raibh maith agat* (guh row MAH-aguth; literally, "may good be with you")

You're welcome *Tá Fáilte romhat* (thaw FOIL cheh ROOTS)

What's your name? *Cad is ainm duit?* (CODH is A-nam gwitch?; literally, "what name is on you?")

My name is Christina *Christina is ainm dom* (Christina is AH-num dum; literally, "Christina is on me")

How are you? *Conas tá tú?* (cunnas TAH too?)

I am fine *Tá me go maith* (tah may guh MAH)

Goodbye *Slán or slán abhaile* (slawn or slawn a-WHY-leh; literally, "safe home")

Please *Le do thoil* (leh doe HULL)

Excuse me *Gabh mo leithscéal* (go mo LESH-cull; literally, "take my apology")

Where are the toilets? *Cá bhfuil an leithreas?* (kah will an LEH-riss)

Where is the nearest _____? *Cá bhfuil an _____?* (djeh-REH foh-ir)

DAYS AND MONTHS

Sunday *Dé Domhnaigh* (djay DOUGH-knee)

Monday *Dé Luain* (djay LOO-in)

Tuesday *Dé Máirt* (djay MOYtch)

Wednesday *Dé Chéadaoin* (djay KAY-deen)

Thursday *Dé Déardaoin* (djay DAYR-deen)

Friday *Dé hAoine* (djay HEE-nah)

Saturday *Dé Sathairn* (djay SAH-harn)

January *Eanáir* (an-AW-irr)

February *Feabhra* (feow-RAH)

March *Márta* (mawr-TAH)

April *Aibreán* (a-BRAW-n)

May *Bealtaine* (BAHL-the-neh)

June *Meitheamh* (MEH-huv)

July *Iúil* (OO-il)

August *Lúnasa* (LOO-nah-sah)

September *Meán Fomhair* (MAHN foh-ir)

October *Deireadh Fomhair* (djeh-REH foh-ir)

November *Samhain* (sow-IN)

December *Nollaig* (NULL-ig)

NUMBERS

1 *aon (een)*
2 *dó (doe)*
3 *trí (three)*
4 *ceathair (CAH-hur)*
5 *cúig (COO-ig)*
6 *sé (shay)*
7 *seacht (shock'd)*
8 *ocht (ockt)*
9 *naoi (knee)*
10 *deich (djayh)*

Suggested Reading

Ireland is a nation of prolific storytellers. Over the years, Ireland has compiled quite a list of fiction and nonfiction books and poetry that have become famous throughout the world.

FICTION AND POETRY

Beckett, Samuel. *Molloy*. New York: Grove Press, 1955.

Beckett, Samuel. *Malone Dies*. New York: Grove Press, 1956.

Beckett, Samuel. *The Unnamable*. New York: Grove Press, 1958.

Delaney, Frank. *Ireland: A Novel*. New York: Harper Paperbacks, 2008.

Fitz-Simon, Christopher. *The Most Beautiful Villages of Ireland*. New York: Thames & Hudson, 2011.

Harbison, Peter. *Spectacular Ireland*. New York: Universe, 2009.

Joyce, James. *Dubliners*. London: Penguin, 1914.

Joyce, James. *Ulysses*. Paris: Sylvia Beach, 1922.

Joyce, James. *A Portrait of the Artist as a Young Man*. New York: B.W. Heubsch, 1916.

Joyce, P. W. *English as we speak it in Ireland*. Toronto, University of Toronto Libraries, 2011.

McCourt, Frank. *Angela's Ashes*. New York: Scribner, 1996.

Stoker, Abraham "Bram." *Dracula*. London: Archibald Constable and Co., 1897.

Swift, Jonathan. *Gulliver's Travels*. London: Benjamin Motte, 1726.

Wilde, Oscar. *The Picture of Dorian Gray*. London: Ward, Lock, and Company, 1891.

Yeats, William Butler. *The Collected Poems of W. B. Yeats*. 2nd rev. ed. New York: Scribner, 1996.

NONFICTION

Boland, Eavan. *Irish Writers on Writing, featuring William Butler Yeats*. Dublin: Trinity University Press, 2007.

Coohill, Joseph. *Ireland: A Short History*. London: Oneworld, 2008.

Lynch, David J. *When the Luck of the Irish Ran Out: The World's Most Resilient Country and Its Struggle to Rise Again*. New York: Palgrave Macmillan, 2010.

McCaffrey, Carmel. *In Search of Ancient Ireland: The Origins of the Irish from Neolitic Times to the Coming of the English*. Lanham, MD: Ivan R. Dee, 2003.

O'Reilly, Emily. *Veronica Guerin*. London: Vintage Books, 1998.

Stoker, Abraham "Bram." *Personal Reminiscences of Henry Irving*. New York: Macmillan, 1906.

Stoker, Abraham "Bram." *Famous Imposters*. London: Sidgwick and Jackson, 1910.

PLAYS

Heaney, Seamus. *New Selected Poems 1966–1987*. London: Faber & Faber, 1980.

Heaney, Seamus. *Opened Ground: Poems 1966–1996*. London: Faber & Faber, 1980.

Heaney, Seamus. *Selected Poems 1965–1975*. London: Faber & Faber, 1980.

Heaney, Seamus. *The Cure at Troy*. A version of Sophocles' *Philoctetes*. Dublin: Field Day, 1990.

Heaney, Seamus. *The Burial at Thebes*. A version of Sophocles' *Antigone*. London: Faber & Faber, 2004.

Shaw, George Bernard. *Caesar and Cleopatra: A Page of History*. New York: Brentano's, 1906.

Shaw, George Bernard. *Three Plays for Puritans, Volume 18*. New York: Brentano's, 1906.

Wilde, Oscar. *An Ideal Husband*. London: Haymarket Theater, 1893.

Wilde, Oscar. *The Importance of Being Earnest, A Trivial Comedy for Serious People*. London: St. James's Theater, 1895.

Index

Acknowledgments

I would like to give my heartfelt thanks to the people of Ireland, who made me feel so welcome when I arrived and who made this book possible. This is dedicated to you. Also, thank you to my Irish girls, Sarah Sweeney, Kelly Roche, and Elaine Hollowed, for your unfailing support and honest opinions; and to Sarah Sweeney, Susan Legg, and John Molloy, who contributed photos for this book. And, most importantly, to Richard and Adam; you both give my life meaning each and every day.